Future Storm

The Dynamics Unlocking the Future

Michael, with
best wishes,
Bill, Feb 4 '08

by William Houston & Robin Griffiths

HARRIMAN HOUSE LTD

43 Chapel Street
Petersfield
Hampshire
GU32 3DY
GREAT BRITAIN

Tel: +44 (0)1730 233870
Fax: +44 (0)1730 233880
Email: enquiries@harriman-house.com
Website: www.harriman-house.com

First published in Great Britain in 2003 by William Houston.
Reprinted in Great Britain by Harriman House 2006

Copyright Harriman House Ltd

The right of William Houston & Robin Griffiths to be identified as the author has been
asserted in accordance with the Copyright, Design and Patents Act 1988.

ISBN 1-897-597-98-3

978-1-897597-98-9

British Library Cataloguing in Publication Data
A CIP catalogue record for this book can be obtained from the British Library.

Printed and bound by Biddles Ltd, Kings Lynn, Norfolk.
Index by Indexing Specialists (UK) Ltd.

to Averil

'History is a series of events repeating each other'
Eugene O'Neill

'The further backward you look, the further forward you can see'
Winston Spencer Churchill

'Chance favours only the prepared mind'
Louis Pasteur

Corroptisima republica plurimae leges
('The more corrupt a republic the more laws it passes')
Tacitus Annals III 27

Contents

About the Authors

William Houston joined the Royal Navy at the end of the Second World War and specialised in weapons. After leaving the Service, he qualified as a Chartered Engineer and in administration before embarking on a career as a 'company doctor' – advising a large range of industrial and commercial concerns. There followed a period acting as industrial advisor to a City merchant bank.

His first book *Avoiding Adversity* was published in 1989 warning businessmen of the coming recession, shortly to be followed by *Meltdown* and *Riding the Business Cycle* that warned of the growing disruption that would take place early in the next century.

Robin Griffiths joined Phillips and Drew in 1966 having taken a degree in Economics at Nottingham University. He went on to be a partner at WI Carr, the first British stock broker to have offices in Hong Kong and Tokyo. Part of this firm was acquired by Grieveson Grant with whom Robin enjoyed a stay in Japan.

In 1986 Robin joined James Capel, which was already owned by HSBC. He stayed there until normal retirement age and during that period travelled all over the world to meet their extended client base.

For the last six years of that employment Robin was resident in New York. He has been a regular on CNN, CNBC, Reuters and Bloomberg TV. Robin was married for 30 years and is now happily divorced. He has four grown up sons.

Also by William Houston:

Avoiding Adversity

Meltdown

Riding the Business Cycle

Acknowledgements

It would have been impossible to write this book without the help of a number of references that I have done my best to acknowledge in the text and in the reading list. I have also received encouragement from a great number of people and am particularly indebted to: Chris Cawthorn, Eddy Choy, Paul Corby, Adrian Davies, Richard Dent, Fred Fox, Ian Gordon, Evelyn Garriss, John Hayes, Sheila Hollis, Lacy Hunt, Paul Mansell, Helen Mitchell, Richard Mogey, William Rees-Mogg, Ian Notley, Marc Nuttle, the late E. Terry Ross, Bill Weavers, Michael White and Chris Woodward.

Any errors are entirely my own.

I have received much encouragement and help from Dick Fox, Christeen Skinner, Stephen Lewis and Stephen Watson, who have provided ideas and comments on the text. I am also most grateful to Stephen Hill, who, as the editor, has provided many helpful insights and suggestions; Alan Robertson has also me given much help in editing and putting the book together. Finally, I am indebted to my wife Averil, who has taken time from her own busy life to be an assiduous proof-reader and editor.

William Houston, Datchworth, May 2004

'Those who cannot remember the past are condemned to repeat it'

George Santayana

Introduction

We are slaves to the times we live in, for the times we live in are determined by cycles.

At 8.45a.m. Eastern Standard Time on 11 September 2001, flight AA011 from Boston crashed into the south tower of the World Trade Center, followed by further planes hitting the north tower and, later on, the Pentagon. Nearly 3,000 people lost their lives in these atrocities, more than in the Japanese attack on Pearl Harbor in 1941. On a smaller scale commuter trains to Madrid were bombed and more recently London. Only in the last outrage were national citizens the terrorists.

These were not aggressions by a state, but by individuals believing, by some satanic perversion, that by killing civilians they were doing the work of their God. There was another terrorist attack in the name of nationalism on 28 June 1914 when the Serbian terrorist Gavrilo Princip murdered the heir to the Austrian throne and his wife in a bizarre shooting incident at Sarajevo in Herzogovina, then part of the Austrian-Hungarian Empire. This atrocity led to the First World War. The 11 September, and subsequent attacks, could have as dire consequences, for the world is threatened by a convergence of six critical cycles. We will call these 'dynamics', for they will have very active and far-reaching effects.

The first dynamic is a somewhat loose religious rhythm of around 700 years that started at the birth of Christ, which gave mankind the hope that the Supreme Being valued each and every person as a manifestation of Himself. Some three centuries later, the Emperor Constantine made Christianity the official faith of the Roman Empire. The next two rhythms were driven militarily by Islamic religious fervour. By AD 732, 100 years after the death of the Prophet Mohammed, the Muslims had created an empire that stretched from the Atlantic to Sind in India, and was only stopped at Poitiers in France by Charles Martel.

Around 700 years later, the next holy war, or jihad, was started by Osman, the ruler of the small Ottoman province in Anatolia, now modern Turkey. This fervour swept across the Bosphorus, occupied Greece, then took the previously impregnable Constantinople. The Muslim warriors then drove up the Balkans to threaten Vienna in the sixteenth century as part of a circling movement around the Black Sea. Remarkably, the Ottoman Empire lasted until 1922, when General Kemal Ataturk drove the Greek invaders out of Anatolia on 11 September of that year. The date of the New York and Washington atrocities was carefully chosen by al-Qaeda, for it also marked the creation of the British Mandate in Palestine in 1922. It is highly likely that the next jihad will continue to be ruled by terrorism in many facets.

The second dynamic has a rather shorter duration of 500 years, but is no less potent. This cycle was last active around 1500, for by then the Ottomans were approaching the gates of Vienna, the techniques needed for the industrial era were available; the voyages of discovery began and the greatest power on earth, the Roman Catholic Church, was shaken by an Augustinian monk called Martin Luther. Now, 500 years later, we are at the start of the 'Information Age'. Whereas the Industrial Revolution caused a concentration of physical, organisational, financial and political power, the new technology is likely to create a decentralisation of energy, talent and political authority. This will be a movement away from cities and nation states to form new centres of excellence that will have a dynamic and life of their own. This technologically driven dynamic will lead to a diminishing role for government, a championship of the individual and a greater freedom for people and groups.

The third dynamic concerns climatic cycles of around seventy years that originate in the Atlantic and the Pacific, to the disadvantage of the Middle East, northern China, Central Asia and a range of Muslim countries. The last time the Atlantic rhythm was operating, Israel and Jordan suffered a drought that nearly caused a war. Now, thirty years later, the eastern Mediterranean lands are likely to become dry but the population in the region has risen by 50%. There is another rhythm of nearly 180 years that probably triggered the great tsunami of December 26 2004 and the Kashmir earthquake and could create very cool conditions in the northern hemisphere later in the decade.

The fourth dynamic largely follows from the third. At times of declining crop availability immune systems are weakened and we are more likely to catch diseases. There is also an eight hundred year cycle coming due when invaders – or refugees – bring with them dangerous pathogens.

The fifth dynamic concerns history's greatest credit bubble, brought about by politicians and central bankers in a vain effort to stave off deflation. It has already claimed the largest ever corporate bankruptcies – Enron, then Worldcom – and Argentina as the greatest national default. The so-called 'cockroach factor' prob-ably means that these will not be the last as global debt dwarfs any previous bubble. This economic cycle usually lasts around fifty years – a successor, perhaps, to the biblical Jubilee – and will surely affect government, corporate and individual finances.

The sixth dynamic is concerned with energy and there is a loose five hundred year cycle from the introduction of coal to the present. Although there are a number of alternative energy sources, the present unreliable sources of hydrocarbon will place tensions on to a strained world.

The power of any one of these cycles could cause major discontinuities in the life of the West, but in interactive combination they could be devastating. Politics, so long seen as a master of events, is now likely to become perceived as the servant.

This book seeks to extrapolate the present trends and then examines historical precedents to formulate predictions. We are optimistic that arising from this convergence of critical cycles, an age is coming which will return us to a greater sense of true values and re-emphasise the individual and the liberation of the human spirit, its ingenuity and creative talent – something not unlike Martin Luther's achievement some 500 years ago.

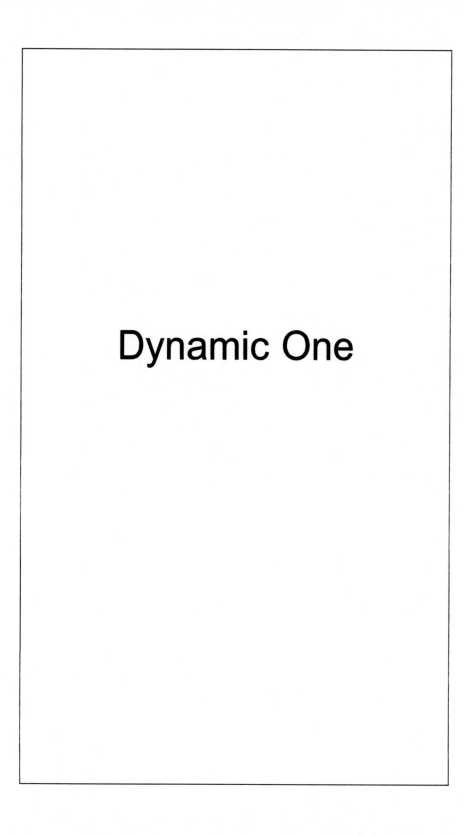

Dynamic One

1

The Threat from Religious Terrorists

The twenty-one terrorists who wrecked the twin towers and a wing of the Pentagon were apparently driven not by economic motives but by a religious dream of 'paying back' the so-called 'Great Satan', who in their eyes had inter alia polluted the sacred soil of Saudi Arabia. The vast majority of Muslims hold that killing civilians (and suicide) is a crime against Islam and it is said that Osama bin Laden commissioned an Islamic scholar to justify the attack on the grounds that those who died were American taxpayers and as such were as guilty as their government. Whatever else may be impinging on this globe, the threat of skilled and deadly terrorist attacks on the West must be included as one of the major factors impacting on the twenty-first century. What is the basis of Islam?

Both the Jews and Arabs claim legitimacy as the descendants of the patriarch Abraham: Jewry through his wife Sarah and her son Isaac, the Arabs from Sarah's maid-servant Hagar and her son Ishmael. Some 3,600 years later, the Prophet Mohammed proclaimed the new faith of Islam – or submission to the will of God.

Mohammed was born in 570 at Mecca into the tribe of Koreish. He became an orphan and was bought up by his uncle aub-Talib as a shepherd boy and camel driver, learning the habits and languages of the Bedouin. That might have been his life, but he worked for, and then married, a rich widow called Khadija and became a merchant. His new affluence gave him time to reflect on the primitive conditions of many Arabs, who worshipped several gods whose effigies they carried around and displayed during battles. In his book The Arab Mind, the scholar John Laffin describes the Bedouins as tribal nomads who had a record of raiding and plundering in minor conflicts where the victors carried off women and camels. The heroes of these skirmishes were those who engaged in single-handed bouts and were immortalised in poems. Mohammed himself led several attacks – the best known was in AD 624 when, with 300 tribesmen, he surprised and vanquished a Meccan caravan at Badr.

The Bedouin language in which these accounts were handed down is one of persuasion, and not given necessarily to perceptual accuracy. An account of a raid may be couched in several different ways depending upon the language used and perspective of the narrator. This does not necessarily mean that truth is unimportant, but words are used more to stimulate and delight the senses than to covey precise information.

This was the verbal environment in which the Koran was recounted by Mohammed as received from the Angel Gabriel to his companions – said to have included a monk and a rabbi. These started from the year 610 until the Prophet's death in 632. The script was written down on palm leaves, leather, stones – whatever was to hand. Just as the language of Shakespeare and the King James Bible became the benchmarks for the English language, so the language of the Koran brought the Arabic tribes together and to nationhood.

To Muslims the Koran is the ultimate word of God, which is why pupils in the increasingly popular Muslim Madrassah schools in the Middle East are required to memorise 'The Word' and to recite whole tracts by rote – often at the expense of a wider education. For example, applicants to the Al Azhar University in Cairo are obliged to memorise all 114 chapters and 6,666 verses of the Koran if they want a place, irrespective of any other qualifications. Unlike the languages of Iran and Turkey, Arabic does not readily accommodate foreign words so any new ideas or facts tend to be expressed within the existing linguistic framework.

In 622, the Prophet fled for his life to Medina, some 290 miles away, for his new faith threatened the centre and cult of the Ka'ba – Black Stone – at Mecca. The journey is known as the Hegira, the starting point of the Muslim calendar and celebrated annually by Muslims at Ramadan, when the faithful are forbidden to eat between sunrise and sunset. Eight years later, his military exploits won him acceptance in his home town of Mecca, which he entered in triumph as the Prophet of Arabia to make the Ka'ba his shrine. He died and was buried at Mecca two years later.

The Encyclopaedia Britannica describes the new religion as uncompromisingly monotheistic, requiring a strict adherence to certain religious practices that control much of daily life. Although there have been many sects, movements and cultures within the religion, among the regions of the Islamic world, all followers of Islam should be bound by a common faith and a sense of belonging to a single community. The West, while bringing a more liberal culture and economic benefits as part of its colonial expansion, is often distrusted for weakening these global ties. The Koran, however, with its attitude to women and its rules for organising a state, seems to be denying its followers similar economic benefits. This is the great paradox for Islam. Muslims want the prosperity that the West generates but are unable to attain the same benefits without deviating from what Muslims hold to be the ultimate word of God. This is why so many of the Prophet's followers find a balance between their temporal and spiritual lives in the West.

The word 'Islam' is used repeatedly in the Koran, in the sense of 'surrender to the will of Allah'. For Muslims, the Prophet Mohammed is the last and most perfect of a series of messengers of God to mankind, from Adam through Abraham to Moses and Jesus. The Bible is rebuked for not foretelling the life of Mohammed, and Christian claims for Christ's divinity are strongly rejected. Despite this, Jews and Christians are accepted as people of the Book. Although Mohammed is only a human creature of God, he has nevertheless an unequalled importance in the Koran that sets him next only to God as deserving of moral and legal obedience. Hence, his sayings and deeds (sunnah) serve as the belief and practice of Islam.

In Koranic theology God is unique, omnipotent, omniscient and merciful. Mankind, as his servants, are exhorted to obey his will (i.e., to be Muslim), and special responsibility is laid on men. The Muslim creed consists of five articles of faith: they should believe in one God, in angels, in the revealed books, in the prophets and in the Day of Judgement. To these was added, during the early development of the creed, the belief in God's predetermination of good and evil. The profession of the faith (shahada) is: There is no God but God, and Mohammed is the prophet of God.

All Muslims are enjoined to obey the Five Pillars of Islam. These are: to recite the profession of faith at least once in one's lifetime, to observe the five daily public and collective prayers, to pay the zakat (purification) tax for the support of the poor, to fast from daybreak to sunset during the month of Ramadan; and to perform, if physically and financially possible, the hajj, or pilgrimage to the holy city of Mecca.

The most important and fundamental religious concept of Islam is that of the sharias – the laws – which embrace a total way of life as explicitly or implicitly commanded by God. These were formulated by religious teachers in the second and third centuries of the Muslim era (eighth to ninth centuries AD), to include both the doctrine or belief and practice of the law, as applied to individuals and the state. There is, however, a paradox. While penalties for crimes and misdemeanours are dealt with much more severely in Muslim states, which enjoy hugely reduced levels of crime compared to the West, it is rigid adherence to the Koran that has held back the Islamic states economically in a rapidly changing world.

Despite the notion of a unified and consolidated community as taught by the Prophet, violent differences arose among Muslims within a few years of his death. The sect of the Kharajis, for example, assassinated the Third Caliph (deputy or successor of Mohammed) for what they regarded as nepotism and misrule. They interpreted the Koran as justifying holy militancy and at least two other caliphs were murdered. The group consequently rebelled and, as a result, were virtually wiped out during the first two centuries of Islam.

In what became the Sunni branch of Islam, the concept of the Caliph was both a spiritual and temporal chief executive of the Muslim state responsible for enacting the Koranic law; unlike the Pope he had no authority for interpreting or creating dogma. Later the break-away sect of the Shi'a held that the iman held the ultimate responsibility for governing and the spiritual guidance of the flock. The Iranian ayatollahs are the latest of a long line of Shi'ite clerics through whom the 'truths' of the Koran are revealed.

Such a doctrine was adopted also by the Sufis, an ascetic movement that arose, largely within orthodoxy, in reaction to the worldliness of the early Muslim dynasties. The Sufis refer to the mujahedin as warriors against 'unbelievers'. These soldiers must perform acts of penance and austerity (such as fasts) as part of a purification of their souls to receive the divine light.

From the very beginning of Islam, Mohammed's requirement of brotherhood and close relationship was driven by the original persecution of the nascent community in Mecca. Islam not only sought to regulate an individual's relationship to God (through his conscience) but also to other people, in various social and state settings. There are different interpretations of Islam, extending from the strict Shi'ia state of Iran to secular Turkey. However, these must be narrowly interpreted because the Koran gives neither latitude for adaptation nor encouragement for experimentation.

Five centuries after the initial spread of Islam under the banner of the first jihad, described later, the Sufis inaugurated a much larger expansion. Long before Ignatius Loyola's Jesuits spread the Christian creed far and wide, Muslim mullahs and merchants spread the faith in India, Central Asia, the Malayan peninsula, present-day Indonesia, Turkey and sub-Saharan Africa. Although there was a loss of political power during the colonial nineteenth and twentieth centuries, the concept of the Islamic community helped various Muslim peoples in their struggle to gain political independence in the mid-twentieth century.

There are two levels of belief: the first is Islam – the act of submission to Allah – and the second, deeper, iman, meaning belief or trust. Thus it seems possible initially to act out the ritual without having the faith, only later gaining belief. The term 'jihad' has many meanings, the most basic being that each must seek to be the best person possible and to show love and kindness. It also means a holy war.

Despite this assertion there is little of the Christian incentive to love one's enemies. In one translation, 'Mohammed is the Messenger of God and those who are with him are hard against the unbelievers.' In another, the Koran advises believers not to take unbelievers as friends. In other words, 'Islam is a delight to believers but a damnation to unbelievers.' On the day of reckoning those in the first category will recline on jewelled couches, 'waited on by immortal youths with bowls and ewers and a cup of purest wine, and theirs shall be dark-eyed houris, chaste as hidden pearls.' The latter shall dwell amidst scorching winds and seething water.

There is little doubt that of the 1.2 billion Muslims in the world, the vast majority are those whose faith requires them to be obedient to Allah by following the laws contained in the sharias. The West may object to their attitude towards women, the medieval approach to punishment and the Taliban's wanton destruction of Buddhist statues, but these can all be justified in the eyes of fundamentalists.

Islam and 11 September 2001

What is less clear is the Islamic attitude towards violence and the West's horror at jubilation in Gaza after 11 September, which set back the Palestinian cause in many quarters. Unfortunately this same jubilation was present among some disaffected young Islamic men in Western countries who felt alienated from what they thought as an unfriendly culture. Unlike the Buddha, the Old Testament prophets and Jesus Christ, Mohammed led troops in battle and there is no doubt that the two jihads, described later, were prosecuted by the sword. Muslims may point to the violence of the Crusades but the Christian Saviour would never have sanctioned these, or later, violent acts.

Despite the protestations of peace, the Koran in sharia 9, verse 5, enjoins Muslims, 'if there are abuses against Islam and its Prophet, to fight the Pagans wherever ye find them. And seize them, beleaguer them and lie in wait for them in every stratagem of war'. The problem is, who decides what constitutes abuses against Islam and its Prophet? It seems that in the event of an attack on defended Islamic soil, Muslims of that country are obliged to wage a jihad. If infidels attack an undefended Islamic country, the jihad becomes an obligation on all Muslims. There is the proviso that if infidels ask Muslim countries for help, and they co-operate or spy, then this is punishable by death. This sounds much like a Western non-aggression pact, but the extent to which the faithful wish to take on America militarily – after successful campaigns in Afghanistan and in Iraq – remains to be seen.

There are precedents of how a jihad may be enacted. Apart from the initial terrorists who murdered earlier caliphs, the next group of murderers were called the 'Nizaris', later the 'Ashishin' (the original 'assassins'), the forerunners of today's fanatics. These names were given to a group of Shi'ia Syrians led by a strange prophet called Hasan ibn al-Sabah – also called the Old Man of the Mountain – who ran a gang of murderers in the eleventh and twelfth centuries. They operated from a stronghold in the valley of Almut, within which was a beautiful garden full of flowers and fruit, and fine buildings with exquisite paintings. Wine and milk flowed freely and the inmates were delighted by houris. This was the base from which the Old Man detailed murders of prominent Sunnis, the sect's sworn enemies. Their most prominent victim was probably Ubayd Allal as-Khatib, the chief of Isfahan who, despite bodyguards, was struck down while at prayers.

The next significant group was organised by Ibn Abdul Wahhab, who preached a totalitarian and ultra-strict Islamism from his tract The Tawhid in the late eighteenth century. He came from the Nejd, the site of present-day Riyadh, and his followers, known as Wahhabis, were fanatics who wanted all Muslim states to be united in their strict observance to Allah. In the First World War the British, in their war against the Turks, encouraged Wahhabi aggression and the sect has continued to this day, still based in Saudi Arabia. It is supported by the Saudi royal family who encourage the sect's dictates to be observed in schools, the police and media.. It is said that Osama bin Laden is a Wahhabi, as were the killers of Anwar Sadat, the President of Egypt, in 1981, and the current suicide bombers in Israel. Recently Wahhabi sages have criticised the Saudi rulers for being too pro-Western and in any uprising, Wahhabi forces could totally dominate the Kingdom. For the US, the real potential fear, apart from dislocation of oil supplies, is that a very large number of American mosques probably have mullahs who are Wahhabi sympathisers.

There are other groups in Central Asia, in the old Soviet states of Kazakhstan, Kyrgyzstan, Tajikistan, Turkmenistan and Uzbekistan. Under Stalin all religious groups were quelled and the rulers have tried to continue this policy since independence. Further east there are many Uighur nationalists in the Chinese province of Xinjiang, where the authorities have tried to dilute the Islamic influence through the emigration of ethnic Chinese. 60% of the region's fifty million people are under twenty-five years old and the population has seen a decline in living standards, despite sitting on considerable oil and mineral wealth. Since the break-up of the Soviet Union, however, Islamic missionaries from Pakistan and Saudi Arabia have helped to finance the building of mosques and have provided copies of the Koran in local languages.

In the revival of religious fervour, at least two ultra-religious groups have formed. The first is the Islamic Movement of Uzbekistan (IMU), a powerful and militant sect formed in 1998 by extremists. Their aim is to topple the often corrupt and authoritarian secular governments in the region and, in an effort to support the Taliban and al-Qa'eda, fought against the Northern Alliance and the US in the north of Afghanisan. Their first aim is to control the verdant Fergana valley, an action that has forced the authorities to mount counter measures.

The second is the Hizb ut-Tahrir al-Islam (HT), which, like the Wahhabis, was started in Saudi Arabia by displaced Palestinians in 1953. Like the IMU it has declared a jihad in Central Asia, seeking to unite first the Central Asian republics, then Xinjiang, then ultimately all Muslim nations. It seeks to return to a period after the Prophet's death when all Islamic nations were united under a caliphate which would have complete authority over the secular and spiritual hearts of the state, ruling though an Islamic council. The HT is quite open in its aims, generates a great deal of literature and has a growing following among college students in the region. Unlike the IMU, it seeks to gain power through a peaceful uprising but will resort to violence if necessary.

It should be remembered that before the Opium Wars of the 1840s, much of Central Asia was part of China before it became part of the Russian Empire. So it is not surprising that in 1996 China formed the 'Shanghai Five' an initiative embracing China, Russia, Kazakhstan, Uzbekistan, Kyrgyzstan and Tajikistan in a group called the Shanghai Cooperation Organisation (SCO). The aim seems to have been economic and mutual security..

Since then there have been riots against the ruling communist oligarchs in the second and fourth of the republics that almost certainly has is roots in religious agitation and the climatic shifts described in Chapter 7. It will also spread. This has caused China to increase security as part of the SCO that has not been helped by the US apparently supporting genuine nationalist movements in the region. This area is undoubtedly a source of instability not just internally but between Russia and China as both nations attempt to control the sources of raw material in an increasingly strategic region.

Osama bin Laden and al-Qa'eda

We can now look at bin Laden's al-Qa'eda through the eyes of history. The organisation is said to have been started after the Soviet invasion of Afghanistan, when bin Laden ran a clearing-house for fighters to take on the invaders. In time the organisation grew to include fund-raising and it also became a focus for extreme clerics and devoted men willing to be martyrs. When the Russians withdrew, the focus moved to America's support for Israel, and the Saudi fighters within the group were appalled when Saudi Arabia gave support to the 'infidels' during the 1991 Gulf War. Bin Laden was expelled from Saudi Arabia and his passport withdrawn.

The exile's organisation now consists of a consultative council where Israeli intelligence believes the operating brains are two officials, one from Hezbollah, the other from Egypt. Also on this council are four groups dealing with military, financial, religious and public relations. Al-Qa'eda has already sent veterans to fight in Bosnia, Kashmir, Chechnya, Algeria, Egypt, the Sudan and elsewhere. In countries like Indonesia, where al-Qa'eda is outlawed, groups under the extremist cleric Abu Bakar Basyir and the Abu Sayyaf organisation in the Philippines, have probably received training from al-Qa'eda. The group was also responsible for the attacks on US embassies in Africa during 1999, the destroyer USS Cole in Aden in 2000, and, indirectly, the Bali bombing.

The group has built up terrorist organisations in most Western countries, which Saddam probably helps with funding, logistical back-up, training in chemical and biological warfare and more advanced weapon training. The US is home to 11 million Muslims: the greatest percentage live in California and the vast majority are loyal citizens. This still leaves many hundreds of potential fanatics, however, who perceive their faith as under threat and are willing to attack to order – among others, there is an al-Khifar organisation which is supposedly a Muslim charity and has offices in thirty-eight US cities; there is also the Muslim Brotherhood. Funds are believed to be generated from the sale of drugs and sent home through money bureaux along with normal remittances from thousands of migrant workers.

There are also cells within Europe, home to around 13 million Muslims. In Britain, the dissident focus is in a few mosques, from where, it is believed, several dozen have received terrorist training in Afghanistan. Al-Qa'eda is one of twenty-one groups outlawed since February 2001. There are also cells in continental Europe, where many countries have welcomed Muslims either to work or as settlers through ex-colonial links; they almost certainly carried out the Madrid bombing. In 2001, police in Italy and Spain discovered unsettling evidence that dissidents had plans for attacking US embassies and the European Parliament. The riots of Muslim youths, though not thought to have been al-Qa'eda inspired, are still a potential threat. There are also reports that al-Qa'eda could have obtained nuclear materials from Russia through Chechnya, reputably in exchange for $500 million in cash and heroin.

Bin Laden is credited by 'Anonymous' in Imperial Hubris as a charismatic and intelligent leader who has scored a number of victories over the US without being seriously inconvenienced or suffering defeats. His complaints against the United States including polluting the sacred soil of Saudi Arabia, invading a Muslim state in the Gulf War, supporting Israel against the Palestinians and dominating other Muslim states.

Bin Laden has learnt from the Viet Nam War the ways in which a weak nation can inflict moral and economic damage on the rich and powerful US and is prepared to use every method. Does this mean the terrorist can prevail over Western nations by relying on the inability of democracy to protect itself? Almost certainly not, but it means that democracies will have to take distinctly illiberal measures to arrest, intern, confiscate – even kill to prevail.

But even these highly dangerous individuals can be thwarted if the West is determined. They need to create counter-organisations able to gain intelligence and protect vital centres of water, food and electricity, as well as essential government and commercial buildings. Does this mean that the West is against Islam? Again, almost certainly not, because religious practice is generally separate from the state, but the West needs to be less politically correct when reporting not only on Islam's peaceful merits but also its capacity for violence.

The first jihad

To many Muslims jihad is first a journey of self-purification by battling against the devil and overcoming inducements to evil. The next journey is the propagation by word that was so successfully carried out by the Islamic merchants as they spread the message by 'tongue and hand'.

However to a militant minority jihad has come to mean a duty of the faithful to wage war against unbelievers and enemies of the Islamic faith. Originally they did not include Christians and Jews, to whom the Prophet gave special consideration as 'people of the book' and they were allowed to practise their faiths. Unbelievers were given a choice: conversion or death. Apart from life there were certain benefits for the former such as relief from paying poll and land taxes and they were excused enrolment as galley slaves or soldiers.

The first of the Prophet's successors was the Caliph Abu Makr, who completed the conquest of Arabia in two years and then advanced north towards Palestine. He was followed by Omar, who in ten years advanced to Damascus, beat the Byzantines at the Yarmuk River, then continued eastwards to Mesopotamia and Asia Minor. By AD 643, Persia was overrun, forcing the forebears of the present-day Parsees to flee south to India, where they settled in present-day Bombay.

Successive Caliphs, Othman and Ali, continued east to what is now Afghanistan, capturing Kabul in 664 and Sind in north-west India in 712. Meanwhile, Arab forces captured Alexandria in 643 then swept along the North African coast. There was some Berber resistance but the Muslim army crossed the Straits of Gibraltar in 711, conquered Spain, and were only defeated at Tours, near Poitiers by Charles Martel in 732.

In an epic battle between lightly armoured Muslim cavalry composed of Berbers and others hungry for loot, and heavily armoured Frankish infantry defending their home soil, the defenders prevailed. Although the forces were equal in number, with some 30,000 each, Martel had chosen a position that could not be outflanked and the exhausted attackers left the field with around a quarter of their number dead, including their commander.

In 100 years, from nothing, the Islamic empire now stretched from the Atlantic to Sind, and shared a single faith and language. However, the empire then split into two centres of excellence. To the west the Umayyad family ruled the Moors and made their capital at Cordoba on the Guadalquiver River, north-east of Seville.

There Abd ar-Rahman and his successor al Mansur established the most advanced capital in Europe, home to 471 mosques, many grand houses and splendid palaces. Under their benign rule the city produced elaborate fabrics, leather-work and jewellery from over 80,000 shops, and scribes produced beautifully decorated religious scrolls; it also had a university of European renown. Cordoba fell to the Christian invaders in 1236, which accelerated its economic and cultural decline to become a city of churches and monasteries. A good idea of Moorish magnificence can still be judged from the Alhambra Palace at Granada.

To the east, Caliph al Mansur, of the Abbasid family, extended a village on the Tigris to the city of Baghdad from 762. Over ten thousand men were employed in building a circular city with walls over 3.5 miles in circumference with 360 towers. After a period of conflict and civil wars, from 786 to 809 Harun al-Rashid became the fifth caliph of the Abbasid dynasty to rule an empire which stretched from the Mediterranean to India in a splendour that is described in The One Thousand and One Nights. He first made his name by organising an expedition against Constantinople that obliged the Byzantine emperor to conclude peace – in the Arab's favour.

As caliph, he required the various governors to make payments to Baghdad in return for semi-independent status. In the period of tranquillity those skilled in textiles, metal working, paper making and traders were attracted to the capital bringing untold wealth to themselves and the Abbasid family. Harun's palace and court was the wonder of the world, its tables loaded with vessels of gold and silver studded with gems; guests were entertained by numerous eunuchs, concubines, singing girls, and male and female servants. The caliph himself was a connoisseur of music and poetry and gave lavish gifts to outstanding musicians and poets. Not for nothing, however, was he a potentate with power of life and death over his subjects. By the time of his death, the walled city had expanded to the south to house the influx of artisans and merchants and by 814 it was probably the largest city in the world.

800 years later the splendour had faded and the Moors were ejected from Spain – something that bin Laden apparently still resents. Mesopotamia (present-day Iraq) was occupied by the Mongols, who destroyed the elaborate irrigation systems to restore grassland for their horses. This merely slowed the rate of conversion of the

infidels, which continued through traders and missionaries encouraged by the crucial victory over the Chinese at the Talus River in 751 (a victory that also brought paper-making to the West). India was the first to be proselytised, followed by the Malay Peninsula, Sumatra, Java, Borneo, Mindanao, the Moluccas, the southern Philippines and the Celebes islands. This was a remarkable feat carried out long before the Christians, a much older faith, made the effort to spread their 'word'.

The second jihad

The second jihad started in a minor emirate in Turkey nearly 700 years after the Prophet's death that became one of the most terrifying invasions of Europe. Its shadow still hangs over us, in the Balkans, in Chechnya and Central Asia and in the enmity between the Greeks and the Turks. While the Balkan Orthodox Serbs and the Catholic Slovenes in the sixteenth century were tolerated by the invaders, they were required to pay taxes and were eligible for military service, often as galley slaves. Those who became Muslims congregated in the towns and became the administrators, while the Christians became the farmers.

After the Mongols retreated from Anatolia in the late thirteenth century, Osman, an aggressive emir of the Ottoman family, successfully occupied the land opposite the Sea of Marmara, in 1326 having declared a holy war against non-Muslims. His followers then captured Bursa to the west and then the Emirate of Karasi in 1345. Ten years later the Ottomans had crossed the Dardanelles and captured the Gallipoli peninsula before occupying Adrianople (present-day Edirna in Bulgaria).

Continuing north, the Ottomans under Bayezid I defeated the Serbs and Bosnians at Kosovo in 1389 before absorbing most of the independent emirates in Anatolia. Hence by the end of the century the new empire stretched from the Danube in the west to the Euphrates in the east. The advance paused in the early part of the fifteenth century after Murad was defeated by the Mongol Tamerlane and there was some attempt in the Balkans to shake off Turkish rule, but the warrior stock was not conquered. Under Mehmed I and his son Murad II, Anatolia and the southern Balkans were recaptured. The next major drive was Mehmed II's capture of Constantinople using an enormous twenty-two-inch bore cannon to batter down the walls. The city's submission brought an end to 1,000 years of Byzantine rule which had absorbed much of north Africa.

Over the next twenty-eight years Mehmed's forces went south to occupy Greece, established a toehold at Kaffa on the Crimean peninsula and advanced further east. By his death in 1481, the Ottoman frontier stretched from Bosnia in the west to Crimea in the east. There was then a pause in the north while the Turks challenged the sea power of Venice to become a force in the Adriatic. In the early years of the fifteenth century the new Sultan Selim I defeated a challenge from the Shi'ites in Iran, occupied Damascus in 1516 and the holy places in Jerusalem, then went south to defeat the Mameluke in Egypt a year later. It was about this time that the elite infantry of the Ottomans, the Janissaries, stormed Rhodes which the Knights of St

John had occupied after being forced out of Acre. The Christians then founded a new base in Malta, where they successfully resisted an epic siege of St Elmo's castle in Valetta in 1565.

While the voyages of discovery were being made by the West, Islam was being actively promoted in Europe and the Mediterranean, in Persia and in India. In south-east Europe the new Sultan Suleiman I (the Magnificent), and now the de facto caliph, attacked the previous Serbian borders by taking Belgrade in 1521 and Bucharest five years later; by 1529 the Turks were besieging Vienna. Like Cordoba and Baghdad hundreds of years earlier, Constantinople's population, which had been 40,000 at the time of its capture, increased tenfold and the city became renowned for the splendour of its public works, the magnificence of its mosques and the soundness of its administration and education. Even more frightening for Western visitors was the strength and discipline of the army which, in the latter part of the sixteenth century, recaptured stretches of north African coast first occupied in the first jihad.

At about the same time, Persia was undergoing a cultural revival in the reign of Abbas I, while further east in Central Asia Babur swept through Afghanistan to found the Mughal Empire in India, which also became renowned for its culture. Once again Islam was divided between the Sunni and Shi'ia sects and was no match at sea against the Portuguese, who had sailed east in search of peppers and spices. The tide was turning in the West too with the defeat of the Ottomans by the Venetians at the great sea battle of Lepanto in 1571. The high-water mark of the Ottoman Empire was probably on 12 September 1683, when the armies of the Grand Vizier were repelled from the gates of Vienna and were obliged to flee south-east to Belgrade.

The defeated Kara Mustafa tried to hide his ignominy by garrotting the commanders who had witnessed his incompetence. However his performance did not escape the Sultan, who sent his chief executioner to throttle him with a bowstring and as proof of his demise was decapitated and his stuffed head sent back to Istanbul. Even then the saga was not over, for the head was captured by the Austrians, who displayed it in Vienna's museum for many years. Remarkably the Ottomans lasted for almost another 300 years, their conquests being gradually rolled back by the advance of the Europeans. First to be liberated were the Balkans, then Greece, Egypt and North Africa. Arabia was the last possession to go during the First World War and the peace treaty was signed at Lausanne on 11 September 1922, when Britain's mandate for Palestine began.

And the third jihad?

The makings of a third jihad were probably sown when Islamic countries were released from semi-colonial rule. In 1920 only four countries – Turkey, Saudi Arabia, Iran and Afghanistan – were independent. This figure had risen to 69 by 1995 and of these, 49 had predominantly Muslim populations, with many mullahs demanding a return to religious purity.

This has fuelled fundamentalist movements, such as those in Saudi Arabia, Central Asia and the Far East, fed by the fanaticism of young people – who form at least 40% of the population – for whom there is little work, and poor living conditions. There also seems to be a natural aggression in the newly liberated Islamic states, where the proportion of people under arms is double that in Christian countries. There have been many instances of clashes between Muslims and other faiths, evident in places such as Chechnya, Palestine, Nigeria, The Sudan, the Balkans, India, Indonesia and elsewhere in the East. China also could be in peril from a Muslim uprising in Xinjiang.

Already the aborted Russian invasion of Afghanistan from 1979 to 1989 is regarded as being the first victory of the third jihad despite the majority of the Afghans' weapons and funding coming from the United States. The next, in retrospect, was the Gulf War of 1990-1 where, although defeated, Iraq had the support of a great many Muslims, despite the governments of Saudi Arabia, Egypt, Turkey and Syria supporting the West. Many deemed that although it was wrong for Iraq to invade Kuwait it was an even bigger sin for the US to lead a retaliatory invasion against a Muslim country. As it is the declared intention of the Bush administration to quell terrorist elements in Syria, Iran and North Korea, this could generate widespread Islamic reaction and militancy, which could suck in many other states and only deepen the degree of religious fervour.

There is a clear danger for states such as Israel – but the West itself could also be in peril from the past high level of migration. By the late-1990s there were 13 million Muslims in Europe, of which 4 million lived in France; in the US there are estimated to be 11 million. After September 11, the West's suspicions that might previously have been directed against those of African descent, are now directed at Muslims. Already some young men who cannot find a job, such as those in France, have drifted towards militant mosques where fundamentalist mullahs have encouraged them to fight for Osama bin Laden or one of his many associated groups.

Should there be further attacks like those on the Twin Towers and the Pentagon and it were shown that indigenous Muslims were the culprits, then the whole community could be under suspicion, and internment or repatriation might be demanded. Martin van Creveld, Professor of Military History at the Hebrew University of Jerusalem, argues that modern armies are almost useless against the sort of war the Palestinians are waging; he believes that physical segregation is the only answer. Creveld gives the examples of the Great Wall of China, and those of Berlin and Nicosia in Cyprus; he could also have mentioned the British policy of strict isolation during the Malayan Emergency.

Samuel Huntington, in his book *The Clash of Civilisations*, may be correct when he argues that the seeds for the next jihad have already been sown, not just between the Islamic extremists and the West but also within Islam itself. The destruction of the Afghan Taliban, largely by American air power, might well have given new leaders pause for thought but the extremists have shown themselves ruthless and cunning in adapting to Western weaknesses, as was shown so tragically in Bali.

This was an attack thought to have been organised by a fanatic called Hambali, in an island that is not Christian but largely Hindu.

On March 11 2004 several bombs were exploded on commuter trains around Madrid killing two hundred people in another apparently mindless attack. Senseless, unless Osama bin Laden still bears a grudge for the ejection of the Moors over five hundred years ago, or as a punishment for Spain supporting the Bush Iraqi coalition. If it was the latter the stratagem worked all too well for it succeeded in electing a socialist prime minister who vowed to remove his country from the allies. This appeasing response to aggression has a long history of failure and it can only redouble al-Qa'eda's efforts to change the West's policy towards Israel and Islam.

What is so sinister for the West is that it appears that attacks are not just originating from Afghanistan or North Africa, but from disaffected nationals who find it all too easy to assemble bombs to be used against their own countrymen in the name of Allah. The third jihad is just starting.

References

Anonymous, *Imperial Hubris* (Brassey's Inc, 2004)

Berman, Paul, *Terror and Liberalism* (W.W. Norton, 2003)

Burke, Jason, *Al Qa'eda* (Penguin, 2004)

Huntingdon, S., *The Clash of Civilisations and the Remaking of World Order* (Simon & Schuster, 1996).

Kepel, Gilles, *Jihad* (I.B. Tauris, 2002)

Kepel, James, *Jihad* (I.B. Taurus, 2003)

Khan, M. Z. (trans.), *The Koran* (Curzon, 1970).

Laffin, J., *The Arab Mind* (Cassel and Company, 1975).

Lewis, Bernard, *What Went Wrong?* (Weidenfeld and Nicolson, 2002).

Palmer, A., *The Decline and Fall of the Ottoman Empire* (John Murray, 1992).

Dynamic Two

2

The Cycles Surrounding the Information Age

In one of the amazing paradoxes of history, the second jihad that swept through the Balkans in the fifteenth century was also mainly responsible for the globalisation of the last 500 years. By interrupting the spice and pepper trade-routes to the east, the Ottomans forced Europeans to create their own supplies for commodities that made living in cities bearable. The voyages of discovery needed their own techniques but, although they did not know it at the time, all the other technologies that made the Industrial Revolution almost inevitable were available by the year 1500.

Something similar happened 1,500 years earlier when Jesus Christ had challenged the priestly class that dominated the Temple Mount in Jerusalem to create a new faith, which of course later became the Roman Church, established by the Emperor Constantine by the Edict of Milan in 313. The Catholic Church was itself successfully challenged in 1517 by an Augustinian monk who questioned the right of the Church to be the sole arbiter of the Scriptures. For those countries touched by the Reformation, it released a powerful energy that dominated the next 500 years and helped generate the political, financial, industrial and social structures that propelled the eighteenth, nineteenth and twentieth centuries.

Shrewd commentators have identified the attacks of 11 September as being the true start of the twenty-first century, for they crystallised in the minds of many the suspicion that a great deal would change, especially in the all-pervasive Information Age. It is highly probable that we are approaching a discontinuity every bit as fundamental as that of around 1500, but this time instead of the events taking place over centuries they may now occur within a generation. The Second Dynamic describes the changes likely to occur to make this a deeply exciting time for some people, but greatly unsettling for others.

A five-hundred year cycle of discontinuity

One of the first to define a 500-year cycle was Raymond Wheeler of Kansas State University during the 1920s and 1930s. He became interested in people's reactions to climate over hundreds of years and recruited a number of students to research all known reliable references (they found that monks and soldiers were the prime recorders in the early days). The climatic data were derived mainly from eyewitness accounts, but by the 1930s tree rings from the ancient Sequoia redwoods in California were recognised as giving an excellent record over many centuries. The tens of thousands of items were duly recorded and filed, and a summary was written in the 'Big Book' at the Foundation for the Study of Cycles in New York.

Wheeler reached two main conclusions. Firstly, people responded differently to varying combinations of temperature and moisture. The most welcome is a warm and wet climate that creates a sense of well-being and abundant food; however this also breeds optimism which can lead to wars of expansion. The next most beneficial is when it is cool and wet, for while people have enough to eat, the cooler weather makes them more energetic. Wheeler held that warm and dry conditions could lead to a state of lethargy and despair, fertile conditions for tyrants and dictatorships; while cool and dry conditions make people energetic and angry – the perfect conditions for potential revolutions. All phases complete in a cycle of around 100 years.

Secondly, there was a 500-year cycle in the affairs of mankind, which can be traced back at least to the years before the birth of Christ, when Confucius and Guatama, the Buddha, were teaching. The first 500 years AD were marked by the fall of Rome and mass movements of displaced peoples in Europe; the continent then plunged into the Dark Ages and only emerged at the end of the second cycle. The second millennium started with the division between the Roman and Eastern churches and ended with the major discontinuities of around 1500 described earlier. Over the last 1,000 years each major event has been accompanied by an explosion of Christian evangelical energy. After the split with Rome, the Orthodox missionaries went north into Russia then 500 years later Luther generated the Protestant Revolution. This in turn stimulated the missionary drive of Ignatius Loyola and the Jesuits. Now there are signs of a new Protestant evangelical zeal among the English-speaking peoples and in Latin America.

The Industrial Revolution

Although the technology was known by 1500, it was over 200 years before Abraham Darby successfully smelted iron using coke instead of charcoal and so released an energy not constricted by the use of wood. Next came Newcomen's first steam pump which made it possible to pump water out of deep coal mines. From then there were inventions in cotton spinning, weaving, in engineering, in power, with Watt's steam engine, and then in transport with Stevenson's Rocket. The pace of manufacture by machines accelerated through the nineteenth and twentieth centuries.

At first most of the inventions were empirical but then the application of science developed away from steam-driven mechanical energy into the internal combustion engine, electrical and chemical engineering. By the end of the nineteenth century it became possible to take production away from the craftsmen and use semi-skilled labour by dividing the work into simple operations using the methods of F.W. Taylor, the ground-breaking originator of work study. These were initially applied by the Ford Motor Company but then later to domestic appliances, transport, military equipment, electronic goods and even ships. By the end of the twentieth century and the start of the Information Age there was excess capacity for basic materials such as steel and manufactured items like motor cars, domestic appliances and even computers. This made most factory production so competitive that only the most efficient made a reasonable return on capital; this may no longer be true in the steel industry where, despite great efficiency and demand from China, European companies are being forced to downsize through international competition.

We can now look back to see how the Industrial Revolution affected nations and peoples, for it took about six generations for Britons to retrain, and the new machines virtually destroyed the old guild monopolies. While women and children were in demand for manning the new equipment, craftsmen had the option of either doing odd jobs or retraining for another skill. There was some disruption from groups such as the Luddites, who smashed the hated machinery that made their skills redundant, but it was not a major political issue. The Germans were not so lucky, as their transition to the industrial age took about thirty years, causing terrible social upheaval and divisions in society that are still present.

In due course the Industrial Revolution created such entities as big government, large industrial organisations, national banks, the capital system and the supporting professions. Most politicians loved it because, through taxation, they had the money and the industrial base to wage aggressive wars. Probably the best organised were the Prussians, who united Germany in 1870, then enriched themselves further by demanding huge reparations after defeating France. Ships were built, armies formed and overseas colonies were created that provided a source of raw materials and markets for industrial goods. During the Second World War industrial organisations in the United States used Taylor's ideas easily to out-produce the combined industries of the German and Japanese empires.

The Information Age

The year 2000 heralded the Information Age, although many of the trends were discernible beforehand. The politicians and bureaucrats, however, whose job it is to use taxation wisely, have difficulty in spotting future trends and continue to spend money on state-run concerns that become increasingly irrelevant. The new trends could also reverse certain patterns of the last 300 years, which will have major implications for the individual. Technology will be the driving force, the equivalent to steam in the Industrial Revolution, and will encompass the same strands as that earlier revolution: transport, energy, data generation, communications, warfare and materials.

The winners will be the wealthy elite among designers and users who, acting in groups or as individuals, can operate free from the constraints of politicians and regulations. These teams are likely to be highly flexible and will come together for a specific project or adapt as the market opportunities arise – often outmanoeuvring large corporations, just as Microsoft overtook IBM. Location will not matter and the new individuals will be able to choose their own lifestyles and taxation regime.

The losers will include those previously holding well-paid managerial and professional jobs, whose skills are being superseded by technology and who may therefore be obliged to take lesser tasks and a diminished standard of living. As perilous as this is politically, the real threat to stability will be the rising numbers of semi-skilled blue-collar workers no longer needed by a dwindling industrial base. By 2010 it is estimated in the UK and US that manufacturing industry will employ only 10% of the population; 2% will be needed in farming, 3% in government and perhaps 35% in service industries. Unless this matter is considered quite soon, internal problems caused by the unemployed in the West could demand a form of Fascism to safeguard the population, raise tariff barriers and control migration.

If history is any guide, not every nation will be able to respond rapidly and positively to these events. However it is likely that the nations where the state exists for the individual, such as the US, Britain, Australia, New Zealand, some of continental Europe and Scandinavia, could lead the changes. English-speaking peoples (ESPs) – which could also include many in India, Holland and Scandinavia – will initially exploit the new opportunities before other nations consolidate the trend. This view is endorsed by Robert Conquest in his book *The Ravaged Century* and by Jeffrey Sachs, Professor of International Trade at Harvard University, who shows that the predominant technical innovators are the ESPs. After all, it was they who initiated the Industrial Revolution.

The democratic welfare state is an institution that an increasing number of thoughtful commentators believe will be obliged to retrench under pressure from many directions, and although politicians' and bureaucrats' instincts for self-preservation mean that they will not give up power easily, the unwinding forces will prove the more powerful. Globalisation will compel nations to become 'friendly' to entrepreneurs who, as suggested earlier, can easily relocate elsewhere. In the US around 1% of individuals provide at least 25% of tax income and such a loss would force governments to retrench. Also peer pressure from international comparisons will force politicians to make more liberal choices and there will be the demand from the electorate for much greater consultation over issues that directly affect their lives – probably through referenda.

Philip Bobbit, the author of *The Shield of Achilles*, came to a similar conclusion after analysing the role of the state from the Italian Renaissance compared to the present. He believes that the nation-state will progressively be unable to defend its citizens or provide social security to the required standard so will be forced to unwind most of its services.

The cost of unfunded pension liabilities will require budgets to be restructured, as most Western countries have an ageing population. For example, by 2030 it is estimated that in Japan the number of those aged over 65 will be 50% of those of working age; the equivalent figures in Europe and America are 40% and 35% respectively. If this were funded by debt then by 2030 Japan will have gross government borrowings of almost 300% of GDP, and for most EU countries the equivalent will be approaching 100%. *The Economist* estimates that by 2020 sovereign debt in most EU countries and Japan would be downgraded to BBB – equivalent to that of Egypt.

Should the impact of the Information Age be as anticipated, then by 2010 the welfare cost of the rising numbers of unemployed in the regime described earlier will become unsustainable. All of these factors will force governments to unwind such functions as health, education and welfare, making the state role similar to that of the nineteenth century, when it was concerned with maintaining external defence, the currency's integrity and the laws of the country. Perhaps nations could be turning towards the Swiss decentralised constitution as a potential model for industrial nations. In addition the present geographical alliances might change on the basis not of economics but of tradition.

One such could be an association between Israel and Turkey; another could be an alliance of the English-speaking peoples. There could also be a reformation of old empires such as those of Austria and Hungary or the Carolingian alliance of France and Germany. This would not bode well for present groupings such as the wider EU or even the UN.

Decentralisation would also reverse the size of organisations associated with the industrial era. They may tend to locate themselves in suburban or rural areas, where they can take more responsibility for such things as security. (Unfortunately, owing to the rising unemployment and climatic problems described later, there will be an increasing number of run-down cities similar to Detroit or Manila.) Like the trade guilds in medieval times these enterprises will form the core of communities – many of which will try to be self-supporting and make use of the growing proportion of older citizens. As central and local governments falter, these groups could generate their own style of administration, which would then attract like-minded people. With women increasingly becoming at least the equal economic partner in a marriage, it is probable that this would lead to an increasing number of family business units. This could have the further effect of reducing the high divorce rates in Britain and America and go some way to reverse the trend towards single-parent families. There are suggestions that migration laws in the industrial world be stretched to attract well-qualified graduates from the East, Africa and South America to provide the skills missing in low-birth-rate countries in the West. Stephen Lewis, Chief Economist at Monument Derivatives, believes this would take the form of a reverse colonisation, where only the most able would be accepted because of the employment prospects projected for 2010.

References

Bobbitt, Philip, *The Shield of Achilles* (Penguin, 2002)

Conquest, Robert, *The Ravaged Century* (W.W. Norton, 1999)

Houston, W., *Riding the Business Cycle* (Little Brown, 1995).

3

The Ages of Innovation

If we wish to understand the timings and changes likely in the Information Age we must first study how similar changes came about in the industrial era and then see how they may be mirrored in the future. This is one of four chapters investigating the new era, and deals with cycles and trends in innovation. The next suggests how these might work out in practice. The third considers the new breed of winners – and the likely losers. Finally, chapter 6 indicates the likely future direction of politics and the role of the state.

In his book *Business Cycles*, published in 1939, the great economist Joseph Schumpeter asserted that the Kondratieff Cycle (an economic cycle identified by the Russian economist Nicolai Kondratieff) was almost certainly controlled by the 'bunching' of innovations at the beginning of the 'up-wave' that gave impetus to each recovery. He went on to argue that once these new innovations pass the peak of growth they decline, and the weaker companies are forced out, so triggering the next down-wave.

The dot-com boom and bust of the late 1990s was a classic example. His ideas were expanded by other economists, most of whom disregarded the fact that the threat of war has often triggered innovations without leading to an economic recovery. For example, the rearming of the 1930s encouraged a number of developments, including the telex, jet-powered aircraft, FM radio, helicopters, the coding machine and radar. None of these generated a recovery then but they considerably assisted the post-war up-wave.

As technology and innovation play such an important part in Western culture, it is necessary to examine whether they work in cycles and how, in combination with other rhythms, they may develop in the future.

The S-curve pattern of technology

In 1890, the French sociologist Gabriel Tarde was the first to suggest that the development of new technology forms a series of S-curves. Anything new starts with a slow advance, followed by a rapid and uniformly accelerating progress which then slackens off, until it finally flattens and probably declines. Plotted on a graph, this pattern of development follows the shape of a flattened S.

The idea was applied to product cycles in 1950 when the economist Joel Dean suggested that the length and shape of a product's performance was governed by the rate of technological change, market acceptance and the ease of competitive entry. Later researchers went one further, arguing that the S-curve has four fundamental phases:

Introduction: A new product has a slow start when first brought to the market; there is no established demand and sometimes it has to be proved technically. Some pharmaceutical products, like thalidomide, were in this category, as was Clive Sinclair's first electric vehicle – both failed at the first hurdle.

Growth: The new product is accepted, demand begins to accelerate and the size of the market grows rapidly. This can happen even during a recession, such as during the 1930s, when refrigerators became popular for preserving food.

Maturity: Demand slackens, products are bought only as replacements, and competitors crowd into a diminishing pool of demand. 'Commoditisation', as it is called, permits only the most efficient companies to continue in developed countries. For example, with continued globalisation it could become very difficult for Western steel-makers to survive without protection or subsidies.

Decline: Sales drift downwards when a product loses appeal. This was the fate of the stage-coach when replaced first by the train and then by the motor car. To ensure continuity the next product should be introduced before the previous one becomes obsolete. For example, Rank Xerox failed to introduce an electronically controlled photocopying machine before the electro-mechanical design patents had run out. The company had the choice either to lose the market or to completely retool their photocopiers.

The S-curve theory also applies to international trade. For example, machine-driven textile spinning and weaving started in England during the eighteenth century and was much in demand overseas. Despite a strict export embargo, machines were smuggled into America but could not be worked until much later when the migration of skilled individuals enabled the plants to be used. Now most industrialised countries can no longer compete with imports of textiles from nations that use the same machinery but have a lower cost base.

With the coming of the Information Age, advanced countries are being obliged to import most commoditised manufactured products while their own companies set up in low-cost areas overseas. This is particularly true in the garment industry, where retailers are now forced to resource from central Europe or the Far East, where labour is considerably cheaper than in the West. In this way domestic firms still retain the marketing, technological and design expertise but sub-contract the manufacturing. This does not just apply to manufacturing. British Airways' computing and many other back-office services are handled in India, and such things as insurance processing, order-handling and even accounting are now sub-contracted to lower-cost areas.

Simon Kuznets (the economist whose name was given to the US real estate and climatic cycle described later) applied S-curves not just to products but also to industries. He found a growth series in agriculture, mining and a range of manufactured products where innovations revived obsolete technology, so creating new life cycles. For example, the principle that power could be transmitted through a piston started with Newcomen's steam engine in 1712, was perfected by James Watt, and found new applications in vessels and locomotives by using higher pressures. Nikolaus Otto then showed how power could be generated in the internal combustion engine, so continuing a cascade of S-curves that has lasted over 300 years. Overall one can detect sub-cycles of around forty years from when the Industrial Revolution really got under way to the development of railways, then steel and electricity, and finally manufacturing, that lasted until the late 1970s.

The history of technology

If indeed by the year 1500 the techniques were known that made the Industrial Revolution almost inevitable, we can trace a number of sectors up to and beyond that date. Around that time, the most important driving force was probably warfare, which created the demand for materials and weapons. When the Industrial Revolution started the emphasis was still on materials, but soon technology became the motivation for the textile trade, then transport, mining and so on. Energy only later became significant when the distillation of oil made the internal combustion engine possible.

While communication became important around the time of the Armada for controlling ships in battle, semaphore did not come widely into use before the Napoleonic Wars. Data transmission only became significant when controlling naval gunfire in the early years of the twentieth century, but then became rapidly important for business and, in the Second World War, for code-breaking. The following analysis does not include the important sector of pharmaceuticals and medicines that could also be related to the rhythm of warfare.

Materials

The Ancient Egyptians were probably the first to smelt copper alloys for use as weapons, household implements and ornaments. Tin was essential for making bronze and it was only when the supply was blocked by invaders that iron ore, previously regarded as a waste product, was smelted – with some difficulty, for the melting temperature was over 1,500°C and required quite sophisticated bellows. In each case the naturally found ores were in the form of oxides that had to be reduced by the introduction of carbon (usually as charcoal) into the melt.

The next fundamental breakthrough was in 1709, when Abraham Darby smelted iron using coke instead of charcoal, so releasing wood to be used in other sectors of the economy, including construction and shipbuilding. The next advance was thirty-one years later when Benjamin Huntsman first added carbon to pure iron to make steel for implements such as scythes and sickles. Later the process was commercialised by Alfred Krupp of Essen, then later by Bessemer and Siemens.

The late twentieth century saw the rise and then the flattening-out of the S-curve for metals and in their place came oil-based polymers for non-strength applications where shape and colour were at a premium. Copper, gold and silver are still used for their electrical conductivity but in the future we can expect many composites to be developed that have the strength of metals but are also much lighter. This has enabled a 7% weight reduction in the areas where composites have replaced metal in the Airbus A380.

Nanotechnology is a branch of quantum mechanics dealing with atoms or molecules with a width of a millionth of a millimetre – the size of ten hydrogen atoms. At this level materials can be made to have quite different optical, magnetic, thermal or electrical properties to generate new types of substances. At some point it will be possible to programme atoms and molecules to form specific shapes without the process of such things as heating, forming, manipulating or changing in a chemical reaction.

Warfare

Warfare is one of mankind's oldest occupations where the aim was either to batter an opponent with a weapon, or even better, to attack him from afar to reduce the risk of retaliation. The metal weapons first used copper-based alloys then the heavier and more durable iron for battering. The Egyptians used bows and arrows which, even at the Battle of Waterloo in 1815, were still regarded as a more potent and accurate weapon against un-armoured opponents than the musket and had a longer range with a higher rate of fire.

The age of medieval knights was ended by the use of gunpowder-based cannon, and gunpowder held sway until the nineteenth century, when more efficient propellants and high explosives were introduced. The process of battering ships from afar was perfected by the time of the Armada in 1588 but cannon range was only a few hundred yards until the nineteenth century, when Joseph Whitworth introduced rifling which spun a projectile in flight and gave it greater range and accuracy. Some of his first rifled cannons were used at the Battle of Gettysburg in 1862, and in the same war the Spencer carbine was the first repeating rifle.

The true ability to strike from afar was perfected in the twentieth century, when aircraft were used initially for reconnaissance then in aerial combat. Later they became powerful enough to carry bombs and torpedoes to make the Battle of Midway to be the first sea combat with no ship action. The use of technology now allows weapons to be directed with pin-point accuracy from miles away, and in future an increasing number of land and air weapons will be unmanned.

The age of mass combat may now be passing as military planners are now obliged to combat the sort of terrorism described in chapter 1, returning warfare almost to the age of individual combat. This will require a completely different form of personal and material security, with a new generation of sensors and weapons able to identify, then later neutralise, individuals – possibly through stunning.

Transport

The horse and later the chariot were used by Egyptians at least 1,000 years before the birth of Christ, as were boats propelled both by oars and sails. There was little innovation by land until the stage-coach, but by the early fifteenth century fully-rigged ships were making an appearance, having three masts and five or six sails to propel more heavily laden vessels. Initially ocean passages were made by galleys in short stages, but by the 1490s the magnetic compass and methods of mathematical navigation were used by Vasco da Gama, Columbus and Cabot for their trans-ocean voyages. After this there was little innovation before the mid-nineteenth century, when ships became steam-driven.

On land, George Stephenson solved the problem of the steam locomotive in 1829, when the boiler draught was pulled through by steam discharged through a funnel that avoided the use of a chimney. Rails were initially made of cast or wrought iron, before the advent of steel enabled long lengths to be joined. The real breakthrough for the modern day was the invention by Nikolaus Otto of the four-stroke internal combustion engine that powered cars, ships and later aircraft. In due course the principle of the pelton-wheel was used to power steams turbines and then the much more compact gas turbine. The next proactical innovation could be a Shuttle-type scramjet that skips around the stratosphere at speeds unheard of commercially.

Energy

To an extent this is the mirror of transport. First there was oats to feed horses then wood was in widespread demand to smelt iron, in construction, shipbuilding and as a fuel until supply ran low early in the eighteenth century. Coal, which had a higher calorific value and was extracted from surface seams, could not be used for heating houses until chimneys were added to discharge the noxious fumes – the pressure on wood was further relieved when coke was first used to smelt iron in 1709.

Coal's abundance in many countries literally fired the Industrial Revolution until unrefined oil was discovered naturally in Java and Trinidad. However, this was not used as a fuel in the West until Scottish shales were distilled in the middle of the nineteenth century. Oil was drilled in Pennsylvania in 1860 but it was not until 1913 that Standard Oil introduced thermal cracking to break down crude oil through distillation.

Lighting first graduated from oil lamps and candles in 1814, when the National Light and Heat Company heated coal to produce the first gas for London street – and later home – lighting; its use was greatly extended by the gas mantle late in the century. The mantle was immediately threatened for, only a few decades earlier, Michael Faraday had discovered that an electric current flowed when a wire was moved in a magnetic field. The practical development of the dynamo, and the turbine that drove it, became possible late in the nineteenth century. It then required the genius of Thomas Edison to construct a filament glowing within a vacuum for electricity to supersede gas lighting.

With the likely depletion of oil and natural gas in the early decades of the twenty-first century there is a crying need to develop alternative sources of energy. Another even more important issue is the need to counter the water shortages described in chapter 7 by evaporating seawater. One approach would be the development of conventional nuclear power but many countries have frowned on this environmentally despite the cost of $0.05 per million BTUs compared to $6 per million BTUs for oil.

There could, however, be a possible re-birth of coal where global reserves are estimated to be three hundred years and the cost is $1.25 million BTUs. There have been many efforts to exploit this source in power stations but the handling and environmental problems have given way to oil and gas. The new initiative uses the possibility of liquefying coal into a form of oil that can be piped to where it is needed – a solution particularly appealing to China.

One new answer to power generation is the pebble bed modular reactor (PBNR). This needs a bed of high temperature graphite balls – around 70% of which have a proportion of uranium. When critical, the heat is transferred through a gas to a turbine and there is an inherent fail-safe system compared to a conventional reactor for it shuts down automatically when the temperature reaches 1600 degrees Celsius. Other benefits are its relative cheapness, compactness and it only takes 24 months to build.

Another future possibility is cold fusion that uses a controlled form of the energy released by a hydrogen bomb. The possibility was first announced by Messrs Pons and Fleischmann in 1989 but the experiment could not be replicated so that interest declined. The nuclear explosion works on the principle of fusing two atoms of deuterium – the hydrogen part of 'heavy water' – together at a temperature generated by a nuclear blast releasing a huge amount of energy. Research is focussing on providing the necessary merging energy without the need for a huge electrical input.

One totally renewable source of energy is ethanol made from distilling corn (maize), cane sugar, grain or straw. Although Rudolf Diesel showed that his engine could be run off peanut oil in 1900, it took the oil-shock of 1973 to make it economical to run adapted car engines off pure ethanol. Now E10 gasohol is often used in America that is a mixture of 90% gasoline and 10% ethanol. Corn growers in the US now hope that of the 255 million tons harvested, more than 30 million tons will be needed. The rise in popularity of ethanol in Europe and the Americas will depend upon competing demands of energy against food should the climatic shifts considered in chapter 7 become a reality.

The fuel cell idea became a reality with manned space craft that required a reliable source of electricity. It works, like a battery, having an anode that is supplied with a source of hydrogen atoms that generate electrons. Oxygen is supplied to the cathode that attracts the hydrogen to produce water. The electrolyte completes the circuit. There is clearly a danger from an uncontrolled mixture of the two highly reactive gases so that elaborate sensing and pumping is necessary. Apart from its compactness, the real advantage of the fuel cell is its efficiency (up to 60%) compared with a steam turbine or an internal combustion engine with a maximum efficiency of 40%. Although the initial separating of the two gases needs a source of energy, the system is regenerative and may be coupled with solar power to make it self-contained.

Thoughts and numbers

It is believed that pictures representing simple ideas and objects were used some 20,000 years BC in widely separated areas such as Java, Egypt and the Americas. However, it was the Egyptians and Chinese who first used patterns to represent particular things or ideas and it is thought that the former were moving towards symbols representing sounds – something that happened in Syria around 1300 BC. Gradually the Roman alphabet came to be the most flexible form of writing in Western Europe although we have to thank the Egyptians and Chinese for the origins of our modern decimal system. The credit for the base-10 system goes to the Hindu-Arabic mathematicians of the eighth to eleventh centuries AD.

Only hand-written books were available until Johannes Gutenberg invented the printing press, with moveable typeface, in 1448. By 1500, more than 1,000 presses throughout Europe had produced about 10 million copies of 35,000 titles – more than all the books produced since the first written work. And this was only possible after the Arabs had learnt the art of paper-making from the Chinese following the Battle of Talas River in AD 751.

Apart from the abacus, which is still used in the East, the first machine to perform calculations was designed by Charles Babbage in the mid-nineteenth century, but it needed the thermionic valve and electronic storage before the first 'Colossus' computer was designed in the Second World War to break the German Enigma codes. The modern computer became a possibility after the invention of the transistor by Bell Laboratories in 1948 and the integrated circuit in 1959. Together these were more compact, reliable and durable than the thermionic valve. With increasingly sophisticated software, a new technology has emerged called 'evolvable hardware' (EHW), which can seek solutions by trying billions of differing possibilities. We can consider the possibility that these machines will increasingly be able to make ever-more business and life decisions, even to the pitch of making inventions.

Communications

The first messages were thought to have been sent through beating hollow logs, then later primitive drums, to convey meaning – even emotions. The same sort of beacons that signalled the fall of Troy in 1084 BC over 500 miles to Queen Clytemnestra, heralded the Spanish Armada's arrival in the Channel in the sixteenth century. Although the Romans had used a simple form of telegraph, it was not until 1792 that Claude Chappe invented the semaphore system using a shutter array capable of being read over six miles. It was used to link the French ports with Paris during the Napoleonic Wars.

The first electrical telegraphs were available for the Crimean and the American Civil Wars, but speech could not be transmitted until Graham Bell patented the first telephone in 1876. However, the range was limited and long-distance calls were only possible after the invention of the thermionic valve just before the First World War. About the same time, Guglielmo Marconi invented wireless communication that greatly increased the speed of sending messages where there was no direct line using Samuel Morse's code.

Now in the twenty-first century we can look forward to extending the power of the Internet to a complete system of voice and data communication using low-level satellites. This will enable individuals, wherever they may be, to communicate securely with anywhere else in the world without needing to use terrestrial-based systems.

Cycles of technology

There are clearly technology cycles, although the rate of innovation has been uneven. Schumpeter argued that inventions such those of Abraham Darby or Thomas Edison come relatively seldom but they trigger others to generate a completely new cycle. For example, the Darby furnace generated the demand for coking coal which, in turn, created the need for Newcomen's steam pump and associated engineering skills. Likewise the railroad network in the US took off after Henry Bessemer developed cheap steel for making rails; in the rising prosperity this probably triggered the rotary press and the discovery of anaesthetics which occurred at the same time.

The weakness in Schumpeter's theory is that the diesel-electric locomotive, synthetic rubber, colour photography, radar, the gas turbine and so on, were all invented at the depth of the 1930s Great Depression but failed to trigger a recovery – in fact many British innovations (as judged by patent applications) have occurred during recessions. This implies that it is not the innovations themselves but the subsequent development that creates the new economic cycle. Another way to view Schumpeter's work is that many conflicts start at the high or low points in his cycle of around fifty years.

Another theory has been put forward by the veteran economist W.W. Rostow, suggesting that as the timing of agriculture and raw-material innovations was necessarily tied to such determinants as population growth, these went in fits and starts over a cycle of some fifty years. For example, innovations such as McCormick's reaper and binder or nitrogen-based fertilisers were encouraged by high grain prices, but their introduction in turn created a huge excess of capacity and prices then fell until population growth caught up and shortages appeared once again, forcing prices up and creating the next round of innovations.

Rostow has also put forward the idea that the type of investment varies between the Kondratieff up- and down-waves described in chapter 9. Consumer-goods investment and production lead the recovery while money is put into the infrastructure during the decline – so aiding the next recovery. For example, canal building in Britain during the late eighteenth century made possible the first up-wave between the 1790s and 1815. Likewise, the investment in railways during the down-wave that ended in 1848 triggered the recovery during the 1850s and 1860s. The American railroad investment in the 1850s and onwards made possible the huge increase in agriculture in the next up-wave and the rapid movement of men and military supplies during the Civil War.

There was considerable infrastructure investment for imports of refrigerated food from the US and New Zealand to Britain in the late nineteenth century. The first successful refrigerated dock warehouse was set up in London in 1882 and frozen stores made it possible to remove abattoirs from the cities. Food conservation took another step forward when tomatoes were successfully canned in California and New York State, making it possible for retailers to offer a wide range of out-of-season fare. There were similar innovations during the Great Depression in the USA, when refrigerated trains made more efficient food distribution possible and Roosevelt's 'New Deal' greatly increased federal funding for new roads, harbours and hydro-electric programmes.

About innovation

As we have seen, most innovations rely on a relatively small scientific content. For example, it was said that the production of the nuclear reactor for USS Nautilus, the first true submarine that could remain under water for long periods, was 90% technology and 10% science. The physics of operating a pressurised water reactor were known and understood but the real skill was making it work within the confines and safety considerations of a manned submarine. When one is considering the cycles of technology it is wise to remember that there have been few really earth-shaking inventions that owe nothing to the past. James Watt's steam engine was a brilliant adaptation of Newcomen's 'atmospheric mine pumping engine', and the gas turbine owed much to the water wheel and Parson's turbine.

There will surely be similar practical breakthroughs in the future similar to those of Darby, Newcomen, Harrison, Whitney, Edison, Otto, Bell and Marconi – among a host of others. Despite large organisations setting up their own development divisions, Du Pont reports that of the seventy most important inventions in the first part of the twentieth century, over half were produced by individuals. They contributed such innovations as cellophane, bakelite, the ballpoint pen, the cyclotron, the gyro-compass, the jet engine, xerography and so on.

Individual contributions continued in the latter half of the twentieth century and will surely dominate the twenty-first century. In many of the rapidly changing modern markets, innovators such as the founders of Apple Computers and

Microsoft will increasingly flourish – putting to shame any large and powerful organisations that are unwilling or unable to change. Perhaps many large companies will find it more economical to sub-contract developments to individuals or small groups, then license these for commercial exploitation. Alternatively, they may simply acquire much smaller innovative companies. For example, Johnson & Johnson has recently bought Bioscience, a company with sales of just $1 million, at a price of $600 million.

Jacques Ellul

In a remarkable book called *La Technique ou l'Enjeu du Siècle* ("Technique, or the Stakes of the Age"), the French sociologist Jacques Ellul argues that the driving force in the technological society is technique. One does not necessarily have to agree with the writer's conclusions to realise the power of this as an analytical tool.

Ellul believed that technologists would be the new elite corps. For example, a scientist might discover minerals on the seabed in the Red Sea, but this knowledge is useless unless a technologist can find a way to mine the ores. Technique is also about rationality, efficiency and repeatability. And it is a continuing process, which applies not just to machinery but to management procedures, the professions, politics and also to society.

Technique as Ellul uses the word first started with the application of machines to society. Using the examples of Abraham Darby, Bessemer and Siemens, he shows how manufacturing techniques can become standardised and repeatable. This means that all associated problems that might impair their application are solved and confirms that individual preferences are irrelevant. This may be summarised thus:

Technique is a group of movements, which may be manual, procedural or artistic, which are known, are successful and can be repeated. Each technique obeys its own laws, is new and does not depend on the one it supersedes. They may be concerned with mechanical productivity or a surgical procedure whereby each technique defines the process absolutely, whether or not it produces poor social side-effects.

When man becomes subordinate to technique, the only way to retain dignity is working within the confines of his master. There will of course be relics of the non-technical age such as artisans, petty tradesmen, butchers, shopkeepers, domestics and smallholders.

The people who least understand techniques are politicians, for they attempt to impose systems from above rather than adapt and learn from what was there already. Ellul cites revolutionary France: when it discarded established Church teaching methods and tried to invent its own, its system failed. He argues that the English Civil War and the death of Charles I created a 'social plasticity' in England that was not present in France until well after the Revolution. In particular the Puritans, who were later to be the Pilgrim Fathers, had a very practical mind-set that helped them absorb new ideas. The result was that the state had less influence in England than France.

Ellul's ideas clearly benefited the military, where the correct technique could raise citizen armies. It also explains why some states see military dictatorships as the only group able to restore order. Unsurprisingly, F.W. Taylor's ideas meet with Ellul's approval, as do settled commercial techniques such as banking, estate management, accounting, the law and distribution. These concepts are not only confined to business; the same methods are used in local government and other administrations. The list goes on to farming, the arts, medicine, economics and so on.

Ellul's analysis shows why nationalisation cannot work, for it superimposes a system on what has grown either naturally or under the direction of different hands. It explains how tinkering with concerns such as nationalised health services to effect improvements is never likely to work, and warns us against such artificial constructions as the European Union and its common currency.

References

Basalla, G., *Evolution of Technology* (Cambridge University Press, 1988).

Betts, J., Harrison (National Maritime Museum, 1933).

Briggs, A., *Iron Bridge to Crystal Palace* (Thames and Hudson, 1979).

Ellul, J., *Technological Society* (Vintage Books, 1964).

Schumpeter, J., *Business Cycles* (Harvard University Press, 1939).

Van Duijn, J.J., *The Long Wave of Economic Life* (George Allen and Unwin, 1983).

Kurzweil, Ray, *The Singularity is Near* (Viking Books, 2005)

4

What the Information Age Could Mean

Three hundred years ago the Industrial Revolution started in Britain. It changed the lives of most people over some six generations with relatively few disturbances, for it gave individuals time to adapt. We are now faced with another revolution that ideally should take place over several generations but could be much more rapid, for any increase in terrorism will make people reluctant to work in cities and prominent buildings, or be regular users of public transport. This chapter identifies the changes that could propel us into the Information Age over a period of about a decade.

Leading up to the Information Age

Fortunately, we are not attempting anything entirely new for we are part of a continuum trodden by our forefathers – something that would be worth studying before setting out to change our own world. We can look at the 500-year cycle described earlier and also apply what Alvin Toffler calls the 'third wave'.

Toffler holds that the 'first wave' occurred around 8000 BC, about 5,000 years before Abraham settled in the Promised Land and the first Pharaohs united Egypt, when nomadic tribes developed tillage and husbandry, growing several varieties of wild wheat and barley. The area encompassed the 'Fertile Crescent' of the Tigris, Euphrates and the Nile valley, and included the Plain of Jezreel, close to the famous site of Megiddo. Other areas such as California, southern China, South Africa and south-west Australia had a similar climate but the eastern Mediterranean was the first to be developed.

As the glaciers retreated after the last Ice Age, it took 3,000 years for the hunter-gatherers to migrate as far as northern France and Germany; they reached England by 3800 BC and Scandinavia 1,300 years later. By the birth of Christ there were cities, but no great physical innovations to replace the building power of human or animal muscle. Iron and the base metals had been smelted but the source of energy had changed little; water wheels and wind-powered mills were to come much later.

There were, however, considerable advances in society. The Greeks created the first form of democracy and the Romans a durable legal system; they also introduced a means of exchange that enabled trade to be carried out throughout their empire. By the early part of the second millennium, the social classes were well established, with power residing in the great families of kings and nobles, who owned the land and retained serfs to work the soil and provide fighting soldiers. Within these societies, trades such as wood and iron-working, spinning and weaving, leather work and the like, flourished. These skills contributed to the growth of the towns, the tradesmen forming guilds to protect their abilities and thus becoming independent of the great houses. The artisans were not the only people to free themselves from serfdom. The Black Death in 1348-51 destroyed over one-third of the European population, creating a labour shortage which slowly broke down serfdom in England. In the aftermath the craftsmen and merchants became even more prosperous and the power of the towns gradually supplanted that of the nobles.

The second millennium also saw the rise of the nation state. Although there was unity in China, Japan and India before the birth of Christ, England was the first country in Europe to become governed by a king in AD 924. France became an entity only in the 1450s, after the Hundred Years War, and Spain after the unification of Castille and Aragon in 1469. Countries such as Germany and Italy were not unified until the 1870s – well into the Industrial Revolution of the second wave.

The other major player in the first wave was the Roman Catholic Church. Gaining its initial impetus and authority from the Roman Empire, it kept its status through the ultimate power of absolution and levied countries and individuals with subscriptions, obliged rites and required observances, and from time to time demanded support to fight wars such as the Crusades.

Although the technology that made the Industrial Revolution almost inevitable was available by 1500, the second wave did not begin until the early part of the eighteenth century and was then driven by the competing demands of wood for shipbuilding, construction, heating and charcoal (needed for smelting iron ore). These demands in turn relied upon exhaustible deposits of coal, oil and natural gas. It was a time of bustling energy, when the ideas of Adam Smith ruled economic and political life.

Adam Smith (1723-90) explained how the efficiency of specialised labour in a needle factory could be multiplied a thousand-fold if craftsmen gave way to machine operators, who, while performing a single operation, were many times more productive. Size was also essential: only one large steam engine was needed to drive thousands of spindles in a textile plant. Fortunately for the redundant craftsman, his wife and daughter became the breadwinners while he had the time to retrain for the new jobs being created – among them millwrights, who were essential for keeping the transmission systems of mills running.

The new industries initially generated two classes of people: entrepreneurs and workers, the latter leaving the countryside in droves to work in the new factory towns, where, for the first time, they were able to earn a steady income. It was this division that was to stimulate Marx's belief that the only cost was labour and that the workers would overcome owners. Of course in most Western countries it never happened; soon it was no longer possible for the new plants to be managed by their owners, and a new class of managers appeared, specialising in co-ordinating the various functions of procurement, production, sales, development and accounting.

The concept of economies of scale did not just apply to factories; it also extended to such institutions as banking, the Government, education, the Church, the police, the armed forces and many other organs of the nation. After the Second World War, governments encompassed health, employment, social and other services as an all-embracing welfare state in European countries. Politicians loved their increasing power and the more aggressive used it to conquer their neighbours or create empires. After all, it was much more efficient to colonise a large grain-growing area that could supply the homeland than to use people and resources that could be more profitably employed in factories. The colonies also became a market for the excess goods produced by the colonial powers. There was part-industrial colonisation when European and American concerns exploited copper mines in Chile, uranium deposits in the Congo or oil in Arabia.

The pinnacle of industrial size and efficiency was first reached by Henry Ford when he started manufacturing the Model T automobile in 1908 using the techniques of the analytical genius, F.W. Taylor. He codified the principle of labour division by breaking down the Model T's production into 7,882 different operations. So famous did Taylor become that Lenin enthusiastically followed his ideas when he forcibly industrialised the Soviet Union. Taylor's ideas extended to armaments, domestic appliances, radios, trucks and telephones.

Hitler, bored by economics, never believed that the US could out-produce a German-controlled Europe, but they did so spectacularly using Taylor's ideas on labour specialisation. By 1944 the US had produced over 96,000 aircraft; the combined total in Germany and Japan was 68,000. Using the same techniques, the US turned out over 2,200 major war vessels compared to only 400 or so by the Axis powers.

The real drive towards economies of scale occurred after the Second World War. In Britain, well-meaning politicians nationalised industries such as coal, steel, railways, air and road transport, electricity, health and gas in the belief that the greater efficiencies would yield rewards for everyone. The industrial era divided political parties in most developed nations between left and right, representing, respectively, labour or managerial interests, and they too became second-wave phenomena. In international affairs, the League of Nations was set up after the First World War to avoid another conflict. Congress rejected American involvement and the League became defunct in the late 1930s, later to be replaced by the United Nations and other agencies specialising in banking, development, food, health, tariffs and so on.

The first signs that the second-wave edifice was beginning to crack came when the nationalised industries showed large losses and generated a record of poor labour relations – something regarded as impossible when the workers owned the enterprise! However, it was not until the 1980s that serious steps were taken in Britain to de-nationalise the state-owned enterprises and control the labour unions. A further stake was driven through the collectivist heart with the collapse of Communism, and at about the same time the computer emerged as a management tool in its own right, capable of handling automatically a whole range of first accounting, then later administrative, functions.

As the demand for brawn subsided even in heavy industries, many more tasks became available for which women were more adept than men and their talents were particularly needed in the rapidly growing service sector. This not only put at risk the ability of many semi-skilled men to find permanent jobs but threatened the family unit itself, for it meant that both parents felt obliged to work. This resulted in many children feeling neglected and the increase in single-parent families contributed to the rise of truancy and crime. Whereas the first wave encouraged several generations to live together, the industrial age stripped away everything that reduced mobility; elderly people and dependent children could now be cared for by specialist groups, leaving the working couple free to earn as much as they could.

We are now entering a new age where many repetitive industries, employing large numbers of people, are relocating to central Europe or the Far East, where economies of scale are cheaper to achieve. This will leave the West to concentrate on higher-added-value products or services employing many fewer people. As previously stated (and confirmed by the Organisation for Economic Cooperation and Development (OECD)), this will leave only 10% of the working population in manufacturing industry, 2% in agriculture, 3% in government and perhaps 35% in service industries.

The scale of the resettlement could be considerable. The US Bureau of Labor Statistics estimated that by 2005 the biggest employers were health services, then computer-related jobs; next will come child-care workers and teachers. The largest losses will be in telecommunications of all kinds as wired telephones give way to satellite links. One can see how the manufacturing figure of 10% is possible when General Motors now need just over 300,000 people to turn out the same number of cars as 500,000 produced in the 1970s. This is not only due to automation; GM is buying a much larger quantity of completed sub-assemblies.

The transition from the present to the future will need to be guided not by politicians, notorious for looking only through the rear-view mirror, but by individuals or groups adapting to new situations, just as they did in the eighteenth and nineteenth centuries. For the moment it is easier to discern the likely result of the Information Age than assess how it is to be managed.

The Information Age

The future of the corporation is central to the Information Age. The corporation's structure and flexibility drove the Industrial Revolution, but in the Information Age, though corporations will certainly continue, they will exist in a very different form. The US firm Monorail, which sells computers, may be typical. It operates from a rented single floor in Atlanta; its computers are designed by freelance workers; to place orders customers call a free-phone number that passes the order to a contract manufacturer, who assembles and ships the parts specified through Fedex, who in turn collects the payment. Dell do something similar.

Another development is the enterprise that works in real time so that when an order is received, the whole system of order-processing, procurement, shipping and collection is updated immediately through sophisticated software. The response time of such a system, which is that of a small firm, will outflank the hierarchical structure and financial firepower that was central to the making and marketing of steel, for example. It will now have to compete with new composite materials.

How then are the mighty billion-dollar companies reaching maturity likely to manage? Many will survive, of course, but in addition to managing their shareholders and customers, governments have given them increasing social responsibility for the health and safety of their employees, the environment and so on. The changes will be difficult for the top managers, who grew up in these great concerns, to organise, for they did not reach their positions just to unwind their inheritance. Their dilemma will be compounded, for they will also have to handle the other three principal dynamics which are unlikely to give them the luxury of managing gradual changes.

We can identify several probable facets to their decisions, for by definition only the most efficient businesses that have reached the mature phase of the S-curve can survive. The remaining companies will either have to shut down or relocate to a low-cost area to compete – and relocation is clearly not possible with basic industries. However there may be opportunities for technical consultancy or contracts to manage nascent equivalent companies in low-cost areas. Then, part of the delayering consists of sub-contracting particularly repetitive functions to low-cost areas. For example, a typical Western bank can outsource 17 to 24% of its cost base – such as back-office work – to a country like India, so reducing its cost-income ratio by up to 9%. A similar opportunity is open to insurance companies in Britain, where 65,000 jobs could be lost to the increasing numbers of Indians trained to speak in English accents, and to be able to exchange current pleasantries, at a cost saving of up to 60%. To indicate the scale of the opportunity, *The Economist* estimates that, should India's 50 million English speakers be able to earn $20,000 per annum, it would double India's GDP. Already, General Electric has expanded its development into India, employing 600 people, nearly one-third of whom are PhDs. By 2018 Forrester Research estimates that 3.3 million jobs and $136 billion in salaries will have migrated from the US, where in 2004 it was a major election issue.

Those made redundant are unlikely to find the same level of government support as those made jobless from the closing down of Britain's coal fields – once the mainstay of the Industrial Revolution and the claimants of public sympathy. This time the enterprises themselves could well find themselves responsible for providing support.

Other stranded whales are likely to be the large concerns whose products or services have reached the maturity part of the S-curve – what economists call 'commoditising'. This implies that for such a business to succeed it must shed all the trappings of a 'great' company to become the most efficient producer of its kind. It can then seek to use its remaining financial strength to generate another series of S-curves – either through acquisition or by sponsoring budding entrepreneurs. But it is a truism that timing is everything. The British GEC shed its old image – and its financial strength – by acquiring a number of expensive hi-tech communication companies that were unfortunately reaching their own mature part of the S-curve. By the spring of 2002 the company, now called Marconi, was obliged to convert its debt into equity reducing previous shareholders' value to zero.

Undoubtedly many companies are still rising on their S-curve and for them the immediate problem is to grow amidst shortening product life-cycles and increasing competition. They will need all their ingenuity to create a 'flat' organisation and to keep their brand-name shining.

The new entrepreneurs and technologists will also experiment with different corporate structures to provide the flexibility and protection for new ventures. One can visualise entrepreneurs either singly or in groups undertaking a particular contract or venture, then selling their 'vehicle' before starting up another – as in the case of Bioscience mentioned earlier. At the same time, the present institutional shareholders and banks are unlikely to be needed to such a degree, for many of the new ventures will have assets in the form of human ingenuity, not finance.

The board of directors was the right structure in the industrial age to bring in experienced and well-connected individuals to advise and take responsibility for the conduct and solvency of a company. Their ability to perform this role is now being challenged by failures such as the Texan-based Enron. Fast-moving technology also means that it may not be possible to maintain the continuity of a board. Instead we could see the shareholders appointing groups of people to act, not unlike a military staff, as advisors on such subjects as finance, product development, marketing or new technology. The unions, once regarded as co-partners with enterprise to safeguard employees' rights, are likely to weaken, as corporations and the state's services are obliged to unwind.

Similarly, the professions which played a vital support function in the industrial age will now need a different focus. As companies grew larger and litigation became more prevalent they were essential not only to provide an external monitor for the shareholders and creditors but also to keep the board within legal limits. If, in the conditions set out in the fourth dynamic (see chapter 9), there are to be more Enrons the ability of the professional accountants and lawyers will increasingly be questioned. A few large professional firms will still be needed but the new entrepreneurs are more likely to need the services of 'one-stop' advisors, who can give counsel on such matters as raising finance, accounting, real estate or the law. The growth of para-professionals is also likely, given their ability to access ever more available information. This concept could also apply to medicine and education, where growth in home-monitoring and teaching devices would take the load off the professionals.

The great engineering institutions built on the reputations of men such as George Stevenson, Thomas Edison and Michael Faraday, have already adapted to new specialisations but there is likely to be much more cross-fertilisation in the future as multi-disciplinary requirements grow. In addition, there are likely to be fewer jobs for engineers per se in larger organisations, so that membership of a learned institute will probably also require some commercial qualification.

During Toffler's first and second waves the individual has gone through phases of belonging to a family, a tribal group, being either a serf or slave, becoming independent, belonging to a guild, then, in the industrial age, becoming an employee. In the industrial era up to 95% of the population could be employed but the proportion is likely to fall to 75% or less in the early decades of the twenty-first century. Male skills and brawn were most in demand up to the late twentieth century, but with the growth of services, women's skills have become steadily more important and, in the Information Age, could predominate.

If the percentages employed in each sector set out earlier are correct then during the first two decades of the twenty-first century it is inevitable that there will be winners and losers. The winners, constituting up to perhaps 20% of society, will be the entrepreneurs and technocrats whose ability to capitalise on new technology and its applications should make them very wealthy. They will also have highly transportable skills, enabling them to live in whichever cultural, fiscal or climatic environment suits their lifestyle. Through new encryption and communication devices they will also be very largely independent of states. Should the taxation regime become too onerous in one country they could readily move, so depriving politicians of large amounts of revenue – as we have seen, perhaps over 25% of personal tax revenue in the US comes from 1% of the population.

The primary losers will be the executives and bureaucrats who previously had secure and well-paid jobs but, made redundant, will now be obliged to retrain for less rewarding tasks. The other major group will be those – primarily unskilled males – whose expectation of working in a repetitive environment has been destroyed by their former jobs going to lower-cost areas in central Europe or the East, especially China. This rather gloomy outlook has been confirmed by a study conducted by the British Henley Centre for Forecasting and Business Training College. It showed that only 40% of those aged between 16 and 24, and 50% of 25 to 34-year-olds, believed they would earn as much as their parents.

The new earning patterns will have a profound impact on consumer choices. There will clearly be no problem for the winners, who will continue to demand the finest and probably the most exotic products and services. They will continue to patronise the arts, send their children to the best schools and live where they like. They will also probably be obliged to sponsor work-generation measures for those less fortunate than themselves. However, for many people life will become more serious and probably utilitarian as they are obliged to learn new skills and perhaps become self-employed. This will create a demand for businesses, tools and a way of working that could model the old guilds of the seventeenth century. It could also provide an attractive way of living for many people, freed from the need to commute and the risk of being someone else's employee.

One can also anticipate an increased demand for locally based activities and services, including those previously provided by central or local governments. These might include education, health care, security, entertainment and leisure activities. There will also be a demand for locally based tradesmen, and outlets such as bakeries, market gardeners and other food suppliers. There could be experiments in local administration, ranging from the socialistic to the laissez-faire, that would attract different people. There are precedents in the examples of the Israeli Kibbutzim, the North American Amish communities, John Calvin's Geneva or the Puritan groups in New England. Undoubtedly there will be many more experiments.

These changes could provide useful outlets for older people who still want to contribute and earn. They might remember how people helped each other previously in times of hardship, especially in wartime, and it is likely that they will create a demand for converting homes into three-generation dwellings that could also be used as a workplace; indeed, some leading house-builders are already selling 'the electronic home'.

De-layering will accelerate the dispersal from cities that is already taking place in the United States. In the early part of the twenty-first century, it is estimated that people in nearly 60 million households work from home. This is double the number in the early 1990s, and the move into the suburbs and country will only accelerate if terrorists attack, say, public transport in an effort to disrupt the economy. Other countries are likely to follow the US trend.

The rising number of refugees from the industrial era will create a new class of self-employed people that governments would be wise to encourage through simplifying start-up procedures and possibly guaranteeing low-interest loans. The process could also solve another legacy from the industrial era, where both partners in a relationship or marriage feel obliged to go out to work – often leading to a breakdown and a rise in single-parent families. The new family unit would work from home; the active life would help reduce obesity and working together could reduce one-parent families. These new enterprises could also take on apprentices.

Unlike 200 years ago, when the age expectancy was around the forties, demographics will play an important part in the Information Age. If present trends continue, then by 2050 in Germany, those over 65 will represent over 50% of the adult population, implying a reduction of the present working population from 40 to 30 million. Japan has a similar problem – indeed any nation where the birth-rate is 1.3 per woman compared with a sustainable 2.2 will have a diminishing working population. One can see some of the implications of this already, with the aged representing a growing constituency, demanding a higher proportion of social security spending and increased pensions. Most Continental countries have unfunded state pension programmes to honour. For example, Italy has future liabilities representing around 200% of GDP and in the US the equivalent debt would be 100% of GDP. It will not be possible to fulfil pension entitlements in Euroland unless there is general agreement either to print money or raise taxation to crippling levels. Another alternative is to issue such a quantity of debt that the EU's rating is reduced to BBB, that of Egypt, by 2020. None of these conditions is likely to be met.

Thus, individuals will be obliged to continue working well beyond their normal retirement date, probably without the present level of state support from medical, social services and pensions. This will encourage specialist services, for example shopping, retraining, job opportunities and other programmes. And it could prove a golden age for older people, with their knowledge and experience put to the service of business, the community and family. It is a truism that wisdom skips a generation and it is likely that instead of being segregated in separate homes, families will accommodate three generations. As suggested earlier, the demographic shift will also have a powerful impact on immigration policy.

The role of defence is likely to change as the primary threat comes, not from big conflicts involving conventional forces, but from individual terrorists. This will increase the need for small groups supported by air power, but the era of pitched battles is not necessarily over, should there be major conflicts in the Middle East, the Indian Subcontinent or Central Asia. There will also be a prime need for intelligence and superior sensing equipment as the numbers of people needed to monitor and protect the state will increase markedly.

Each generation deserves the politicians it elects. In the early years of the twenty-first century this has meant that instead of telling us the truth, for many their purpose has been to make us feel better about ourselves by bending the facts and avoiding reality. In political terms, this means that we no longer know when we are deceiving others (and ourselves). Moral values also become blurred as the churches lose their authority and politicians blame everyone but themselves for not delivering on campaign pledges. In economic terms we seem to believe that the greatest ever creation of credit by the central banks is justified – to keep the illusion of prosperity going.

As will be apparent from previous analyses, the ability of politicians to fund the social security system is being increasingly eroded. Unlike industrial-age managers, who were obliged to work within the confines of their corporation, the new powerful individuals will have the capacity to migrate to low-cost and congenial areas where the power to tax the rich will be severely curtailed. This would leave the remaining 80% to take up the burden of taxation to pay for their own welfare. Indeed this group could need every tax inducement to keep them solvent.

Another bar to transfer spending will be the need, through international pressure on governments, to provide a congenial business environment for the new corporations, which will want the maximum support and minimum bureaucracy for start-ups. Somehow it is difficult to see most Euroland countries adapting quickly enough to the new circumstances. There are also considerable doubts about the ability of politicians and public servants to deliver. For example, in Japan government support after the Kobe earthquake was meagre and the 1990s found the authorities totally unprepared to relieve the economic slump. The public services in that country, which were once a source of pride and admiration, are now regarded with scorn and despair. In the early twenty-first century, the British electors are becoming aware that their politicians are incapable of running public services efficiently.

Any diminution of a government's ability to maintain social security spending would create terrible disillusionment in the West and lead to a reaction not dissimilar to the early 1930s, when political parties divided to the left and right to the exclusion of the centre. Many countries in Continental Europe turned towards totalitarianism, nationalism and religious bigotry.

There are parallels to the present position from nearly 500 years ago, when the Roman Church was challenged by an Augustinian monk who had access to the printing press – the communication network of the age. The Church, which had done so much to foster learning and artistic creativity in the Dark Ages and during the medieval period, began to rot from within, generating the sort of disdain, distrust, and cynicism created by the present generation of politicians. Half a millennium ago the Church adopted ever more insidious fund-raising ruses that have a familiar ring today. It had a monopoly on certain legal areas such as registering marriages and probate, titling land, and regulating terms and conditions of commerce. For example, it was forbidden to conduct any business on the same weekday as the anniversary of the Slaughter of the Innocents, 28 December, had fallen in the previous year.

Nowadays, new regulations in the EU restrict the creation of enterprises, and employment rules make it costly to hire people. In addition, the Church levied regular tithes from congregations and hit upon the marketing idea of selling indulgences, which enabled the buyer to remit graduated periods in purgatory. So successful was this that a beneficial remission could even be bought for deceased relations. Now, politicians extract taxes from individuals that often oblige them to work up to half their time for the state. It was this flagrant misuse of the Scriptures that prompted the professor of theology Martin Luther to nail his ninety-five theses to the Castle Church door at Wittenburg.

Like the Roman Church at the end of the sixteenth century, the social security state has exhausted its possibilities and left many countries potentially bankrupt. These countries have built up huge debts to finance their social spending and have created liabilities for future pensions that they are not capable of delivering. This not only obliges them to increase taxation to keep from running up even bigger deficits but also makes them extremely vulnerable in the event of an economic downturn. Politicians will not be thanked for their present passion to regulate everything, just as 500 years ago the Roman Church attempted to order the lives of the faithful.

Luther's remedy was to return to the truth of the Scriptures and to establish a new Church. On this basis he downsized the bureaucracy, almost eliminated the impositions of the Church on people's lives, reduced wasteful feast days to a minimum, permitted money lending and disbanded the monasteries and convents. The result was an immediate increase in working productivity and a release from petty rules and regulations, which greatly helped commerce. He also increased the power of the individual through the doctrine of 'every man a priest', which made the clergy much more accessible and responsive to the needs of the laity. It is no accident that Henry VIII's Act of Supremacy in 1533, which severed links with

Rome, had the stimulating effect on the English economy that could later be seen in the Elizabethan age, when the Protestant Church was finally established.

If we apply an equivalent revolution to our current situation, two significant patterns could emerge. The first is a move to a kind of hi-tech first-wave structure, with regions becoming more self-sufficient and entrepreneurial, perhaps on the model of the Swiss cantons. Politicians will not be a separate class but become part-time, also on Swiss lines. In addition, the cost of government would fall drastically as the present social security system is privatised. At the same time corporations will become smaller, more responsive and probably form some sort of focus for the community – as did the guilds in the first wave. Within this, individuals will be working either singly or in groups using modern communications to provide a global reach, and will be more self-reliant.

The second pattern, which hardly bears thinking about, is some form of totalitarianism brought about by the speed with which the Information Age might take effect, leaving millions without jobs. One can discern potential powerful movements in Continental Europe to raise tariff barriers, stop migration and impose discipline in an effort to protect jobs – not unlike the forms of Fascism that mutated in the 1930s. Whether this would be successful is doubtful because the power of communications would create a clamour for freedom.

It is difficult to see the West being displaced as innovators in the new technological age, although repetitive manufacturing will migrate. The early advances will be made by the English-speaking peoples, who have displayed the greatest flexibility in the past, to be followed by nations, like France, Germany and Japan, that have a more centralised state and proven records as consolidators of techniques.

Whether China or India will become the second most powerful Eastern nation is a difficult question. At face value the former will become the most dominant, but India has many advantages through its constitution and rule of law. English is widely spoken and the Subcontinent is already being used by the West as a skilled resource.

In an age when manufacturing is less important than information, and communication is instantaneous, alliances may also change from geographical to cultural. For example, there might be a grouping of nations for whom English is the first language, and who also happen to be the greatest innovators. Another union could be between France and Germany, or between the old Austro-Hungarian countries, and there are other possible alliances that could be determined by climate, described under the third dynamic (see chapter 7). Equally, countries that have only been united relatively recently, such as Italy and Germany, could become divided.

References

Davidson, J., and W. Rees-Mogg, *The Sovereign Individual* (Macmillan, 1997).

Drucker, P., *The Next Society* (*The Economist*, 3 November 2001).

McRae, H., *The World in 2020* (HarperCollins, 1994).

Peters, G., *Beyond the Next Wave* (Pitman Publishing, 1996).

Schwartz, P., *The Art of the Long View* (Doubleday, 1991).

Sparrow, O., *Unsettled Times* (Royal Institute of International Affairs, 1996).

Toffler, A., *The Third Wave* (Pan, 1981).

White, M., *The Cybernetic Age*, unpublished paper (August 1996).

5

The End of Politics

'It is the highest impertinence and presumption, therefore, in kings and
ministers, to pretend to watch over the economy of private people, and to
restrain their expense, either by sumptuary laws, or by prohibiting the
importation of foreign luxuries. They are themselves always, and without
exception, the greatest spendthrifts in the society. Let them look well after
their own expense and they may safely trust private people with theirs. If
their own extravagance does not ruin the state, that of their subjects never
will.'

Adam Smith, *The Wealth of Nations*

Each of the principal dynamics is a major force that has a huge influence on human
society. When they coincide in the early years of the twenty-first century, their
combined impact will have implications that are hard to assess unless we
understand both the cycles and their influence on history.

One of the greatest changes we are likely to see is in political structures. By the end
of the twentieth century they were showing the same degree of Byzantine
complexity, centralisation, corruption and venality that was present in the Roman
Church 500 years ago or the Jewish priestly class at the time of Christ. As we have
seen, in the sixteenth century the Church was confronted by Martin Luther, who
challenged the Church's authority and returned power to the individual. Now, the
four dynamics are likely to challenge the same forces and this chapter argues that
there would be huge benefits to the individual by emulating the work of Luther.
While the terrible events of 11 September were not directly associated with the
transformation, they are likely to accelerate changes that were already under way.

The Ming Dynasty eventually fell when, in 1664, starving crowds led by the rebel
Li Tzu-chan'g, overran Beijing and drove out the corrupt civil servants and palace
eunuchs who had plundered the country. The ability of the authorities to protect us
and our savings has changed little since those days. Since the Second World War
the US dollar, the currency of the most powerful nation in the world, has lost 90%
of its value. In addition many Western states run enterprises – often not very well
– as diverse as railways, health services, road programmes, the armed forces,
education, pensions, unemployment insurance, air traffic control, prisons, the
judiciary, the mail, industrial subsidiaries and the like. Each requires a bureaucracy,
paid for by individual taxpayers, which spends more than 40% of national income.

When they have overspent, politicians and central bankers have resorted to borrowing – not in penny packets, but in high proportions of GDP and far in excess of what would be prudent for an individual or enterprise. For example, there are several nations (e.g., Canada, Italy, Sweden, Japan and Belgium) that have borrowed well over 90% of their annual national income.

Before 1914 it was deemed that everything belonged to individuals, with the state taking enough to pay for defence and to maintain law and order. Now politicians have become so arrogant that they talk about tax loopholes as if the government graciously allows individuals to retain a proportion of their income. In the European Union some bureaucratic functions are being farmed out to inspectorates that enforce European directives, charging business-scale fees which the luckless 'clients' have no option but to pay. Like the Roman Empire and the Ming Dynasty before them, politicians and their ministers meet at expensive conferences and make fine declarations but achieve little for the people they are supposed to serve.

There is no good reason why politics, like technology, economics, disease and climate, should not conform to cyclical rhythms. History is full of instances where lawlessness, incompetence, venality or other sins were replaced by equally long periods of benign, competent and frugal government that induced peaceful behaviour and showed rectitude in public affairs. For example, at the end of the 1970s who would have dreamed that in ten years, the power of the unions in Britain would be quelled, the economy placed on a sound footing and the end of the Cold War symbolised by the collapse of the Berlin Wall?

The biblical Jews understood these cycles and legislated for them. At the end of every half-century, strains on the economy were excised by the chief rabbis calling a jubilee. Leviticus 25 tells us that debts to fellow Israelites were to be forgiven, land that had been bought should be offered back to the original owners and any Jew sold as a slave could return to their families. Would that we had the same legal methods of encouraging people neither to lend nor borrow excessively!

A similar cycle worked well in the nineteenth and twentieth centuries, when three readily identifiable rhythms of around fifty years can be identified that had a remarkable influence on political perceptions of the time. Now, in the early years of the twenty-first century, we can learn how politicians are likely to behave on both sides of the Atlantic for there have been remarkable points of convergence.

The long-wave cycle – described in more detail in chapter 9

The long-wave cycle is the maker and destroyer of politicians and has probably had the greatest influence on the politics of the US and Britain over the three complete cycles that began in around 1793. There are generally three phases: an up-wave expansion, a mid-point and a down-wave, when all the pent-up excesses are dispelled. The first cycle, 'K1', ended around 1848 with a deep recession, the next, K2, reached a low point in about 1897 with another slump. The last full cycle, K3, incorporated the Great Depression and only ended after the Second World War.

Each phase has its own political impact. The expansion phase is a good time to be in power, for almost anything is better than the dreariness of the previous depression and politicians can take chances. During the first up-wave, Thomas Jefferson made the Louisiana Purchase for America, and Britain, after shaking off the effect of the American Revolution, started a new colonial empire after the victory of Waterloo. In later up-waves, America opened up the West after the Mexican War and subsequently Theodore Roosevelt's 'Roughriders' captured San Juan Hill in Cuba during the Spanish-American War. The up-wave might have been made for the president: he completed the Panama Canal, built a modern navy and initiated an era typified by Henry Ford's Model-T and the age of mass-production.

In the expansion phase that followed the Second World War, politicians developed the role of government through a social security programme, financed by economic growth, in an effort to protect people from another slump. This period ended in 1976-80, when rising interest rates and commodity prices caused an economic crisis that ended in a short recession, jolting those who believed that growth could continue for ever. Something similar happened in the other two completed cycles, and in each case it was not a good time for a liberal or socialist to be in power, for not only did they have to deal with a crisis but were obliged to be unpopular when cutting back public expenditure.

The mid-cycle recession has quite often been accompanied by wars, for example the American Civil War and the First World War, which stimulate great leaders such as Abraham Lincoln and David Lloyd George, and later Ronald Reagan and Margaret Thatcher, who were instrumental in ending the Cold War. During the 1920s conservative politicians were in power in America and for most of the decade in Britain. Similarly, during the 1980s conservative politicians were in power on both sides of the Atlantic, but in the 1990s this changed. A prolonged boom, fuelled by rising debt, encouraged the electorate to vote into office more liberal politicians in the belief that the good times would continue for ever.

The last and final stage is a period of contraction that takes up less than a third of the cycle but it is exceedingly uncomfortable – particularly for politicians who have assured voters of their commitment to public services. Unlike the expected Jewish jubilee, few now believe that the expansion will – and probably should – go into reverse and are always taken by surprise. This is a time when previous financial excesses and accumulated debt are unwound, which is most uncomfortable for those who have over-borrowed. As economic activity declines unemployment rises, many people have to adopt a lower standard of living and a considerable number have no regular employment. As Japanese politicians during the 1990s and into the twenty-first century have discovered, there is little to be done during a period of deflation except attempt to provide an environment in which entrepreneurs can thrive. All the panache and supposed omnipotence of politicians and public servants built up in the earlier part of the cycle turns to impotent dust.

Clearly this is not a good time to be in power, for much of past government spending needs to be severely trimmed and austerity reigns for the majority of people. The 1930s down-wave destroyed the political career of Herbert Hoover in the US and the Republicans were then out of office until 1952. In the UK the Labour Party failed to agree on action to counter the depression and was out of office from 1931 to 1945.

At the low point of K1, in 1848, there were revolutions in Germany, Austria and France that forced many countries into increased nationalism. In the 1930s most Continental European countries moved decisively to the political right, while the centre parties were squeezed out. Then it was fear of unemployment and Communism; now there is a rising belief that liberal politicians have little understanding of the immigrant threat, as shown in the spring of 2002 when parties of the right gained just under 20% of the vote in both France and Holland.

And this is without a recession. Any recurrence of the 1930s would find highly indebted governments unable to afford recovery programmes because of the previous build-up of debt and the high level of taxation. Rising levels of unemployment and uncertainty would foster even more political unrest, moving the political spectrum considerably further to the nationalist right. It should be recalled that under the system of proportional representation Hitler's National Socialist Party gained power with just over 30% of the vote.

Patterns in political cycles

We can now look back to see whether there are themes that occur regularly in the US and UK, and which could spread to many other nations in the increased globalisation of ideas.

The long wave generates a range of changing ideas: expansions are clearly inflationary and driven by optimism, while down-waves (on their own) are deflationary. This has been true for each rhythm, although the latest cycle could prove more difficult to predict as it coincides with three other dynamics. Liberal reforms, including a greater degree of government involvement, are introduced during an up-wave expansion, but it becomes increasingly obvious that state spending can no longer be afforded in the down-wave. For example, environmental, minority, health and safety legislation, and EU rules enacted during the up-wave will become a costly encumbrance in the down-wave and are likely to be severely trimmed. This then becomes a major problem. The electorate, expecting protection from, say, unemployment that can no longer be afforded, become disillusioned and resentful of politicians and civil servants – the very issues Bobbitt raises, see chapter 2.

Similarly, international co-operation is encouraged enthusiastically during the up-wave but is likely to suffer during the down-wave in a tide of rising nationalism and protection. The League of Nations came apart during the 1930s but the more grandiose United Nations considerably expanded in the up-wave of K4; there are some signs that the UN may not survive the early decades of the twenty-first century.

Barriers and regulations are swept aside in the expansion phase while large organisations expand to meet rising consumer demand. Conversely, many large organisations will break up when demand falls giving individuals the chance to buy their own businesses. In a curious paradox politicians can do even more damage to business in a down-wave by applying well-meaning regulations that stifle business. In the 1930s President Roosevelt introduced the New Economic Plan (NEP) a semi-Fascist measure to control the US economy; fortunately for the US, it was ruled unconstitutional by the Supreme Court. Latterly, politicians like Lionel Jospin – the former premier of France – have called for even more regulations to help 'integrate' the EU.

The latest cycle has shown that corporatist states such as Germany and Japan are most successful during the expansion phase but both are already faltering during the contraction phase. One can expect that the more individualistic nations, such as the US, Britain and Italy, will be relatively more successful in the down-wave.

One can expect tariffs to be lowered and free trade to rule in an up-wave, but tariffs to be raised in the down-wave. The farming lobby in the US called for the Hawley Smoot Act in 1930 to protect commodity prices, which triggered Commonwealth Preference at the Ottawa Conference in 1932. During the early years of the twenty-first century the US was applying tariffs on imported steel and one could anticipate increasing strains within unions such as NAFTA, the EU, the Russian Federation and possibly even the USA. Others groups could follow – particularly relatively recently united countries such as Italy and Germany.

Unfortunately measures and ministries that were introduced during times of crisis often linger when they are no longer required. President Carter created the Department of Energy in the 1970s oil crisis, but it was still in action when crude oil dropped to $10 a barrel. We never seem to learn. Japan's increase in state borrowing and budget deficits during the 1990s, in an effort to reverse deflation, has left the country no better off and made it even more vulnerable should a down-wave become global.

Most electors, being non-savers, vote for moderate inflation to keep them in employment. Conversely, when the mood of the electorate is more likely to favour the right, it will be easier to sell ideas and a policy of low inflation to protect the value of savings.

These are not the only political cycles. There is evidence that other forces may be operating as well. For example, the writer Ralph Waldo Emerson believed that political parties alternate between consolidation and innovation. He said, 'we are reformers spring and summer, in autumn and winter we stand by the old.' (His divisions are not necessarily between the Republican and Democratic stereotypes; several Republicans such as Theodore Roosevelt and Ronald Reagan were reformers.) The historian Henry Adams described the pattern as like the beat of a twelve-year pendulum, swinging between centralisation and diffusion of national power, the basis of the original dispute between Hamilton and Jefferson in the early stages of the union. President Woodrow Wilson commented that each generation can only raise its sights above material things once, before reverting to an easy life. This is why the radicals are in power for only a third of the time. Wilson's remark was borne out by his successors Warren Harding and Calvin Coolidge – both archetype conservatives. Finally, the philosopher Arthur Schlessinger Jnr observed that consumer goods investment had priority during the up-wave while the infrastructure took precedence in the down-wave. This is exactly the story of Japan since the Second World War, but unfortunately infrastructure investment has been not only ineffective but also wasted.

The current political cycles

The earlier analysis suggests that people on both sides of the Atlantic could want more big government in the early twenty-first century because of the terrorist threat and the migration of jobs to low-cost regions like China. If this coincides with the K4 down-wave, then highly indebted states could not increase spending without printing money – as the Weimar Republic did in the early 1920s. A counter to this is the demand for much more direct consultation between governments and the people on matters affecting voters' lives.

So there could be at least two forces at work: a movement towards the centre and a centrifugal drift towards local communities. The real political danger perhaps could perhaps come from the roughly 40% of the working population who, with the advent of the Information Age, will have little regular work and will expect to be supported by the state. However, as we have seen, a government's ability to raise more revenue will be severely limited; not only will raising taxes above a certain level be unacceptable, but politicians' ability to raise debt at low coupon rates will be severely curtailed by investors' fear of default or a currency collapse.

How will the status quo change?

There have been few recorded examples of a ruling system giving up its power voluntarily; it may be forced to relinquish the reins through enfeeblement or violence but seldom by choice. The same is true of other institutions such as the Church, which has only ever been reformed by outside pressure. When theorists encourage those in power to change by giving up their authority voluntarily, they are actually expecting a form of political hara-kiri.

Ironically, the modern state may have inadvertently sown the seeds of its own downfall through its spending excesses – not unlike an alcoholic who needs even more liquor to achieve oblivion. When politicians feel they can no longer raise taxes they have to increase borrowing to make up the spending shortfall. As Professor Bremner of Canada's McGill University recalls: 'The difference between Baring's inability to control Nick Leeson and the Canadian government is that in Baring's case, the bank's mismanagement forced the firm to default. In government there is no such responsibility: politicians can impose taxes to cover losses, print money when they can raise no further debt and wipe out their obligations by allowing their currencies to collapse.' He goes on to report on a survey which stated that unless Canadians were able to take control of their own affairs, many would migrate to a more benign tax regime.

Perhaps the state will, like the Church, be forced to change from outside. If a modern country like Argentina has borrowed so much that it must default on its debts, then no institutions will buy its bonds; if treasuries can no longer sell their debt they can either print money or reduce their own spending. Despite protestations about 'keeping a lid on inflation', most politicians would rather inflate than fail at the ballot box through unpopularity, hence the preferred alternative would be to 'keep the game going'. Eventually the government would be forced into painful retrenchment – having wrecked the nation's savings.

A collapse in public spending would devastate the welfare state in most Western countries, leaving millions who rely on the government with no support. If most counties were forced into a spending cutback, it would torpedo the European Union's drive for federalism, with its huge agricultural support and petty harmonising regulations – leaving nothing, except possibly a free-trade area. It would be difficult also to continue other international treaties, such as the World Trade Organisation and the North American Free Trade Area, as each country would erect barriers in an attempt to arrest the rapid rise of unemployment. And the cutbacks would almost certainly reduce the United Nations and associated agencies such as the World Bank, the International Monetary Fund, the Food and Agricultural Organisation and so on.

Could a war on terrorism have a destabilising effect? Possibly, for it tends to divide political parties between those on the left, who worry about civilian casualties, and those on the right, who become more determined to proceed to a successful conclusion. Something not dissimilar happened in August 1931 when the British Labour government of Ramsay MacDonald was split over the decision to cut public spending in the face of a mounting budget deficit. Unable to make a choice, the Prime Minister and a few others joined the Conservatives to form a coalition government which handsomely won the next election. The political dilemma can only be resolved by going back to first principles – as did Martin Luther about 500 years ago.

Returning to fundamentals

In Western countries, education is accepted as a state responsibility on the grounds that future economic growth is dependent upon the skills of the people although until the 1870 Education Act, these ideas did not mesh with the English tradition. This holds that the government should restrict itself to essential matters such as defence, the rights of property, the rule of law and a stable currency. Unfortunately, what seemed to be a good principle has fallen foul of bureaucracy. In his book *What Comes Next*, political thinker James Pinkerton coined the phrase 'the Bureaucratic Operating System' (BOS) – an assumption by bureaucrats that they can manage all affairs better than the private sector. This arrogance was believed by many politicians after the Second World War, but it did not stop unemployment rising, nationalised industries becoming economic stranded whales and state education systems costing more and delivering less. Pinkerton calculates that each function disentangled from state control, including education, costs 25 to 30% less for the same quality of service, which means that if this happened across the board, the state could unwind at least a quarter of its costs in the event of the economy slowing down.

One of the first to introduce general state education was Friedrich Wilhelm III of Prussia who, early in the nineteenth century, decreed that all children should attend schools where available. In a flash of inspiration the king appointed the explorer Friedrich von Humboldt to direct the course of education. One of his first acts was to require the secondary-education gymnasium school-teachers to extend the curriculum by including the humanities, mathematics and sciences. The modern programmes were given a considerable boost when Kaiser Wilhelm declared that the 'duty of the state is to teach children to become young Germans, not Greeks or Romans'.

Unlike Britain and France, where the focus for scientific work was the learned societies, Humboldt decreed that this work should be undertaken by the universities, where professors taught while conducting research. By the third quarter of the nineteenth century students were flocking to Germany to sit at the feet of the sages. Although this led to some fragmentation it encouraged experimentation – one of the key ingredients of innovation – and the ideas spread around the academic world. The tragedy for any organisation is that once they enter the BOS, experimentation virtually ceases – just as Jacques Ellul predicted.

In the tradition of English empiricism, primary schooling was started either by the churches or benevolent institutions. For those who could afford it the fees were ten shillings a year; for the remainder it was free. Most unfortunately, Mr Gladstone's Liberal administration, believing that the Anglican Church was the 'Tory party at prayer', introduced the Elementary Education Act of 1870. Initially unpopular because of poor teaching, the schools were placed under local authority control and made free of charge, to be financed by a flat-rate tax. Unwilling to pay the rates as well as the church school fees, parents moved their children to the state schools, so forcing most of the 11,620 private establishments to become nationalised. Fortunately the Act did not eliminate the traditional private agencies, the fee-paying grammar and public schools. The ethic of the private sector was led by outstanding men such as the Reverend Thomas Arnold, who, after being appointed headmaster of Rugby School in 1828, is credited with changing the face of education in England. He instilled a spirit of moral responsibility and intellectual integrity grounded in Christian ethics, a basis that was to have an enduring influence on private schools in the English-speaking world. In due course his principles were also applied to grammar schools.

Initially in the United States, elementary schools were run by parishes or through philanthropy, and absorbed local traditions such as a strong Puritan ethic in New England. Later, the Articles of Confederation laid down that in every prospective township there should be a plot of land reserved for education, and since then some twelve million acres have been allocated. One of the first universities was founded in Charlottesville by Thomas Jefferson, who held that democracy can be effective only in the hands of an enlightened people. It was the most up-to-date secular institution of its sort in America and was the model for later state universities. As the nation expanded, alongside the growth of each township was the common school – free to all and provided by the state. This was the forerunner of the present-day American public school.

Education in America

Socialised education has not developed well for much of the USA; in the late 1990s an average of 30% of pupils were dropping out of high school – nearer 60% in urban areas. Twenty-seven million Americans over the age of seventeen were illiterate and another forty-five million were barely competent. One study showed that illiteracy was costing the US nearly $230 billion a year – almost 3% of GDP. Where learning is discounted, schools have become centres of violence and drug-taking, with an estimated 15% of students carrying weapons. As a result, 29% of all children are sent to private schools – the teachers in the state establishments leading the pack – because of parents' concerns that religious or moral subjects are being neglected. A growing number of children are also being taught at home: in 1998 an estimated 1.2 million – or 2% of the student population – were being taught in this way and the number is growing at around 15% a year. These ideas are being carried through to college level, where 5,000 students at a Virginia university are taking their courses through distance-learning – the material being transmitted to a number of community colleges.

In 1999, nearly $530 billion was being spent on private and public education but on present trends the state system is bound to decline. James Pinkerton reports that out of 4.6 million people employed in state schools, only about half were teachers. At some point tax-payers will become restless paying for an incompetent, declining and expensive system which fails to deliver results. The same is likely to be true of other state-run organisations. Why not, he suggests, turn the running of the schools over to the teachers, just as the Tory government were doing in the mid-1990s. With the consent of parents, schools would then be run for the community and it would surely be possible to make savings of at least a quarter so that better teachers could be recruited and more be spent on books and equipment. Ways could then be found to cut the costs of administration further and reduce taxes. A refinement of this would be the use of vouchers. After a long period of gestation, the city of Cleveland, Ohio, petitioned the Supreme Court to introduce a voucher system, which is particularly supported by poorer parents who are condemned to send their children to bad schools. The idea is that every parent receives a grant to pay for basic schooling with the option of paying more out of their own pockets.

61

Pinkerton suggests how the economics might work for America and Britain: assuming an average school of 1,000 pupils in the US spends $6,000 per student, which gives it a revenue of $6 million; with a pupil-to-teacher ratio of 17:1 this means nearly 60 teachers. If the average salary cost for teachers is $42,000 then the total cost is $2.5 million, leaving $3.5 million for overheads *and* bureaucratic supervision. Surely, he argues, much of this could spent for the greater benefit of both teachers and students.

The removal of bureaucratic control from the education system would revitalise the experimentation that was the mainspring for the German revival in the early nineteenth century and is still present in private schools. One can visualise how this could develop. By making teachers educational entrepreneurs, the profession could expand into areas such as adult education, develop specialisations to attract pupils from other areas and become centres of literacy.

Seeking the right model

If Toffler is correct in identifying the trends of civilisation, then the dynamic of the third wave will mean that the centralised governments that grew out of the Industrial Revolution will have to be replaced. Given the long wave described earlier, just devolving the same amount of government spending to regional authorities will not be possible for the revenue will not be available. It is the time not to nibble at the margins but to go back in history and rethink the whole role of government.

If the history of education described above is to be a yardstick, then one might apply the same ideas to other government functions such as unemployment benefit, health and social security and care for the aged. For example, local security and work-creation programmes described under the fourth dynamic could well provide not only employment but also care within the community – something that was implicit in the first kibbutz in 1910 (long before the creation of the State of Israel in 1948). These collective agricultural or industrial settlements held all wealth in common and profits were reinvested in the settlement after members had been provided with food, clothing, shelter and with social, educational and medical services. Members were elected to set business and internal policy then administer the group and consult others weekly.

The kibbutz is one model but there are many others and it is quite possible that voluntary organisations such as the Salvation Army, together with more local groups, could look after some of those previously provided for by the central state. This could be organised through a type of Conservation Corps network paid for through local bartering groups. Like the education example, it could be achieved at a fraction of the cost of state-run organisations, with their associated central and local bureaucracies.

Another example that might be followed is the principle of the Swiss cantonal devolution leaving the Federation spending only 18% of GDP. Altogether public spending is 38% compared to well over 45% for most continental European countries. The central state has little borrowings but not even the prudent Swiss have lived within their budget since the early 1990s because the growth rate has been much below the USA and even below the EU average. This has caused them to drop behind in GDP per head coming fourth after Norway, the US and others. Swiss unemployment is a fraction of most European countries at 4%.

A role model for the third wave

The Swiss Federation has an enviable record of stability and efficiency, and a high level of decentralisation implicit in its history and constitution. Unlike the US today, they have implemented the spirit of the Tenth Amendment ('The powers not delegated to the United States by the Constitution, nor prohibited by it to the States, are reserved to the States respectively, or to the people'). This means they retain a high degree of local authority and devolve only necessary powers to the federal government. In contrast, the EU only pays lip-service to decentralisation.

The present republic goes back to 1291, when the 'forest cantons' of Schwyz, Uri and Lower Unterwalden formed a league in defence of their liberties against their Habsburg overlords and successfully broke away in 1389. The entry of Lucerne, Zurich and Berne, amongst others, brought the number of cantons to eight by 1353, just when the Black Death was ending. Switzerland's neutrality was guaranteed after the Treaty of Vienna in 1815, when Geneva and other territories joined. There are now twenty-six sovereign cantons (subject only to federal laws) which compete to make themselves attractive to business by keeping taxes low; they do not charge capital gains tax, and estate duty is 10% in most of them. The Swiss are some of the highest savers, encouraged by a stable, virtually gold-backed, currency.

In an enviable method of consulting the people, the Swiss have the right to a referendum dating from 1874. Under this rule, 100,000 citizens can submit a written proposal to add to or change the constitution. The initiative is then discussed by the Berne Assembly, who may accept, reject or modify the request before it is put to a referendum. Likewise, a group of 50,000 citizens can challenge laws and treaties that have been on the statute books for more than fifteen years. This means that 1.5% of the Swiss population (6.8 million in 1992) can demand that the Assembly debate their requests; the equivalent number of electors in Britain would be about 900,000 and in the US just under 4 million. Unsurprisingly the Swiss saw Brussels' bureaucracy and the European Assembly as flawed and voted against joining the EU by a large majority.

The basic economic and political units are the 3,000 or so Swiss communities, not unlike the New England townships of the 1830s. Their rights and responsibilities differ, but the local units tax their residents through the community town or district councils; in addition they look after such matters as schools, local traffic, refuse collection and sport. Above them, each canton has an elected assembly and an executive of between six and nine people. Their size varies: for example Zurich was the only canton with over 1 million people in 1999 and there are eight, such as Jura, with below 70,000.

The powers delegated to central government are controlled by the Federal Assembly of two houses: the 'lower' house is the Federal Council, which runs the government and the federal judges. Members are elected every four years, and the Council meets for several weeks, four times a year. Unlike most other countries, members are not professional politicians and receive only expenses. The upper house is the Council of States, which, like the US Senate, has two members from each canton. The seven-member Federal Council is elected from the Assembly for a four-year period, with one of the seven elected annually as president. It is hardly surprising that few Swiss know the names of their federal representatives – let alone their president.

The cantons provide free primary schooling, for which attendance is compulsory, plus fee-paying higher education. After leaving secondary school pupils go on to qualify either at vocational or academic establishments. There are only two federal universities, at Zurich and Lucerne, the others being shared by cantons with a common language or faith. These are obliged to conform to national standards but are otherwise autonomous; they decide the types of school, the length of term, teachers' salaries and the like. Social security is based on a principle of a minimum wage that continues through to old age. These services are funded through various pension and insurance schemes, paid for by the individual, employers and, to a lesser extent, cantons and the federal government; there is strong opposition from the elected centre-right majority to a full-blown welfare state, which could dangerously inflate the federal deficit that has been growing since 1972.

The Swiss run a remarkable citizens' army, whereby all fit males are required to attend a seventeen-week basic course at the age of twenty. This is augmented by eight refresher courses up to the age of twenty six. After completing military service some men transfer to the civil defence corps. As an object lesson for other states terrified of citizens owning weapons, the men eligible for active service keep their equipment, weapons and ammunition at home. They are also required to maintain a certain proficiency at regular compulsory target-practice sessions, and have their kit inspected.

The various systems described would fit in well with the ideas expressed by the veteran management guru Peter Drucker in his book *The Post-Capitalist Society*. Here he urges 'the abandonment of the things that do not work'. In Toffler's third-wave terms this means dumping the second-wave ideas of political management of health, education and welfare services. It could also include the failure to relieve poverty through social engineering, redistribution of income and political management of pork-barrel political initiatives. Governments have also failed to maintain the value of people's savings and increasingly to keep up law and order. These moves would also be in line with Adam Smith's famous quotation at the start of this chapter, where he states that individuals are far more capable of managing their affairs than any politician is.

Drucker believes that the state should then concentrate on 'the things it does well', which could perhaps include the armed services in most Western states – probably the only segment of the modern state that has not fallen into disrepute. Perhaps with fewer other distractions governments might be more capable of managing currency and providing security.

Another view

Alexis de Tocqueville was a French aristocrat who, in the early nineteenth century and in despair over the excessive centralism of post-revolution Jacobin France, sought to rediscover individual rights by researching early-nineteenth-century America. Like present-day conservatives in the West, he was appalled by the growing power of the state and wanted to create a more compact and less costly method of government – a return to days when people took responsibility for their own affairs. The Frenchman noted that France had a degree of local autonomy before the guillotine eliminated many of the nobility to be replaced by bureaucrats. The Jacobins, the revolutionary leaders and later Napoleon, followed Jean-Jacques Rousseau, who held that the happiness of the individual was inferior to the wants of the majority. Rousseau stated that it was the duty of the French state to create a set of rules for its citizens. These rules challenged private ownership of property and reserved the right to dictate opinions – as Tocquville quotes, 'making people a flock of timid and industrious animals with the state as the shepherd'. The Christian tenet of equality in God's eyes was despised by politicians who themselves became the sole source of wisdom in a centralised state – and the only means of social progress. The Jacobins had a lot to answer for: Lenin based his Communist state on the same principles.

The French aristocrat's ideas help us with another model for adapting today's centralised state. Tocqueville discovered that American principles of local responsibility (where the public interest was a sum of individual interests) was adapted by the Founding Fathers from Benthamite ideals. Holding that religious freedom was the most basic of all institutions and that all were equal in the sight of God, people could work out their own ideas within the context of shared civil and religious beliefs. The first responsibility was within the family, then outwards to the town; later these were grouped into counties and then states in a series of widening concentric interests. In the Jeffersonian concept, central government was to deal only with matters of general concern.

This shared belief was the ultimate source of social stability without which there could be no sense of justice. This gave the New England middle-class settlers a sense of equality, the confidence to run their own affairs and to deal with public needs as they arose. It also provided an agreed standard of morality and self-interest which was quite contrary to Tocqueville's experience in French Canada. There the people, still wedded to the idea of a centralised state, lacked the passion for self-government and the independent commercial drive of the Anglo-Americans. This independence gave the Americans a spirit of local sovereignty enshrined in the Tenth Amendment.

Sovereignty in New England thus stemmed not from the state but upwards from private citizens. Each individual authorised the introduction of new taxes, and the supreme court of each state not only applied laws but judged whether basic rights were preserved from the tyranny of the majority. The importance of local autonomy meant that laws were created, and if necessary were changed, to suit the people, who became willing observers – or even magistrates. Quite different from the bureaucratic megastate where many people regard the law as their enemy.

The civic spirit fostered by local autonomy was the final guarantee against the encroachment of the remote and bureaucratic state that Tocqueville had observed in France. The American blueprint might not have bred uniform behaviour and administrative tidiness but it created something much more powerful. It generated not only their well-founded schools and a sound local administration but people who had a self-interest in their local community, concerned with such matters as crime prevention, education, condition of local roads, halls and churches. Whereas an autocratic society imposed obligations without choice, a democratic society created a series of unwritten or undefined contracts which bound people of different talents. Tocqueville admitted that individual ambition could run rough-shod over the rights of others but observed that free societies spawn a myriad of associations starting with the family. Within these, people could receive confirmation of their own judgements and re-enforce their moral or intellectual convictions; people like this do not look for the state to 'brush away every danger from their path', and can enjoy 'the power of a great republic and the security of their community'.

Towards a new political agenda

The USA and UK are reaching the stage by 2010 at which better public services may no longer be an election issue. Then it is likely that political and economic pressures will have persuaded electors that politicians are incapable of managing cost-efficient public services. There will, of course, be questions of competence, but one of the most important issues will be the poor rate of return from taxation. For example, the average US citizen can expect to receive a return of around 1.5% on their social security payments to the government, when they could achieve at least twice that amount if the money was invested by the individual in US Treasury bonds.

Once people believe they can provide better health, education, pension and welfare services for themselves, it needs only the political will to make it happen. (This is exactly what Martin Luther achieved nearly 500 years ago when he convinced the German people that they could create their own relationship with God without the intermediary of a Catholic priest.) With this in mind we can begin to attack the very basis of the second-wave government edifice – not unlike when Winston Churchill set up his own intelligence network to challenge the British government's policy of appeasement and disarmament in the 1930s.

It is easy to identify the programmes that do not work. In Britain and America these are likely to be health, education, welfare, law and order, or pensions, distribution of transfer payments and care for the elderly. These will then be rated inter alia as a cost to the taxpayer, the seriousness of the problem, the private sector alternatives and so on. Some, like care for the homeless, could probably be immediately undertaken by the Salvation Army and both countries are well endowed with competent voluntary services.

Then, emulating Luther, as many services as possible should be returned to local control. This could include primary education, preventative policing, primary health care, putting the unemployed to work. Churches could also have an important welfare role – as they did before their work was taken over by the state. In addition, it would be interesting to examine the role of the seventeenth-century guilds to discover whether local firms could provide the kernel of a needed organisation.

There are a number of examples of how much power local states, cantons, provinces, counties or regions can take over from central government. As Switzerland shows, the opportunity for the English-speaking peoples is clearly considerable. Other countries rely more on central government but increased globalisation will help each nation to explore the opportunities. The worst 'solution' would be for additional layers of bureaucracy to be imposed without any reduction in the cost of central government.

Other dynamics such as terrorism or rising disease will need to be tackled both nationally and locally. It is also probable that a Swiss-type army, the US National Guard or British Territorials will be required to deal with external and internal first-line defence and possibly for peace-keeping duties in countries such as Afghanistan ravaged by wars. These are unlikely to be popular duties but they could have other effects such as improving fitness and health, reducing obesity, improving basic education skills and reducing unemployment.

The twin pressures of the cybernetic revolution and the collapse of the credit bubble will place much more responsibility on individuals to run their own affairs wherever possible, including paying for their own social services. For those unable to afford the charges at least part of their services will be provided through some form of state insurance.

To assess the savings, one might begin with Pinkerton's calculations that privatisation of state services and reduced bureaucratic control could cut costs by 25%. Assuming that at least 15% of this is spent in improving salaries, repairing buildings and enhancing amenities, this means that UK government spending of 42% of GDP could decline to 38%. This is about the Swiss figure, so clearly the cost-saving potential is much greater. Nevertheless, it would allow lower rates of taxation, the abolition of taxes on savings or inheritance, an increase in economic activity and a government concentrating on essentials. Should the virtuous spiral continue, quite soon one could be talking about real savings.

References

Cohn, N., *The Pursuit of the Millennium* (Secker & Warburg, 1957).

Conquest, R., *Reflections on a Ravaged Century* (W.W. Norton, 1999).

Cook, Chris, and John Stevenson, *Modern British History* (Longman, 1988).

Houston, W., *Through the Whirlwind* (Little Brown, 1997).

Murray, C., *What It Means to be a Libertarian* (Broadway Books, 1997).

Pinkerton, J., *What Comes Next* (Hyperion, 1995).

Schlesinger, A., *The Cycles of American History* (Andre Deutsch, 1987).

Siedontop, L., *Tocqueville* (Oxford Paperbacks, 1994).

Willett, T. (ed.), *Political Business Cycles* (Duke University Press, 1988).

6

The Information-Age Winners

It was the failure of religious dogma to provide answers to the looming industrial age in the 18th Century that encouraged enlightened thinkers to provide rational explanations for the new philosophical and moral questions that were being raised. Now, two centuries later, when churches no longer have the courage to speak on moral questions we seem to have turned a complete circle, for only secular answers to all the great questions of life appear acceptable.

Today there are changes that will also need rationalising as mankind adapts to the Information Age, which initially will benefit only the minority who realise the potential. Unfortunately it could also bring distress to the many steeped in the customs of the industrial age and who are unable to change. This chapter describes the sort of people who could do best in the new environment and the need for them to create new ways of working.

Unsurprisingly the people most likely to thrive in the conditions of the dynamics described in earlier chapters will be specialists in deriving, processing and using information. But what sort of individuals will they be? Will they be the New Men so beloved by dictators in the 1930s, the strong pitiless warriors committed to Fascist dreams? Perhaps they might be the heroic Soviet model fighting for a socialist people's paradise. Then there are the manly James Bond, Captain Scott, John Wayne or Lawrence of Arabia role models beloved by post-war cartoonists. Perhaps they might be the caring, brave people like Nurse Edith Cavell, who was executed by a German firing squad for helping Allied prisoners in the First World War, or indeed Florence Nightingale, who totally revised the army's approach to medical care. Maybe the world will have moved on to an age where individuals, either singly or collectively, will seek their own path almost independently of their politicians.

Profiling the New Persona

We may be helped in this quest by a survey carried out in the late 1990s by the magazine *Wired*. In an article called 'The Digital Citizen', American correspondents were rated from those who were 'super-connected' to the new electronic highway, through the 'connected', to the 'semi-connected' and the 'unconnected'. The super-connected used e-mail at least three days a week, had a laptop, a cell phone, a beeper and a home computer. By contrast the unconnected used very few of these technologies. When the survey was conducted the super and connected made up 9% of the sample, the semi-connected 62% and the unconnected 29%. If the survey were conducted in 2006, the proportion of the most connected group would probably be nearer 20%, the semi-connected perhaps 50% and the unconnected 30%.

All the correspondents believed in the principle of democracy. However, this belief was most fervently held by 60% of the most connected group compared to 50% of the others. Over 90% of the most connected group believed in free markets while the less connected were nearer 70%. Among the unconnected, the free market ideal was shunned by over 20%. Similarly, over 65% of the most connected group had faith in the future, compared to just over 50% of the least connected. In the latter category 37% believed they would be worse off in the future.

On attitudes towards change, nearly 70% of the most connected believed that they were in control; only 40% of the unconnected believed they were in charge and the same number thought they were not.

There was little difference between all groups in their political affiliations but there was a greater desire among the connected group to see the social security system re-organised than among the unconnected. There was also much less enthusiasm among the connected group for public education than the unconnected, where nearly 70% had confidence in the system.

The 'New Connected Persons' believe that free markets and technology are highly positive forces that thrive within democratic freedom. They are knowledgeable, tolerant, spend up to twenty hours per week reading books, are civic-minded, radically committed to change and are optimistic about the future. There is a degree of the libertarian about them which makes them sceptical about the ability of a centrally directed government to change what is wrong in society and they believe in decentralised self-help. They are more likely to be in their forties than twenties, there is little difference in attitude between the genders, and the great majority are white and live in the suburbs. However, they believe strongly that those less fortunate than themselves should have support and encouragement.

By contrast the survey appears to show that the least connected people are likely to have negative feelings about politics, change and the future. They lack control over their lives but are positive about the government's role in public services.

I am my brother's keeper

Of course, this survey doesn't tell us everything about these different categories of people. Any winners of the Information Age will still require leadership skills, with the associated mental, emotional, moral and physical stamina needed to guide not only themselves but others. They will also have to take responsibility for the least connected majority, for unless these are given hope for the future there will be a huge divide in society that could be the recipe for civil unrest.

Unfortunately the time to make the adjustment could be short and there will still be many steeped in the principles of the industrial age who will feel completely adrift.

They will be like those who crammed into St Margaret's Wall Street church after the crash of 29 October 1929 who had lost not only their jobs and their capital but also their status, obliging them to look for menial work. They would be like the British officers after fighting in the First World War selling matches on street corners wearing masks – ashamed to be recognised by their friends. During the early 1930s, very respectable people in the US would politely ask passers-by whether they could 'spare a dime'.

One helpful guide might be the hierarchy of needs proposed by Abraham Maslow, a psychologist and a disciple of Carl Jung. It is made up of seven levels, ranging from the basic homeostatic (food, clothing and shelter) through to the highest aesthetic level. The psychologist argued that once the basics had been satisfied, people would then require safety and security – hoping, presumably, that they themselves would never have to return to the lowest level. The next level is love and belonging, then esteem – something that was obviously the main concern of the frightened people in St Margaret's and the officers selling matches. After esteem, Maslow believed people need self-actualisation, a process of inner attainment, then above that the more cultivated levels of understanding and, finally, aesthetic appreciation. In essence, people are given the opportunity to promote themselves through the up-wave part of a long wave, and they worry about sinking during the conversion to the Information Age and to the down-wave.

Maslow was describing primarily an industrial-age phenomenon when most people were employees; it is probably unsuitable for analysing those working in medieval guilds – and may not be appropriate for the Information Age. To be sure, human nature does not change, and, to use a military metaphor, there will still be a modern equivalent of the successful general, the able staff officer, the reliable non-commissioned officer and the foot soldier.

If the earlier figures on the proportion of those connected is correct, then the new elite will comprise some 20% of the population and embrace both leaders and staff officers. Unlike most of the top people in the industrial age, only a relatively small proportion will need to be able administrators for there will be fewer large concerns; instead they will work either singly or in groups. They will need to be widely educated and be the intellectual and probably the cultural pace-setters of society. By definition their scope will be international and they will be able to draw upon and apply the latest technology. Like it or not, they will also have a wider social role, taking up some of the responsibilities of those less fortunate than themselves. This group would include what Jacques Ellul would describe as technologists, the individuals who bring order to society.

They will also be leaders who, having identified a challenge, will set up the necessary resources and timetable and go for it – often with the guile of Sun Tsu, the Chinese general who won battles by stealth. They are intelligent, industrious and aggressive individuals capable of communicating their ideas very clearly and leading others towards a goal. They are likely to work for wealth, power and prestige but they can also be the leading light of charities and good causes. They will often be highly cultivated individuals capable of working in several areas such as politics, business or the professions; one might hope that some would be successful clerics. A number of their qualities will be interchangeable with those of staff officers.

The semi-connected group might comprise over 50% of the population and in the sixteenth century would have been the mainstay of the guilds. In his book *The Theory of Moral Sentiments*, Adam Smith describes what he calls the 'prudent man':

> *He studies seriously to understand what it is he professes, he is not cunning or arrogant, he does not assume airs and is not ostentatious or quackish to preserve his reputation; he believes that only the superficial have vanity. He never exposes himself to the accusation of falsehood and restricts his friends to a few well-tried companions; likewise he is not guided by showing off but by modesty, discretion and good conduct. The prudent man is frugal, never sacrificing the future for the present. He always lives within his income and does not go in quest of new adventures or enterprises – preferring the life of secure tranquillity. He is also a man of principle and honour, adhering steadily to maxims.*

Today our men of principle need to have additional qualities. They will be professionals working in many different fields, able to implement the plans prepared by the staff officers and directed by the leaders. Most of them will be self-employed, acting in a sub-contracting capacity within their specialisation. They will be completely dependable, averse to taking risks and will not put a foot wrong. They will need to be set tasks and are natural contractors. Smith then goes on to identify his prudent man as an object of proper respect, deserving and obtaining credibility among his equals. Smith believes that it is of the utmost importance for a younger man to maintain his health, fortune and reputation – this is what he calls 'prudence'. Older men appear to need a different agenda!

At first glance there would seem to be little future for the unconnected comprising some thirty% of the working population and consisting of primarily unskilled males. But this could be an error because technology is increasingly making it possible for work, previously the province of a tradesman, to become a possibility for those without a trade. For example, a replacement wooden window could be manufactured by a machine set up to precise digital specifications and there are a number of franchises where application and good sense are more a requirement than training; of course there is also the possibility that the standards of living for many will decline in the West for manufacturing to start a recovery. For those unable to find a niche.

The new qualities

None of these qualities is necessarily new, it is just that the Information Age will need the following in greater abundance than before. Flexibility is obviously a key attribute, whether moving up or down Maslow's hierarchy, and it is an essential quality during the down-wave. To quote Adam Smith in *The Wealth of the Nations*:

> *The speculative merchant exercises no one regular, established, or well-known branch of business. He is a corn merchant this year, and a wine merchant the next, and a sugar, tobacco or tea merchant the year after. He enters every trade when he foresees that it is likely to be more than commonly profitable and quits it when he foresees that its profits are likely to return to the level of other trades.*

This flexibility was not just applied to trading; Smith suggests that a carpenter 'is also a joiner, a cabinet-maker, a carver of wood, a wheel-wright, a plough-wright, a cart and wagon-maker'.

Now it will not be so much a question of switching professions although many entrepreneurs have the ability to apply their skills to many enterprises. We can at least anticipate the next moves by thinking through the various scenarios described in the final chapter, make contingency plans, monitor progress then implement policies when needed. We will also need strenuous retraining. In Smith's *Theory of Moral Sentiments* he encourages his readers to adjust to different levels of success (moving up or down Maslow's hierarchy), citing 'the never failing certainty with which all men, sooner or later, accommodate themselves to whatever becomes their permanent situation. This may, perhaps, induce us to think Stoically.' He illustrates this principle by telling of the Count de Lauzun who, when incarcerated in the Bastille, occupied himself by learning how to feed a spider.

Integrity is probably the most important of all characteristics. Described by the Oxford English Dictionary as having the quality of being complete and of having high moral principles, honesty and uprightness, integrity also requires a firm adherence to a moral code. Adam Smith typically suggests a market-driven approach: 'that the real and effectual discipline which is exercised over a workman is not that of his corporation, but that of his customers. It is the fear of losing their employment which restrains his frauds and corrects his negligence.' But integrity need not only be imposed by the market place but have an inner source. In *The Protestant Ethic and the Spirit of Capitalism*, Max Weber explains how John Calvin and his followers were obliged to live out their faith in diligence to God's laws and in hard work. They could become wealthy provided this was not frittered away with hedonistic delights; their gain was to be either accumulated or given away. Weber explains how some of the most ascetic sects make the best businessmen, citing the Mennonites in Prussia during the reign of Frederick the Great. The story goes that despite their steadfast refusal to fight in his armies, Frederick was obliged to excuse them on account of their hard work and industry.

Benjamin Franklin made a similar point about personal habits when he reminded his readers that time and credit is money. A creditor might well extend a loan if he hears 'the sound of your hammer at five in the morning or eight at night. But if he sees you at the billiard table, or hears your voice at a tavern, when you should be at work, he sends for his money the next day.' He goes on to observe, 'for six pounds a year you may have the use of one hundred pounds, provided you are a man of known prudence and honesty'.

Weber cites statistics to explain why pupils with a pious background can be trained to have a good understanding of work, the ability to concentrate, an application to their jobs and a natural frugality. These attributes are obviously not confined to Christians, for other groups such as the Jews and Confucians, also have a powerful love of learning, a respect for their elders and an application to hard work. Adam Smith would agree with Weber when he discusses the basis of morality. Covering such topics as merit, justice, judgement, duty, virtue and so on, he lauds the religious man whose faith enforces a sense of duty. He is not grateful for the sake of gratitude, not charitable from spirit of humanity or public-spirited from love of country nor generous for love of mankind.

We have seen already how our national perceptions change during the long wave: in the up-wave we become international in our thinking and are prepared to enter treaties for mutual benefit. These principles become strained in the down-wave as, amid accusations of competitive currency devaluations and the dumping of goods, we are inclined to think nationally. Again, Adam Smith writes:

The man of public spirit is prompted by humanity and benevolence and will respect the established power and privileges of individuals within the great order and societies within a state. Therefore he will accommodate, as well as he can, his public arrangements to the confirmed habits and prejudices of the people and remedy, as well as he can, the inconveniences that flow from adverse regulations.

Interdependence is the quality of being mutually dependent, or to put it in a different way, to be able to network with many different groups. Adam Smith's *Theory of Moral Sentiments* would have provided an ideal model of interdependence but he approached the matter in a different way in *The Wealth of Nations*. Here he suggested interdependent relationships were in reality self-interest when he expressed his famous dictum: 'It is not by the benevolence of the butcher, the brewer, or the baker that we expect our dinner, but from their regard to their own interest.'

74

Courage is vital but more indefinable, for it covers everything from the heroic charge on the battlefield, to the quiet quality of the uncomplaining mortally wounded individual who thinks only of others, to the brave death of a Jesus or a Socrates. In today's terms it is more likely to include qualities such as intelligence, the ability to plan, to formulate a message and communicate, the charisma to lead from the front, empathy with others and determination. Martin Luther would clearly come in this category, as would latter-day heroes such as Winston Churchill and Mother Theresa.

We saw earlier that ability alone might not carry people through a crisis. In the critical atmosphere described in chapter 9 most individuals will be content to have an income rather than worry about status or job titles. As they respond flexibly to the changes, probably their greatest asset would be the inner drive associated with the Mennonites or Puritans so admired by Max Weber. This inner force need not necessarily be Christian – it could also be the zeal of Islam that has proved so potent over the centuries. The political skills for leading such people will require a combination of qualities seldom observed at present. Those aspiring to be leaders would be wise to heed Adam Smith's strictures.

National characteristics

History may also provide clues as to how we might cope with discontinuities. The following is a brief digest of how the three major European nations have dealt with crises in the past.

During the history of the English-speaking peoples (ESPs), stretching from the Saxon invasion to the American Civil War (1860-5), eight out of thirteen discontinuities have occurred during the climatic extremes described in chapter 7. It seems that people become aggressive towards their rulers in cool climates, when they demand a greater degree of freedom and independence. The most prominent was during the seventeenth century, known as the Little Ice Age, when the winters were exceptionally cold and food scarcity forced prices higher. Of the thirteen major changes, four occurred in England during this century: the succession of the Stuarts, Cromwell's Commonwealth, the Restoration and the Glorious Revolution in 1688.

Perhaps because ESPs have experienced change so often, they have a considerable adaptability. A report by *The Economist*, based on work by Lehman Brothers early in 2001, confirmed that of the industrialised nations ESP policies came top in generating long-term growth, increasing labour-market performance and wider market competition. The US headed the list, followed by Canada, New Zealand, Britain and Australia. Among those at the bottom were Greece, Italy, Austria and Spain.

Although the ESP states are not as effective as others in mobilising peacetime economies, an emergency such as war throws off any reluctance to change and seems to produce a leader who stirs the country. As we have seen, in the Second

World War Britain out-produced Germany in aircraft every year except 1944, and the US produced many more planes than the combined Axis powers. This is probably because these are bottom-up societies that allow considerable social and economic mobility, as exemplified by the American Dream. Unlike the more centralised French, German and Japanese systems, the ESPs perform relatively poorly during economic upturns but outperform during downturns because individuals take much greater initiatives.

With the French-speaking peoples (FSPs), the climatic cycle seems to have created fewer changes, although Louis XIV seized the opportunity to profit from the Thirty Years War which left Germany desolate. Later the Revolution occurred during an economic trough, with the violence made worse by climatically driven food riots. The 'Sabine Minimum', the period of extreme cold that occurred at this time and is described in the next chapter, was undoubtedly the cause of Napoleon's icy defeat during the 1812 invasion of Russia.

Remarkable people have appeared at each stage of French history, starting with Clovis, then Charlemagne, Joan of Arc, Louis XIV, Napoleon and de Gaulle. Some have come from humble beginnings, others from a line of kings or military men. Unlike the ESPs, for whom gradual changes happened over centuries, the overthrow of the *Ancien Regime* and the following wars happened over twenty-five or so years which created a huge discontinuity and left a legacy of volatility from the nineteenth century onwards. The talents of the FSPs seem to become most developed during economic upturns, when the public and private sectors work closely in unison. Unfortunately this may reverse in the event of a future down-wave to cause grave divisions within the nation – as it did in the 1930s.

Lastly, the German-speaking peoples (GSPs) experienced their worst discontinuity during another cold period, the Maunder Minimum, when the Thirty Years War desolated the country and left it divided into some 300 different principalities and city states. It did, however, leave the field clear for Frederick the Great, who energised Prussia, then Bismarck who finally united the country in 1870. In less than 150 years this energetic, industrious, artistic and organised people have stamped their mark on history. Their discipline as a nation has stemmed largely from the old Prussian idea that the citizen's highest ideal is to serve the state, as espoused by philosophers such as Hegel and Nietzsche. It makes the GSPs a formidable economic power during an upturn but perhaps vulnerable to disassociation in the event of a downturn.

In conclusion, history shows that the English-speaking peoples are the most likely to be in the forefront of steering the world through the problems that lie ahead. Once a new configuration has become settled this could be consolidated by the French and German speakers.

Awareness of cycles

Training for expected scenarios is seldom included in the curriculum of either business or military staff colleges, on the assumption that running a business or a war in the future will be much like that of yesterday. Cycles, however, teach that discontinuities often confuse those in charge so that for a business to avoid failure (or an army a defeat) new leaders are needed. For example, during the Battle of Britain those commanding RAF squadrons were regular officers. Out of an original intake of sixty young men in 1920 only two or three survived the onslaught and became air marshals.

It is obviously undesirable that companies should be allowed to fail or armies lose battles just to train future leaders. However, there is now enough evidence that the cycles are working as before to build case studies around anticipated scenarios. Business schools, universities and staff colleges should then consider courses to describe and understand lessons from appropriate moments in history, so that students can at least recognise similar conditions should they recur. For business leaders these might include how to manage a business during the up-wave and down-wave. For example, how to finance a business after a period of recession, the dangers of over-trading and types of organisation best suited to inflation. The examples might include the events leading up to the hyper-inflation of the Weimar Republic and how companies dealt with the great commodity explosion of 1972-4, how prices changed, and how governments and businesses responded.

Conversely, managing a business in a recession needs quite a different sort of organisation, a concentration on balance-sheet stability, not profit margins, and on reducing the break-even point by turning fixed into variable costs. Again, managers could, for example, be taught about the events leading up to and following the Great Crash of 1929, how businesses were run during the subsequent Great Depression and the response to it of countries such as the United States, Britain and Germany. More recent events might include those leading to the crash of many US savings and loans during the 1980s and the lessons learned from the Resolution Trust Corporation.

It would then be possible to convert past and modern situations into case studies in order to analyse what happened and to learn from the mistakes. They could be taught the warning signs of these conditions recurring, planning for contingencies – possibly in the form of scenarios and implications for political, economic, financial and industrial pitfalls; in addition the courses should include the leading indicators for recovery, the action of customers, suppliers, bankers and shareholders. Most universities and business schools would find it difficult to adapt their present courses to the suggested topics, for most lecturers are used to teaching subjects suitable for Toffler's second wave.

Military staff colleges are probably closer to dealing with dynamic situations, for they teach 'what if' situations as part of a strategic plan around which the forces are trained and organised. Likely future case studies might include such matters as dealing with the mass migration of people, coping with a pandemic disease, building and training citizen forces, and disaster relief from conditions such as earthquakes, acute flooding and so on. It is more likely that these new subjects will be taught as post-graduate courses, possibly from new departments of existing institutions. Staff courses, like business schools, are also geared to tackle the staffing and planning aspects of past operations in the anticipation they will illuminate the future. Instead of straight military operations such as the Falklands War or the Gulf Wars, students might learn the intelligence operations behind terrorist operations after an atrocity, the hunting for bin Laden or rounding up potential trouble makers. Unfortunately peacetime students are naturally considering their next appointment, hence will tend to offer 'acceptable' solutions and avoid innovations which might brand them as possibly 'unsound'.

The effects of 11 September

In mid-2003 it is possible to detect a new seriousness in life, particularly in the United States, where there is a quiet determination to revenge the attacks on the twin towers and the Pentagon. There is a heightened sense of patriotism and a desire for the administration to succeed. These realities are obliging many to look outside their previously 'cosy' world and a number of people are reconsidering what America actually stands for. Perhaps Hollywood will respond, as in the 1930s, by making brilliant musicals, or films glorifying sterling individuals such as Sergeant York or the title character of *Mr Deedes Goes to Town*.

When a country assumes a near-war footing priorities change. Stephen Lewis, the Chief Economist of Monument Securities, suggests that where the 'objective is victory, political leaders cannot afford to allow resources to be distributed on the basis of the free market. The celebrity culture of the 1990s was the natural result of the untrammelled satisfaction of mass demands. In a war, governments will see more value in professors than in television celebrities or baseball players.'

In the US there is a retreat from political correctness, feminism and the multi-cultural and liberal agenda; as it becomes easier to talk about faith, more people are seeking inspiration – and consolation – in churches, synagogues and mosques. If terrorist attacks continue then demands for closer integration of migrants into the dominant culture will increase. How each of us will react to new, and possibly fraught, situations even with training is still problematic; like troops going into action for the first time nobody quite knows how they will react and often the apparently macho individuals are not necessarily the bravest.

All this will come at a time of increasingly rapid change now that the demands of the Information Age are upon us and society is obliged to face in many different directions at once. Despite the need for central direction when fighting a war there will be the counter-centrifugal tendency as people increasingly shun travel and cities, and wish to live and work in the suburbs or in the country. Perhaps politicians will be obliged to focus the state less to help the disadvantaged but more to encourage new entrepreneurs.

Should we worry about the future? Mankind has recovered from difficult situations in the past and no doubt will do so again – although it does help if at least some of the likely scenarios have been thought through previously. Probably the most important result will not be the transition itself but how we deal with the next up-wave, for it will be quite different from anything experienced over the last 500 years. One must be optimistic that the Information Age will not only be fascinating but extremely rewarding; the individual could be provided with a sense of freedom, a renewed faith and a dignity only possible for the minority in the industrial age.

References

Sun Tzu, *The Art of War* (Shambhala Publications, 1991).

Covey, S., *The Seven Habits of Highly Successful People* (Simon & Schuster, 1989).

Drucker, P., *Post Capitalist Society* (Butterworth Heinemann, 1993).

————, 'The Next Society' (*The Economist*, November 2001).

Katz, J., 'The Digital Citizen' (*Wired* magazine, December 1997).

Kinsman, F., *Millennium: Towards Tomorrow's Society* (W.H. Allen & Co, 1990).

Smith, A., *Inquiry into the Causes and Nature of the Wealth of Nations*, Books I-III (Penguin Books, 1972).

————, *The Theory of Moral Sentiments* (Henry Bohn of Covent Garden, 1861).

Weber, M., *The Protestant Ethic and the Spirit of Capitalism* (Routledge, 1992).

Dynamic Three

7

The Changing Climate and Water Wars

Of all the water in the world only 3% is fresh. Of that only half of one% is readily available for in lakes and rivers; the others are divided between glaciers and the poles (78%) and groundwater (21%). To illustrate this, it takes 1,000 tons of rainwater to produce a ton of wheat, 6,000 for a ton of rice and 105,000 gallons to make a car.

Already a quarter of the world population lives in only twenty-three cities, and the numbers could grow should the climatic cycles described in this chapter function as they have done in the past and at the same time imposing terrible misery on those that are least able to look after themselves. This is also the West's problem, for it could cause the world's greatest refugee crisis, bringing with it disease and famine.

History abounds with wars fought over water, as people have tried to access rivers or aquifers at another's expense. This is dangerous for one of the first symptoms of malnutrition is aggression. One of the reasons behind the Israeli drive for settlements on the West Bank of the Jordan is the limited access to water in the region, but as we will see later, there is the same amount of water now as in 1974, but the population has risen by 50%. Other areas such as swathes of northern China, Central Asia, north Pakistan, Afghanistan, Arabia and East Africa are in a similar position.

For centuries, much of the history of Western Europe has been subject to the vagaries of the Atlantic and the Gulf Stream, which have made it possible for people to live and sail in waters as far north as the Arctic Circle; it has also caused famines and civil wars. Being a continent, the US weather is more reliable but even there it only replicates around 25% year on year.

Weather has also shaped industries. Humidity and terrain made Lancashire the ideal place to spin and weave the cotton fibres shipped over from the southern US states; initially the machinery was powered by mill streams but then abundant coal and the invention of the steam engine created a much more reliable source of energy.

Climatic changes, which occurred over long periods, were largely ignored in the West until scientists were able to measure secular changes over thousands of years from studying such things as tree rings and ice cores. From this data, and much better recording on earth and from satellites, it was possible to deduce trends.

The best known of these is the Greenhouse Effect, which is held to cause global warming through the rising quantities of man-made carbon dioxide. In fact records show that there was a medieval warm period from about 800 to 1200 when there were no exhaust fumes. In the twentieth-century most of the measured warming occurred before 1940 – prior to the times when 80% of the present gases were emitted.

Actually the temperature in the northern hemisphere has a very high correlation with the length and intensity of the eleven-year sunspot cycle which, from a number of sources can be traced back to around 1500. These show a secular rise in the sun's output since around 1670 – the low point of the 'Little Ice Age'. Mankind has always blamed itself for changes for which nature has been responsible. The ancient Egyptians, for example, believed that shooting arrows changed the weather.

Politicians, seeking 'to be doing something', love to be seen making common cause and condemning scepticism on issues which are of natural concern to many. But they are likely to be looking in the wrong direction, for it has been the natural climate changes that have caused mankind such grief in the past – and will undoubtedly do the same in the future. For us, living in the early part of the third millennium, four major weather cycles, ranging in length from almost 180 years to under ten years, are beginning to dominate – particularly in the most disruptive areas like the Middle East.

The 178.8-year weather and lunar cycles

In 1975 a paper co-authored by Dr Iben Browning and Dr Robert Harrington was published in *Nature* magazine that dealt with a 178.8-year climatic cycle. It described how an examination of ice cores, taken from the Cape Century research station on Greenland, showed a dominant 178.8-year temperature cycle over several thousand years. It appears that an isotope of oxygen is preferentially absorbed into cooler water which then freezes in layers like an onion skin; when analysed year by year, this provides an accurate record of temperature and atmospheric dust.

Browning and Harrington argued that the cycle was caused by a long-term oscillation of tidal forces, which moved from the northern to the southern hemisphere and back again over the period. These caused exceptional friction and pressure on the sensitive tectonic plates that predominate around the Pacific Ocean and in turn trigger earthquakes and volcanoes. While the former are locally very destructive, a large volcano often ejects millions of tons of gas and rubble into the stratosphere, where it spreads around the earth, shielding the sunlight and making the earth cooler. Over at least the last millennium, there has been a strong correlation between these cyclical tidal peaks and cool periods.

Another paper, written by Dr Rhodes Fairbridge and James Shirley, showed how these tidal forces could be driven. It happens that every 178.8 years there are planetary imbalances in the solar system which primarily reduce the sun's output but also could add further stresses to the earth's most moveable material – the ocean waters described earlier. The last cycle peaked on 20 April 1990 and due to lags in the system this could occur around 2008 from the same set of unbalances that caused the December 26th tsunami, described later. The previous imbalances could give us a flavour of what we might expect.

The first cold peak in the second millennium AD was the so-called Wolf Minimum, that occurred just before 1300. It was almost certainly responsible for the increasingly cool weather which caused European harvests to fail in the terrible years 1317-8, when wet and stormy weather rotted the grains and made harvesting nearly impossible. Thirty years later The Black Death hit people weakened by the previous malnutrition, which reduced immunity to diseases. The terrible weather also caused the devastation in the European mainland during the One Hundred Years War, so ably described by Barbara Tuchman in A Distant Mirror. Tough though that period was, there is always an upside to hard times – then, it brought freedom for the serfs.

The Sporer Minimum was in 1500 and lagged some thirty years from the high tidal forces of that cycle. It was responsible for several famines in England in the 1500s, and co-incided with the defeat of the Moors by Ferdinand and Isabella, and the fall of the Yorkist dynasty in England. Cool dry periods tend to generate civil discontent so it is no surprise that Martin Luther's rift with Rome in 1517 gained so much support in Germany, helped by the invention of Gutenberg's printing press some sixty years earlier. It enabled Luther's complaints to circulate around Germany in three weeks, triggering the greatest political and ideological upset in Europe.

The Reformation spread to northern Germany, Holland then later to England and Scotland. It released the dynamic energy of the island people and there is a strong argument that something similar could be achieved should Britain free itself from restrictions applied now, not from Rome, but from Brussels.

The third cold peak, the Maunder Minimum, occurred around the middle of the seventeenth century and caused the most changes for those of European descent than any in the whole millennium. Not only was there considerable volcanic action but the sunspot cycle, was hardly detectable by the instruments then available. The cold weather had a desperate impact at about the same latitude around the world. The Thirty Years War was one of the most tragic conflicts, reducing the German population in the seventeenth century by at least one-third.

The war that followed involved Austria, the German princes, Italy, Spain, France, the United Provinces, Denmark and Sweden, generally along the Protestant-Catholic divide, although Cardinal Richelieu of France sided with the Protestants. Armies lived off the land and quartered with the population, so that in the ebb and flow of battle, a region might be completely denuded of the increasingly short supplies of food. With the appalling harvests of the mid-seventeenth century, thousands died of famine and diseases such as typhus and the bubonic plague.

By contrast, the English Civil War started in August 1642 and was over in four years, but it continued the erosion of the king's power that had started with the Magna Carta. Some hundreds of miles south-east, the power of the Ottoman Empire was threatened when the population was hit by crop failures towards the end of the seventeenth century. This caused mounting disorder among the population, and farmers fled the land into the cities, so further reducing agricultural output. As the caliph's income fell, increased taxes fuelled a rising spiral of disruption. In despair, peasants formed rebel bands, gaining control of large parts of the empire and retaining taxes and food supplies for themselves. Although two caliphs were assassinated for the failure, the empire held together for around another 300 years.

In China, crop failure and famines also caused civil unrest. The revolt started in the south, then, in 1643, moved north to Beijing, where starving crowds rampaged through the streets and killed the corrupt eunuchs and officials. The Ming emperor, seeing the collapse, committed suicide. (There are similarities here to the bread riots in Paris that helped bring down Louis XVI.) This was the signal for a general to call in the powerful northern Manchu tribes and to capture the mainland. The island of Taiwan was the last Ming stronghold to fall.

Across the East China Sea, Tokugawa Ieyasu consolidated the Japanese Shogunate regime in 1635 by quelling with great severity an uprising of rebellious Christians. Although history does not relate whether the riots were famine related, the parallels are too close to be coincidental. After this, the only contact allowed with foreigners was with a few Dutch traders in Nagasaki. Amazingly, the regime lasted until 1867, when the Shogunate were unable to counter the 'Black Ships' of Commodore Perry's American squadron and the regime ended in disgrace.

The seventeenth century was also a period of overseas colonisation. The Pilgrim Fathers landed in America in 1620 and the Dutch founded Fort Amsterdam at present-day New York six years later. The Plymouth colony nearly starved to death in 1640 from the terrible cold that was blighting the northern hemisphere. The Dutch founded the Dutch East India Company in 1602, creating its base at Batavia, and Java seventeen years later. Cape Colony in South Africa was formed in 1652 as a supply base for the East and the Portuguese were ousted from their previous settlements at Colombo, Cochin and Malacca.

The fourth cold peak, the Sabine Minimum, was arguably responsible for the downfall of Napoleon, for it is not too fanciful to suggest that the extreme cold of 1812 destroyed the greater part of Napoleon's *grande armée*. The same minimum caused his defeat at Waterloo: on 9 April 1815, after the volcano Tambora erupted in the Sunda straits off Sumatra with the force of around 100 hydrogen bombs, it ejected some 35 cubic miles of dust and nearly 200 million tons of acid droplets into the stratosphere, which drifted northwards and caused the battlefield of Waterloo to be drenched on the eve of the action. Napoleon, who liked to attack at dawn, was obliged to wait until 1.30 p.m. to start his bombardment, a delay which allowed Blucher's Prussians to join the battle.

The year of 1816 was known as the 'year without a summer' because of the terrible weather, and the cool conditions released revolutionary energy in the Balkans and the freedom movement in Latin America.

Now, 180 years later, we have so far not been bothered by the fifth minimum, but the cold weather has been delayed, not eliminated. Sunspots were at their peak in 2001, so the low point could be expected in 2006. This could nearly co-incide with

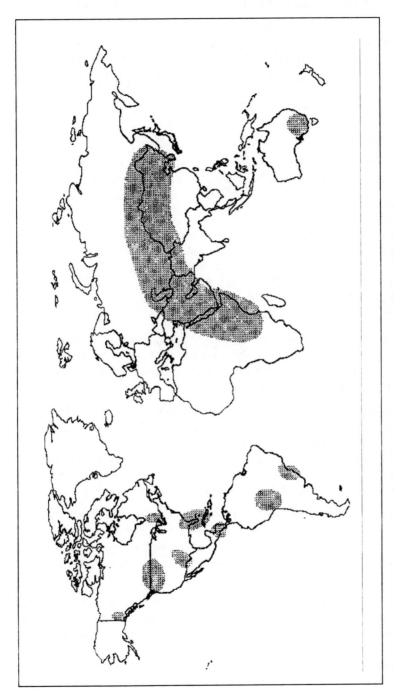

Diagram 1: Impact of La Ni a on weather conditions in Asia, the Middle East and Africa.

Courtesy of the Browning Newsletter

the low point of a much shorter cycle of 18.6 years when the moon precesses around the earth and in 2008 will be at its closest for around 200 years.

As the pull of the moon is some four times that of the sun, this will place the earth's crust under considerable strain. It is likely that the Richter 9 earthquake causing the tsunami on December 26 2004 and the Kashmir disaster is the precursor of rising seismic activity that, by early 2006 is evident on the Kamchatka Peninsula and in mid-Pacific.

Ocean oscillations

Seismic action may have very dramatic effects, but two oscillations in the Atlantic and the Pacific may have even more influence on mankind. These are described in a paper produced by the University of Arizona – see references at the end of the chapter.

The Pacific Decadal Oscillation (PDO) describes a long-term see-saw pattern of temperature variations in the Pacific Ocean with a cycle from warm to cool and back again over sixty to seventy years. In its positive phase, the Tropical and East Pacific are warm while the West Pacific and polar regions are unusually cold. In the negative phase, the West Pacific and polar regions are relatively warm while the Tropical and East Pacific are cooler.

During a positive PDO, El Niños are large and frequent. This phase brings warmth and moisture to the western states of the Americas and frequent droughts to South East Asia. Further north, except during extreme El Niño years, northern China has adequate moisture and growing conditions.

The reverse occurs in a negative PDO. El Niños become milder and cool while La Niñas are prolonged. This leaves the West Coast of the Americas unusually cool and dry while there is often flooding in South East Asia and Bangladesh. Northern China becomes drier, causing problems for both agriculture and hydroelectricity. These conditions seem to benefit India's monsoon in the east but less moisture penetrates into Pakistan and Afghanistan. Its impact is shown on Diagram 1.

The Atlantic Multidecadal Oscillation (AMO) combines the North Atlantic Oscillation (NAO) with other lesser phenomenon. Instead of there being differential cooling east and west, the whole of the North Atlantic is either cooler or warmer than normal; a warmer ocean is known as a positive AMO, a cooler, negative.

Normally the greatest impact of a positive AMO is to move the storm tracks further north so creating drought conditions in south-eastern parts of the USA and the Mediterranean (including portions of the Middle East) during the winter. In summer, very little moisture reaches the interior of North America. The warmer waters generate more hurricanes and Europe is more likely to experience heat waves. The summer of 2003 is typical of this condition if there are not external events that destroy the equilibrium.

With a negative AMO, the rain belts move further south so providing good growing conditions in the eastern and central USA, southern Europe and the Middle East.

There are clearly four combinations of the PDO and AMO due to the periodicity of both that do not necessarily work together and must be considered along with other influences.

The most benign for the US and many places elsewhere, is a positive PDO and negative AMO. Much of the south and west of America has above average rainfall leaving only a few dryer pockets to the north and west. Elsewhere southern Europe and all of the Mediterranean have good rainfall although parts of South East Asia will have droughts. These conditions were particularly prevalent from the late 1890s to 1914 and from 1976 to 1995.

With the AMO still negative and a negative PDO, the south and east of the US and north-west has good rainfall although the central states are hit. Elsewhere northern China and Central Asia has become unusually cool and dry with flooding to the south. Europe and the Mediterranean still has adequate rainfall. This was the pattern from 1916 to the early 1920s and for the 1960s and the very early 1970s.

The combination of a positive PDO and AMO leaves most of the north and west of the US dry, and the East Coast particularly the Southeast, suffers from the positive AMO. However there is rain in California, the Southwest, Texas and the southern Mississippi. Elsewhere the rain belts will be further north in Europe making the Mediterranean dryer than usual. On the western rim of the Pacific it will be dry in the south and rather better conditions in Northern China and Korea. These were the patterns from the late 1920s through the 1930s and the early 1940s. This combination was probably responsible for the dustbowl in a number of mid-Western states and the chaos during China's civil war.

The most dangerous condition for America is a negative PDO and a positive AMO – the PDO dries the West and reduces North America's winter moisture while the AMO leaves the interior of the continent dry and increases the risk of hurricanes along the East Coast. The wheat, corn and western cotton belt are left dry. It is particularly dry in heavily populated California, Texas and Florida, America's primary fruit and vegetable growing areas. This is a similar condition that caused the 1930s Dust Bowl.

Elsewhere the positive AMO will bring drought conditions to the Mediterranean including many parts of the Middle East. In the western Pacific, the areas most affected by drought will be Northern China, Central Asia and much of the Middle East and Eastern Africa. Depending upon the seriousness of the PDO, Korea will become dryer than normal while southern China can expect flooding. The Indian monsoons in the east are likely to be good. This pattern was last encountered in the late 1940s and lasted until the beginning of the1960s and is likely to prevail for the first two or three decades of the twenty- first century.

This is a summary of how individual countries are likely to be affected:

Positive PDO, negative AMO

Benefiting: North and South America, Europe, Northern China, Central Asia, the Middle East.

Suffering: India, South-East Asia.

Negative PDO, negative AMO

Benefiting: Canada, the Pacific Northwest, the Rocky Mountains, Texas and the South-East, Midwest, South-East Asia, Europe, Eastern Mediterranean, India.

Suffering: Southern California, the Central Great Plains, South America, Northern China, Central Asia.

Positive PDO, positive AMO

Benefiting: Southern central USA, California, Northern Europe,

Suffering: Canada, remainder of USA, Mediterranean, South-East Asia, Middle East, India.

Negative PDO, positive AMO

Benefiting: East coast and north-east of USA, Northern Europe, South-East Asia. India.

Suffering: Rest of USA, Canada, Northern China, Central Asia, Mediterranean, Middle East and East Africa.

An arctic oscillation (AO)

There is also a little understood oscillation in the Arctic which, in conjunction with the PDO, can cause an unusually deep area of high pressure over Siberia. Because of this Central Asia, Pakistan, Afghanistan, Iran, and southern Arabia suffered terrible droughts early in the century; for example, in 2001 Afghanistan received only 46% of its normal rainfall, causing 7.5 million to be undernourished (although one suspects the food production could have been better had the country not grown 70% of the world's opium). The result is that as many refugees fled the drought as the fighting.

The AO also caused Siberia, northern China and Central Asia to become exceptionally cold which also affected Canada. It is not a coincidence that Krasnoyarsk in Siberia reported temperatures of $-45°C$ in January 2001, when they would normally expect $-36°C$. The impact of this was felt first in China, where, as we shall see, the water table under the Beijing area is exceptionally low. To add to the problems the Yellow River, which normally supplies northern China, is now often dry before reaching the sea.

Associated religious and disease cycles

It seems that cool periods often trigger religious movements. St Paul's journeys took place in the first cool minimum AD and many of the heretical dissentions of the embryonic Christian Church took place late in the next minimum in the third century. As we saw earlier, the cool period around the death of Mohammed propelled his followers to spread along North Africa into Spain; they also invaded Arabia, Mesopotamia and later India, in the process destroying many of the flourishing Christian settlements weakened by the previous minimum. The Moors were only stopped in Europe at Tours when, in the next minimum, Charles Martel defeated their army in 732.

The Christian Church underwent its greatest changes in the second millennium. The first major setback was during the second Islamic jihad, when Ottoman Turks took the previously impregnable Constantinople in 1453 and severely diminished the scope of the eastern Church. The next cool period, the Sporer Minimum, which spawned the Reformation, was just as devastating.

Since then it could be argued that revivals in the Church occurred during the Maunder Minimum, with the rise of the Puritans and the Counter Reformation led by the Jesuits. John Wesley's mission created Nonconformism and forced reforms in the Anglican Church, which then flourished in the Victorian era after the Sabine Minimum. From this one could suggest that the onset of the next minimum would see a resurgence of religious faith. Although difficult to quantify, a number of religious cycles are due during this period.

The next chapter describes the effect of an 800 year disease cycle that would make even more lethal the mass movements of people likely following the PDO described earlier. Historically, the three mass movements out of Central Asia from 400BC to the Mongols in 1200 have brought the bubonic plague to those who had no immunity to the scourge killing a high proportion of the population.

Now, 800 years later, we are due for another mass movement of people but this time the bubonic plague may not be the killer. In the early years of the twenty-first century half the world's population are living in twenty-three crowded cities – most of them within the tropics – and with the PDO, this proportion could rise much higher. These desperately unfortunate people will be prey to water-borne diseases such as cholera or typhoid fever, sexually transmitted scourges such as AIDS, and probably typhus spread by lice.

In 2001 *The Economist* reported that the number of HIV-positive sufferers is increasing at the rate of 15,000 every day, and that over 7% of the population in 21 countries tested positive; it is estimated that when 25% are infected, GDP drops by at least 1%. Should this cycle arrive as expected, the toll on these poor, increasingly undernourished people would be catastrophic.

What can we expect?

The events described earlier are all driven, not by man, but by powerful forces within the solar system and within the earth's structure over which we have no control. As the combination of events has not occurred for some forty years we have little historical precedent and mankind can only try to anticipate what may happen and take contingent precautions.

Water supplies: Water is essential to life. We can possibly live without oil but in the first two or three decades of the twenty-first century, water supplies in certain vital areas could be highly uncertain should the conditions of a negative PDO and positive AMO, described earlier, prevail.

After the most benign combination lasting for twenty years from the mid-1970s to the mid-1990s, the northern hemisphere has entered the least benign combination of oceanic oscillations. As the most productive grain production areas in North America are likely to be curtailed, the grain excesses of the past decades will cease and the price of growing commodities will rise. Although food constitutes less than 20% of an individual's incomes in the West – and a much higher proportion in less-developed countries – a major price hike would be highly deflationary unless central bankers increase the supply of money – an inflationary action – see chapter 9.

A rise in the food sector is likely to affect all commodities and as many of the deficit areas are oil producing, they could bid up the price of all the grains even more highly. One can expect some alternative supplies to become available from the Southern Hemisphere but in the north, land not normally cultivated could produce crops such as oats and rye requiring less moisture; cattle feed could be in short supply and diets will have to change. One might anticipate a considerable investment in genetically modified crops, cultivating previously poor land and techniques such as hydroponics.

While the West usually has adequate supplies, around 40% of the world's population suffer from shortages and over 80% of Third World diseases are water-based. The UN estimates that by 2025, forty-five countries, including China and India, will suffer chronic freshwater shortages and the disease rate will soar. Put in another context: at present, the world uses 25% of the available rainfall. If the global population continues to grow at its present rate, then by 2020 this proportion will need to rise to 70% – often from the most innacessible rivers. The water is skewed away from the centres of population.

Water positive states such as Canada and Turkey could become highly important economically. There will be a demand for desalination plants and cheap energy such as cold fusion and an increase in nuclear power. Shortages of water leading to conflicts and migrations of people will be considered later.

Potential for war in the Middle East

There have been many conflicts over water in the Middle East. In modern times the first Zionists fought for water supplies in 1948 and the 1967 Arab-Israeli war was directly about water. The problem for the Arabs is that 85% of their supplies arise from non-Arab sources: the Nile, Jordan, Tigris and the Euphrates. For example, Egypt has said it will go to war should there be a threat to the Nile, which could come should the Numidians to the south build a dam restricting the Blue Nile; Israel has made threats to Syria should the Jordan be interrupted. Turkey is in a particularly strong position, for it controls the source of the Euphrates and Tigris – the first flows through Syria before reaching Iraq and both are essential to life in these countries.

There are additional problems from the AMO and PDO described earlier, for it is likely that in the twenty-first century the Middle East will be hit by the AMO deflecting the jet stream further north. As mentioned earlier, the Jordan is estimated to have a similar amount of water as in 1974, when the AMO was previously positive, but since then the population has risen by nearly 50%.

Furthermore, 70% of Arab lands, including the Arabian Peninsula, are virtual desert, with an annual rainfall of around twelve centimetres a year. Even some of the arable lands are being rendered infertile through over-pumping such as the Euphrates Valley where excessive use of irrigation and incoming contaminated water has left a salt deposit which sours the land.

Apportioning the River Jordan is one of the critical issues for peace between the Arabs and Israelis. The river is formed by the Banias, the Hasbani and the Dan; the Dan rises in the disputed region with Syria, from springs that are heavily protected by Israel. They all meet about four miles inside northern Israel, and after 1948 the flow was accelerated when Israel drained the Hulek Lake and marshes in Upper Galilee. This caused friction with Syria when villagers were expelled from the demilitarised zone agreed by the 1949 peace between the two countries.

The continued work included building the E. Gore Canal from the Sea of Galilee to the Dead Sea, which is primarily used by Jordan, although under Israeli control; there is also the Israel National Water Carrier, which flows west then south towards Gaza and the major Yarkon-Taninim aquifer. At one point there were plans to connect this to the Nile. The use by Israel of 95% of the renewable water resources was the main cause of the 1967 war. Since the last NAO 'high' in the 1970s, the demand for water has gone up by well over 50% and water levels in the Sea of Galilee and the Dead Sea are declining.

The conflict with Jordan focuses around the difference in water consumption, with Israel using 300 litres per person per day – about the same as in Europe – compared to 80 litres per person per day in Jordan; there are also complaints that the Arab water is of a lower quality and more saline than that available to the Jews. Jordan could also face conflict with Syria over additional demand from the E. Gore.

Further south the conflict with the Palestinians in the Gaza Strip is probably the most contentious for as the aquifers are pumped lower, the water quality falls, the incidence of disease rises and the land becomes saline. Several solutions have been suggested, but these would only be possible within the context of the overall political and financial settlement for the Strip. One solution for the region is to build desalination plants, but these are fuel-intensive and could only be part of an Arab-Israeli settlement to make cheap oil available. Another is to divert the Latani River in southern Lebanon to connect it with the Hasbaiya and thus augment the total water supplies.

It is possible that Turkey could make more of the Euphrates available to Syria, which depends upon the river for the greatest part of its needs; this could stop the proposed building of the Mukheiba Dam that would have reduced the Israeli take from the Jordan by 35%. Finally, the Arabs could make better use of water. Unlike the Israelis, who reduce evaporation through covered conduits and trickle irrigation, the Arabs use ancient methods of open ditches, where some 70% is lost through evaporation. These are important factors should Israel decide to occupy the whole of the West Bank if Palestinian terrorist attacks become intolerable.

Turkey holds the key to Syria and Iraq's water supplies: the South-east Anatolia Project (GAP) is the largest hydro-electric project in Turkey and was opened in 1992 when the giant Ataturk Dam started to flood. By 2015 it will be adding 20% to the present electricity generated in the country and could irrigate an area the size of Israel and in theory double agricultural output. Before the dam was built, the Euphrates delivered about 7,000 billion gallons every year to Syria, but this could halve and the water be made much more saline after irrigating Turkish soil. In the mid-1990s pessimistic forecasts in Syria and Iraq estimated that the GAP could reduce the Euphrates flow by 40% to Syria and 90% to Iraq.

The penalties for Iraq could be even greater after Syria's own irrigation plans are implemented. This has united the two countries, previously sworn enemies, with support from the Kurdish Workers Party (PKK), a group who claim a homeland in Turkey and who opposed the construction of the Ataturk Dam, obliging the Turks to deploy detachments of their army in the area. This could have dire consequences for peace between Israel and the Arabs.

The Tigris runs through Baghdad and joins the Euphrates at Basra, after the latter river has absorbed a considerable amount of salt from irrigation upstream. In Saddam's time a canal was dug at the junction with the ostensible purpose of washing salt from the soil, but it also drained the area occupied by the Marsh Arabs, a Shi'ia people hostile to Saddam Hussein. This project is in the process of being reversed with the victory of the Shi'ias in the recent Iraqi elections.

Potential for conflict around China: The negative Pacific Decodal Oscillation (PDO), considered earlier, is already having a powerful impact on north China and could be a major source of conflict with her neighbours and also internally.

Before 1995, and the advent of the Negative PDO, there was adequate moisture to irrigate fields using rainfall and pumped water but since then the water table has been depleting by 3-10 feet a year so that now some wells have to be dug half a mile to find aquifers of fresh water. This has meant that water supplies for the mass of people has declined by nearly 40% – although one suspects this does not apply to the Chinese bosses.

Although much of industry will be forced to migrate south, the real problem is the grain harvest that has contracted by 66 million tons – an equivalent amount to Canada's total output. One thousand tons of rainfall is needed to grow one ton of grain (3,000 tons are needed for rice) which makes it is easier to import water in food form from a world that is becoming progressively short of water.

How they will deal with the 2008 Olympics is anybody's guess! The reported solution is to build huge pipelines from the south that would cost over $60 billion and, starting in 2010, would take 40 to 50 years. This does not get over the immediate problem and is likely to cause a huge migration south. It has happened before in similar circumstances.

Drought brings dust clouds like those that occurred in the 1930s Dust Bowl. The trouble for China's neighbours is that they combine with one of the most prevalent sources of pollution in the world and would be a huge cause of concern for anyone downwind. The problem for China is how deal with adjacent states such as North Korea, the Central Asian Republics and with their own countrymen.

Other conflicts apart from the Middle East and China: disputes could break out between any country or area that attempts to deny others the water they deem theirs or, if they are strong enough, to appropriate it. Among these could be India, Pakistan and Afghanistan, among the Central Asian republics and East Africa.

Russia is one area that could be in great difficulty should major volcanic eruptions occur from the close proximity of the moon in 2008 described earlier. Northern latitudes could become extremely cold from high seismic activity making it very difficult to survive. Unlike the USA or China that have a long crossable north/south axis, Russia's southern border is formed by series of mountains stretching from the Caucasus, the Hindu Kush to the Himalayas and Mongolia to the east. If this were to happen, tensions between Russia and its neighbours could become very strained.

Refugees: Mass movements have occurred around every eight hundred years bringing disease and real problems to the host area as described in the next chapter, the last being Genghis Khan in 1200. By early in the twenty-first century the rise in population that has occurred in the last forty years will be experiencing much reduced food production and potential host areas such as Australia, parts of Africa, South America and the southern European countries will be facing demands for resettlement. They will not be alone. Countries like the USA that have been a magnet for economic refugees for many decades may have to reverse their policies as California, and other southern states bordering Mexico, become unable to support their own populations and millions may be forced to move back to their homelands.

Political priorities are likely to move away from international agreements and political and economic unions into domestic matters and security – particularly from militant refugees. Dr Iben Browning commented on conditions such as this by suggesting that those countries that had previously excess food provisions would have sufficient, and those that had sufficient, would starve.

Some implications

This chapter so far has considered only the weather factors impinging on the early decades of the twenty-first century. But other major disruptions are likely to occur related from oil shortages, the threat of terrorism and the likely bursting of the credit bubble. All these are likely to distort and alter an already critical situation. What can various parts of the world expect?

The oil-rich areas affected by the negative PDO – particularly the Middle East and parts of Central Asia will at the same time be short of water. This will create threats to the ruling authorities who are likely to force up the price of oil to pay for the rising price of food. This will create major refugee problems for southern Europe made worse should al-Qa'eda decide to infiltrate those on the move. The alliance between Israel, Turkey and America's allies could be strengthened.

Northern Europe should not be short of water. It will also be relatively warm, and Russia should therefore receive additional moisture unless there is major volcanic action that would cause it also to be a source of refugees. Western Europe may not prove helpful to the refugee problem, should the bursting of the credit bubble described in a following chapter, cause individual countries to become increasingly nationalistic and protectionist. The need to provide additional security could seriously reduce the ability of the West to fund welfare and state run programmes; it could also create new alignments.

In North America, the West Coast could be in some difficulties with extremes of precipitation and drought, while elsewhere Mexico could receive excess rainfall. This could mean that California will be unable to support as many people, and numbers of Hispanics could drift south to find work. If dust bowl conditions apply to the central regions there will also be a drift south by farmers seeking land elsewhere – possibly into Mexico. Any bursting of the credit bubble could seriously reduce the ability of the US to assist in funding the refugee problem although there would still be extensive military commitments.

The areas most likely to benefit are those in the Southern Hemisphere will be Australia, New Zealand, South Africa, the Andes Republics, Brazil and Argentina. All these countries should be able to export food and have adequate moisture. This might make them prey to predators. These areas of stability should be able to attract investors towards energy, commodity based companies and food production.

During the 1920s and 1930s Raymond Wheeler, professor of psychology at Kansas State University worked on the relationship between events and climate, and became interested in people's reaction to changing weather conditions. After analysing the available data, he concluded that we behave differently depending on how hot or cold, wet or dry it is. In particular he argued that a cool, dry climate, which occurs during the various climatic minima, increases levels of human activity and makes people discontented, as they were during the Maunder Minimum.

As we have seen, there is much cause for potential unrest in the early decades of the twenty-first century but there is also cause for optimism for there is always a silver lining after a cold spell. After the Black Death came the freeing of the serfs in England and the Italian Renaissance. After the chaotic seventeenth century, Britain was the first to industrialise, and the dynamism dominated the world – an energy that continued despite losing the American Colonies. The Dutch, freed from Spain after the Treaty of Westphalia in 1648, became one of the greatest trading nations the world has known, and France under Louis XIV became the dominant nation on the Continent. After the chaos of Thirty Years War the Prussians seized the opportunity to stamp their authority in the east while in the north Hamburg's maritime trade boomed.

References

www.paztcn.wr.usgs.gov/rsch_highlight/articles/200404.html

Browning, Dr I., and Nels Winkless, *Climate and the Affairs of Man* (Fraser, 1975).

Browning, Dr I., and Dr E. Garriss, *Past and Future History* (Fraser, 1981).

Browning Newsletter, The, Fraser Publishing, P.O. Box 494, Burlington, Vermont 05402 (November 2002).

Bulloch, J., and Adel Darwish, *Water Wars* (Gollancz, 1993).

Clarke, R., *Water, The International Crisis* (Earthscan, 1991).

Diamond, J., *Guns, Germs and Steel* (Jonathan Cape, 1997).

Fagan, B., *The Little Ice Age* (Basic Books, 2000).

Hackett Fisher, D., *The Great Wave* (OUP, 1996).

Hobhouse, H., *The Forces of Change* (Sidgwick & Jackson, 1989).

Houston, W., *Riding the Business Cycle* (Little, Brown, 1995).

Dynamic Four

8

The Battle Against Germs

Since 11 September, the West has been increasingly concerned about the use of biological or chemical weapons. As the last chapter showed, the world might be faced with an even greater risk of diminishing water supplies in relation to a rise in population; water shortages cause malnutrition, particularly among the poorest, and ill-fed people are at greater risk from disease. Drought forces people to choose between starvation and moving, and as we have seen, Dr Iben Browning believed that conditions in the twenty-first century will create a real conflict. Ploughing up new pasture to grow more food might only make things worse, for many of the deadly ebola-type diseases come from disturbing uncultivated land.

Browning also drew attention to the regular 800-year cycle of disease going back to at least 1200 BC caused by a period of extreme cold forcing whole tribes to move. It is now 800 years since the last major outbreak of bubonic plague, brought by Genghis Khan's Mongols, struck in the early thirteenth century, and the world could now be faced by another refugee problem aggravated by conflicts in central and other parts of Asia. Any new displacement of peoples will add to the overcrowding of the twenty-three cities – most within the tropics – where half the world's population now lives. The risks will not just be confined to the Third World; modern jet travel can spread infection within hours.

It's amazing that the human species survives!

Left to themselves, every creature reproduces at a greater rate than is needed to maintain its numbers, and until the twentieth century disease regularly wiped out a high proportion of youngsters with measles, whooping cough, enteric fevers and tuberculosis. Throughout history many more people have died from disease than ever perished from war or famine. The most notorious killer was the bubonic plague, first brought to Egypt in around 1200 BC. Next it came to Greece via the steppe nomads from Central Asia in 443 BC. 800 years later the nomadic Huns swept all before them, again bringing the plague. Under Alaric the Visigoth, the invaders stormed Rome in AD 410, but failed to take the almost impregnable land-defences of Constantinople. Unfortunately the defenders caught the bubonic plague, in company with the rest of Europe, whose population fell by nearly a half. Finally, Genghis Khan's warriors once again brought the plague to Europe when a besieged fort at Kaffa in the Crimea was defended by, amongst others, Genoese sailors. The attack failed but, as a parting shot, the Mongols catapulted in the diseased corpse of a slaughtered prisoner which infected the garrison. Once the siege was lifted, the sailors, accompanied by flea-carrying rats, returned to European ports, spreading the disease at every stop. The plague took three years to surge through Europe from 1348, destroying, once again, over one-third of the population.

800 years later we should be very fearful. Conflicts lead to massive numbers of displaced people and cause disruption of water supplies, sewerage and other public health arrangements that keep modern cities free from disease. Apart from the bubonic plague, the main scourges of conflict in previous generations were typhoid, cholera and typhus. Wars also bring malnutrition, which reduces the body's capacity to resist disease; this is almost certainly why the outbreak of Spanish Influenza in 1918 caused more deaths than the Great War. Researchers claim that flu pandemics work in 60-year cycles, the virus arriving each time in a form that overcomes the immunities built up in the population despite many having been inoculated.

Some of the worst outbreaks have followed 178.8-year climatic low points. The very low solar output and high volcanic action causes unusually cool and stormy weather conditions and crop failures. Famine provides people with a choice: either they stay and starve or they leave. However, moving also has its hazards, for they may be travelling to an area that has a disease for which they have no immunity. The classic case was the Spanish invasion of the Americas after their discovery by Columbus, where they introduced smallpox and measles; the returning Conquistadors in turn were thought to have brought syphilis to Europe, as discussed below. They also brought tobacco.

The diseases we can catch

Infectious diseases cause grief when foreign organisms enter the body and cannot be dealt with by its immune system. Like other animals, the human body is composed of cells which require the intake of proteins in the form of amino acids to keep them in good repair; immunity declines with malnutrition, which is why epidemics often follow poor harvests. Apart from a healthy diet the immune system is assisted in repelling disease through exposure to the virus, either through surviving the illness itself, or a small quantity of the virus being introduced through vaccination. Providing smallpox immunity is not new. Infected matter had been injected into people in the East and in the Arab world for centuries before Edward Jenner introduced a much safer vaccination based on his observation that the harmless cowpox gave dairymaids immunity from smallpox. Wellington had his army inoculated, as did Napoleon several years later.

The body's immune system works on the principle that it can detect and produce material to counter a foreign body or antigen. At its heart are complicated proteins called immunoglobulins which, when stimulated by antigens, replicate to generate antibodies. These then usually envelop and destroy the interloper. If the balance of the immune system is compromised by disturbances such as malnutrition, chemotherapy, HIV or severe stress, then this mobilises microbes that were once harmless into becoming active and virulent. For example, in the days before antibiotics, lobar pneumonia could only be cured through the immune system. An infected patient often became extremely ill for six or seven days before staging either a rapid recovery or dying. The survivors had a marked fall in temperature and disappearance of delirium as the immune system generated an antibody quickly enough to overwhelm and kill the infecting bacteria. This was called recovery by crisis.

Bacteria are living organisms shaped like small rods or spheres some one-thousandth of a millimetre across which multiply rapidly in a propitious environment such as a cell; they can also copy their own genes. They are essential to life, aiding the digestion system of mammals, for example, and reducing detritus back to basic matter. Bacteria live naturally in the gut of animals without having the slightest ill-effect on the creature; other less propitious places are in the mouth and genitals. The more well-known bacteria are responsible for cholera, tetanus, the bubonic plague, typhus, chlamydia and syphilis. Protozoa, the smallest animal organisms, are responsible for diseases such as amoebic dysentery and malaria. Like any living being, bacteria need food for production of energy which, unlike plants, cannot come from sunlight and carbon dioxide in the air. They are great survivors (in his book *Power Unseen: How Microbes see the World*, Bernard Dixon reports how some bacteria are able to exist in volcanic larva or in glaciers), with a powerful ability to change their composition, or mutate, making them resistant to main-line antibiotics. It is said that Alexander Fleming's discovery of penicillin immediately set in train its own antidote, for even if a few organisms survived they would multiply to form a resistant strain. This is now becoming evident in cases of gonorrhoea, tuberculosis and malaria, where mutations continue to defy antidotes. One particularly resistant staphylococcus called MRSA causes sores over the human body and infects wounds. Penicillin used to be effective but a mutation produced an enzyme that dissolved the antibiotic. By the early twenty first century, only the drug Vancomycin remained effective against some of these resistant organisms. Furthermore, bacteriologists have found that drug-resistance can be transmitted within bacteria species.

The main causes of infections other than bacteria are viruses. These are tiny organisms that can only live and duplicate within cells; they are also able to mutate 1 million times faster than human cells and cannot be killed by antibiotics. Viruses can only be seen under an electron microscope and are spherical in shape. They are versatile enough to grow within insect cells, which helps propagation via mosquito-borne sickness such as yellow fever. They are also responsible for smallpox, herpes, some forms of pneumonia, measles, influenza, mumps and AIDS. In addition, some of the haemorrhagic plagues such as lassa and junin fever are caused by viruses carried by mouse droppings. However the most deadly of all, ebola, has no known carrier.

The body's main natural defence against viral infections is a substance called interferon, which is synthesized and liberated by cells in the course of infection; it then diffuses through the body fluids into unaffected cells to render them immune from viral damage. Immunity against a virus can be increased by inoculation and by stimulating the body's own immune system through the introduction of a substance called viral nucleic acid. Past infection with an epidemic such as measles can also create immunity.

The body is exposed to many childhood viral diseases, such as measles, which are often caught directly through droplets – or aerosols – carried by breath. There is then a pause (of up to ten days in the case of measles) before there are catarrhal symptoms then a skin rash. During the initial period the virus is carried around the body to the lymph glands, gastro-intestinal tract, the tonsils and appendix. The cell sites where the virus lodges also indirectly generate an antibody, which then destroys both the infected cell and the virus. Immunity for the future is achieved through the antibodies that remain in the blood.

How we catch these dreaded bugs

Many deadly diseases are imported. When the Spanish invaded Mexico and Peru, infinitely more Aztecs and Incas died of smallpox and influenza than by force of Spanish arms. Apart from mass movements of people, diseases can be caught in several other ways. Ploughing up new land often disturbs an environment that has its own reservoir of potential pestilence. One such is the bacteria anthrax, that can be latent in soil for many decades. Another haemorrhagic virus, junin, is carried by mice attracted to new sources of food; the mice then infect people through via their droppings and urine. Like other viruses, junin causes bleeding, shock, then death.

Insects are responsible for transmitting a number of terrible scourges. Fleas carried by black rats initially carried the bubonic bacteria; however, its deadly pneumonic form is carried through breath aerosols. Lice carry typhus, while mosquitoes carry malaria and yellow fever. Animals and birds also carry diseases and act as reservoirs for transmission to people: dogs can carry rabies, monkeys carried the haemorrhagic Marburg virus to Germany, Yugoslavia and America. Green monkeys are thought to have harboured the original AIDS virus, mice carry lassa fever and it is known that some wild game carry tetanus, brucellosis and salmonella. Humans also have an awesome ability to spread disease.

Sexually transmitted diseases (STDs) such as syphilis, gonorrhoea, herpes and chlamydia are not new. Syphilis killed many people in the sixteenth century before its transmission was understood; only then did people change their habits. From 1947 many STDs could be cured with antibiotics, but the options are narrowing as new mutations appear. While it seems that the AIDS virus may have been contained in the West, there has been an increase of other sexually transmitted diseases, including Hepatitis B, which, in chronic forms and over a period, can cause cancer of the liver. Chlamydia, though easily treated, is on the increase.

There are several ailments transmitted through the aerosols of human breath, including the common cold, influenza and tuberculosis. Doctors believed that the latter was almost always curable but it has now become more problematic with the mutation to a highly resistant form of the tubercle bacillus. Modern travel is another problem, for not only can diseases be caught through an aircraft's air system but someone can carry one of the deadly haemorrhagic afflictions to the centre of a crowded metropolis. It nearly happened with lassa fever during the outbreak of 1976, when a resident from Chicago visited Nigeria to attend a funeral and caught the disease. Once his condition had been diagnosed all his contacts were kept under strict observation but luckily none succumbed. The story might have been different had he returned to the slums of Rio de Janeiro. Cities have been a focus for diseases from at least Roman times. Potentially the greatest danger to modern man is the rapid growth of conurbations such as Bombay and Calcutta in developing countries

Evolving diseases

Scourges have beset man from the earliest days, when he came down onto the plains and hunted game; often it was the weakest – and possibly infected – prey that was first caught and killed. The next stage was when people settled in villages and, in closer contact, caught new pathogens in an environment where waste would attract predators, and newly cultivated land would release its own diseases.

The rest of this chapter covers the major killers that have struck the West since the fifth century BC.

Bubonic plague was thought to have first infected ancient man when he ate a diseased animal. The first recorded outbreak, however, was in Athens where it was a major contributor to the city's defeat by Sparta. It was carried by the Halstatt invasions of Europe from Central Asia, which indirectly spread from the Ukraine to Spain. The next incursion was when the Huns brought the plague into mainland Europe and the Mediterranean early in the fifth century.

The plague is caused by an egg-shaped bacterium called *Yersinia pestis*, spread by fleas which are in turn carried by rodents – both of which are energetic travellers. Left to themselves the microbes stay in the rodent community and need not attack humans. However when the bacteria infect the black rat they not only play havoc with the animal but are attracted to the refuse normally associated with human dwellings or ships, where the fleas then spread the *Y. pestis*. In a warm climate the sickness begins with a fever; then buboes – swollen lymph glands – appear in the armpits, groin and neck. As the fever rages the nervous system becomes infected, causing a manner similar to drunkenness, and at least half the victims die within five days. Even more die during the winter when the disease, carried by the breath, moves to the lungs and becomes pneumonic, and the patients often die from choking on their vomited blood. In the fifth-century outbreak, the plague also spread eastwards to India, China and Japan.

The next invaders to bring the disease were the Mongols early in the thirteenth century. Europe's natural immunity had been impaired by the famines following the atrocious weather in 1317-8, so many people were no match for the Black Death of 1348. The plague was regarded as a divine punishment for past wrongdoing and even the Pope's exoneration did not help; millions died and had to be buried in mass graves. The story of *The Flying Dutchman*, a ship manned by corpses condemned to sail the seas for ever, might well have originated from reports of vessels drifting around the coasts with dead crews.

Some, however, came off lightly: the city of Milan was almost untouched, as were Jewish people, whose religious food practices required them to have higher cleanliness standards than others. (It did them no good, for they were demonized as poisoners and the ensuing pogroms drove them into Eastern Europe.) There were occasional outbreaks thereafter, the best known being the Great Plague of 1665, which hit London particularly badly and was thought to have been finally eliminated by the Great Fire of 1666. However, the ending is likely to have been more natural, for it is believed the black rats were killed by their brown cousins who did not carry fleas.

There was however a silver lining to the Black Death – or Great Dying, as it was called. A shortage of manpower led to the freeing of the serfs in England and, perhaps unfairly, a weakening of the church's power – after all nobody apart from the Jews could stop the disease spreading! There were some other benefits. The energy of several individuals who survived such as Dante, Petrarch and Boccaccio were prominent in creating the Italian Renaissance.

In 1812, typhus killed more men during Napoleon's invasion of Russia than the cold. It is carried by fleas and ticks that thrive in the cramped, unsanitary conditions found in prisons, slums and some armies. It is thought that typhus was responsible for pestilences in Greco-Roman times, but it is difficult to separate individual diseases, such as dysentery, typhoid, smallpox and scurvy, when they thrive in similar conditions. A new epidemic was noted when Spain employed Cypriot mercenaries in 1489 to fight the Turks. The soldiers went down with a headache, high fever, body rash and swelling in the face; the end came after delirium, sores and gangrene that literally rotted the victims' bodies. In the campaign against the Turks, of the 20,000 who died, only 3,000 were lost in action.

Typhus was rife amongst the Spanish and French armies in the sixteenth century. In one case the French siege of Naples had to be called off when half the attacking troops died within a month. During 1577 in England, one typhus-infected prisoner in an Oxford court wiped out 510 people, including two judges, a sheriff, an under-sheriff, six magistrates, most of the jury and hundreds at the university.

The disease probably took its greatest toll against Napoleon's *grande armée* in the Russian campaign of 1812. Starting out with 500,000 men, over 350,000 were infected by the battle of Borodino, and only 90,000 made it to Moscow, where thousands succumbed to disease and hunger. By the end of December 1812 only 35,000 returned to Germany and of these only 10,000 were capable of fighting. Typhus killed many more allied troops than the Russians in the Crimea and on the Eastern Front in World War I; out of 20 million Russian soldiers, over 3 million died from the disease. By the Second World War the armies had learnt their lesson but even so there was an outbreak among soldiers in Italy and many allied prisoners held by the Chinese died of the disease during the Korean War.

Opening up new pastures for additional grain and beef has introduced mankind to diseases that were previously dormant. One such was in Argentina during the Second World War when ploughing the pampas disturbed the natural habitat of a field mouse *Calomys musculinus*, which harbours the junin virus (named after the nearby Junin River). The disease causes high fever, internal and external bleeding, shock and death. It is caught from inhaling contaminated air or from infected food. Every so often these mice surge in population, only to crash with the virus. In this state the junin spreads to humans, who breathe in the dust from dried faeces and urine.

A similar outbreak occurred in Bolivia when, in an effort to grow more corn and vegetables, the country people cut down dense jungle in the flat areas above the Machupo river floodline. The cultivation again released the *Calomys* mouse which thrived with the increased food supply. As in the Junin outbreak, mouse urine infected both food and house dust. An American research team was asked to investigate and narrowed the vector to the mice, which had spread rapidly after the demise of cats from DDT poisoning. The problem was solved when cats were re-introduced into the village.

Another rodent, a rat *Mastomys natalensis*, carries a similar virus that was discovered in a village hospital at Lassa in Nigeria where several patients were found to have encephalitis (fever, headache, inflammation of the brain, lethargy, seizures), haemorrhage and shock. It was partly cured after the antibodies of someone who had resisted the disease were injected into others and the spread was halted.

Perhaps the most deadly outbreak occurred almost simultaneously in Zaire by the Ebola River and southern Sudan in August 1976. In the centre of Zaire was a mission hospital in the village of Yambuka, where a man was admitted with terrible diarrhoea and was given an injection of antibiotics with a needle that had been used several times. After two days the patient discharged himself, despite haemorrhaging and dysentery. Unfortunately many of the other patients started exhibiting similar symptoms of acute diarrhoea, terrible headaches and bleeding from the gums, bowel and stomach.

The sisters in charge of the mission (there being no qualified doctors) treated the patients with antibiotics but nothing worked. Of those who contracted the symptoms, some 90% perished. Soon the hospital was engulfed by a scourge that turned apparently healthy people, including the nursing sisters, into bleeding convulsing wrecks within a very few days. Ebola was identified as the most lethal disease in the twentieth century after rabies. Samples of the victims' infected blood were sent to the world's top high-security laboratories, where again antibodies were isolated.

Despite a huge effort, including clearing scrub and spraying DDT on swampy ground, malaria has still not been eradicated. In fact, growing crops on fresh ground has created new opportunities for the female mosquitoes of the genus *anopheles gambiae* to lay their eggs in untreated stagnant pools. There are several thousand species of mosquitoes and this is one of the 10% that infect people. Before laying, the female needs to gorge herself on sucked blood and in the process infects her victim.

Malaria is a protozoa that attacks the red corpuscles in the blood, causing feverish paroxysms. Tremors follow which become violent, the face becomes a livid colour and the shaking of the limbs and jaws become uncontrollable. The body then begins to sweat and the patient either dies from exhaustion or falls into a deep sleep before recovering. Once infected the victim can suffer recurrent bouts which cause anaemia, darkening of the skin, or enlargement of the spleen, sometimes leading to liver cancer.

Mosquitoes can only fly two miles; they seek prey at night and prefer not to fly high above the ground. This is why local people build their houses on mounds wherever possible and the surrounding land is drained; upper storeys are used for bedrooms and they sleep under mosquito nets. Over the course of time mankind has had to come to terms with malaria – or swamp fever – which was endemic in Italy during the Roman era. Rome itself was malarial until around 1900 and was only rid of the disease when Mussolini cleared the Pontine Marshes. The disease badly hit the colonial Jamestown settlement in 1607 but was still a grave problem in the southern states of the USA in the nineteenth century. During the summer, the cotton plantation owners either went abroad or moved to the coast, deputing the management of the plantation to the head slave, who was often immune to malaria.

The only known cure before antibiotics were discovered was quinine, prepared by grinding the bark of the cinchona tree and mixing it with white wine. Originally grown in the north Andes, the bark was shipped in small quantities at very high prices to Spain, where the disease was rife. Shrewdly the Jesuits had procured a monopoly of the bark, which enraged some Protestants, who called it 'the devil's powder'.

Malaria strictly limited the advance of colonialism, for only a few white people were immune. Henry Hobhouse in *The Seeds of Change* reports that to remain on station, the British army in India alone needed 750 tons of bark a year – more than was available from the Andean supply. To cure all those infected in India would have required many times that amount. The solution was to plant the smuggled cinchona plant in the Nilgiri Hills of India and in Java, regions with a similar climatic profile to the Andes. By 1880 quinine production was greater than the total produced elsewhere and was mainly used in the subcontinent. The Dutch, however, were more commercially minded and the bark was sent to Europe for processing in Amsterdam and London.

Between 1958 and 1963, $430 million was spent on failed attempts to destroy malaria, and a further $793 million up to 1981. Malaria was slowly eliminated from many areas but then the programme broke down. The expansion in agricultural production opened up new lands and provided ample opportunities for mosquitoes to breed. Although these and other pests were attacked strenuously with DDT and similar pesticides, the inevitable happened and chemically resistant bugs emerged. As insects became immune, in South America and Thailand the disease itself became resistant to the then universal cure of chloroquine and doctors went back to the old staple, quinine.

Man is solely responsible for sexually transmitted diseases (STDs), of which venereal diseases have been one of mankind's greatest scourges, eliminating whole swathes of the population from around the sixteenth century. Humans are particularly good at spreading these germs because our eroticism is unmatched in nature except by dolphins; both species apparently have a similar sexual excitability, not limited by season, which can continue through pregnancy.

The syphilis bacterium was the greatest sexual scourge before AIDS and struck indiscriminately, irrespective of class, gender or race, through the sixteenth century. Although the Holy Roman Emperor Maxmillian III proclaimed it a penalty for blasphemy the Puritans knew better and changed their habits to the strict moral code of John Calvin. These standards were then carried to New England by the Pilgrim Fathers.

Once widely believed to have been brought by the Spaniards from the West Indies, syphilis is now thought to have existed for several thousand years in Europe as a complaint called 'yaws'. This ancestor of the bacillus first lived on decaying matter, then passed to primates, and on to children and young adults, who suffered a disfiguring skin infection and sometimes infected bone marrow. The wearing of clothes reduced direct infection but the germ gained access by the mouth and genitals and spread more rapidly with increased opportunities for coitus in urban life. With more rapid transmission, the disease progressively attacked the nervous system and other organs.

The link between syphilis and the West Indies was originally made in 1495 when Charles VIII of France besieged the Spanish in Naples with 50,000 mercenaries supported by camp followers. His troops, from many parts of western Europe, overcame the defences then sacked the city and raped the female population. Syphilis spread throughout Europe via the returning troops and their 800 women followers. The new plague was horrible and could attack within months or years. It first appeared at the genitals then spread as a general rash over the body into abscesses and sores; it went on to destroy the nose, lips, eyes, genitals and finally attacked bones. By 1500 it had spread to France, Switzerland, Germany, Denmark, Sweden, Holland, England, Scotland, Hungary, Greece, Poland and Russia. It was also carried by troops and sailors to Calcutta, Africa, the Middle East, China, Japan and later to the Antipodes. It felled hundreds of thousands but was not confined to the laity; many priests including bishops and popes are reported to have succumbed as well.

Gonorrhoea, a less heinous disease than syphilis, may also have been present several thousand years ago in Europe and Asia. It affects primarily the urinary tract (and for women their ovaries) but the infection was not identified as an independent bacterial disease until 1827. Before 1947 over 10,000 Americans were dying every year from syphilis, but with the advent of penicillin, which cures both diseases, the number dropped to 6,000 per year by 1949 and in the 1950s was still declining.

But these two diseases were not eradicated. The advent of the birth-control pill increased promiscuity and by the early 1980s over 2.5 million were contracting gonorrhoea annually, with syphilis ranking behind chicken pox as the third most common infectious disease in the USA. Another complication arose in the late 1970s when a penicillin-resistant mutation of gonorrhoea appeared amongst Americans serving in the Philippines, which then spread back to the US, where strains even more resistant to whole families of antibiotics were reported.

The numbers of what were known as pelvic inflammatory diseases (PIDs) were increased by two organisms – herpes and chlamydia. Herpes (HSV 1) has a long history of causing cold sores, and had infected over 90% of older residents in the US and Europe at some time. By 1980 antibodies had been developed but in the same decade a more dangerous strain of herpes appeared called HSV 2; this is a sexually transmitted virus infecting nerve cells and causing painful sores around the mouth and genitals. Between 1966 and 1981 the numbers of HSV 2 sufferers treated by American doctors had increased ninefold and by 1986, 60% of men living in key US cities were infected. By the early 1990s another PID, chlamydia, which can cause female infertility within a year if not treated, was the most infectious disease in the USA after the common cold.

Venereal diseases were not confined to heterosexuals. The gay community was becoming more sexually active, and by 1974, 80% of the 75,000 San Franciscans being treated for STDs were homosexual men. From 1974 to 1979 the incidence increased by 250% and a random survey reported that 20% of homosexuals had gonorrhoea, 10% carried herpes and a smaller proportion were infected with syphilis. There was also a three-fold increase in Hepatitis B (HPV), which can lead to liver cancer. In one form or another, hepatitis has infected humans throughout the centuries but today it infects some 5% of the world's population (over 300 million people), mostly in South America and Africa but increasingly in the United States and Europe.

The AIDS virus was first identified in the early 1980s when a San Francisco general hospital was asked to treat a young male homosexual prostitute with purplish-blue splotches on his skin; a survey showed that twenty-six men from California and New York had the same complaint. Within a relatively short time apparently normal healthy men had died, a number of them from pneumonia. One of the West Coast researchers plotted the rise in the number of men back to the first reported similar case in 1977, forecasting that by 1985, 40% of gay men would be similarly infected. By mid-1982 it had been established that the US epidemic was contracted mainly from two sources: male homosexual activity and intravenous drug users. Equally tragically, haemophiliacs had also caught the disease through infected blood. It is thought that Gaetan Dugas, a promiscuous Canadian flight attendant, was the main link in the spread of AIDS between Africa and North America.

Research as to the origins of AIDS continues but it is thought that the mutating virus could have been carried for centuries by green monkeys in the Lake Victoria region encompassing Rwanda, Uganda, and Tanzania. It was harmless to the monkeys but, possibly through a bite, it spread to humans; it must have stayed local

110

until the region was disrupted by wars following Idi Amin's dismissal in Uganda and the invasion from Tanzanian troops. Every disease needs a period of 'amplification' before it becomes a pandemic and this was the virus's opportunity.

In Africa AIDS initially spread via troops and then by prostitutes along the trading routes. By the late 1990s the growth rate of AIDS in the West was diminishing as people learnt to change their habits. By the early 1990s two-thirds of the world's 13 million carriers were African, but it has now spread to India, the Far East and China. It has also spread to central Europe and Russia. By the early twenty-first century, 10,000 new cases were being reported every day.

Cholera and other water-borne diseases such as typhoid are carried by polluted water and thrive in conurbations with poor sanitation and crowded living conditions. Cities like Calcutta are prime candidates, with rapidly multiplying, ill-nourished people, piles of dung and rubbish from animals and humans, and putrid air conditions. The first cholera outbreak, reported as a new disease, infected the Ganges delta region in 1817.

It is believed that the bacterium *vibrio cholerae* has been around for over 2,500 years. The bacilli transfer from dirty water to the human gut and are then recycled back into the water. The disease can also be caught by eating infected fish, vegetables washed in contaminated water, from flies or soiled towels. Once swallowed, the bacilli multiplies in the intestine, releasing a strong toxin causing violent vomiting and diarrhoea, which rapidly depletes the body of fluids; this in turn causes muscle spasm, circulatory collapse and often death. If untreated, cholera causes up to 50% fatalities within days – even hours. An epidemic can be sparked off by a carrier's faeces being absorbed by fish or water. From the first outbreak in Calcutta, which felled hundreds of thousands including 5,000 British soldiers, it then spread throughout India, the Far East, Arabia and Africa, but at that time stopped short of Europe.

After a decade with only a few fatalities, cholera struck again in 1848, taking 11,000 lives in England. This time the scourge prompted reformers, led by Edwin Chadwick, to overcome insanitary conditions. Chadwick, a zealot for cleansing the unwashed multitude, was appointed commissioner for England's Board of Health. By the time the next epidemic struck in 1868 Chadwick's health reforms, preventative medicine and public refuse collection saved many lives. They were widely copied in Europe and the USA, which markedly reduced cholera and other diseases, including typhoid fever, caused by the bacterium *salmonella typhi*, which causes diarrhoea, headaches, intestinal inflammation and dysentery. It was not until Louis Pasteur, Robert Loch and others led research to isolate the bacteria that it could later be treated by antibiotics. However, cholera is still a danger; in 1991 bilge water thought to have been pumped from a Chinese freighter in Peruvian waters first infected the marine environment. Within two years of the release there were 500,000 cases of the disease in Latin America, which cost the Pan-American Health Organization $200 million improving sanitation, sewage treatment and cleaning the water supplies.

Warfare

The West became aware that it is vulnerable to suicide attacks after 11 September. The initial attack was physical but it was soon realized that chemical, biological and even nuclear attacks could be used as well. Quite suddenly stocks of war-surplus anti-gas respirators and protective clothing were being bought by civilians in anticipation that these weapons could be used. The threat is not new. Although perhaps unintentionally, the Black Death was started when Mongols catapulted a diseased corpse into the Kaffa fort in the fourteenth century.

Since then this type of warfare has become primarily a military weapon first used on the Western Front in the First World War. However the Russians, and later the Iraqis, spent considerable sums on various toxins for only state-backed terrorists can produce the most effective results. Fortunately, most biological weapons are quite difficult to use for conditions have to be almost perfect in order for them to be effective. As with the anthrax attacks in America and the possibility of chemical weapons, both can be effective as a means of creating apprehension and fear. The following is a brief summary of this type of warfare.

Chlorine was first used on the Ypres front in April 1915 when the Germans released the gas from massed cylinders against unprepared French troops. Chlorine attacks the eyes and lungs, which in this case incapacitated the defenders, although the attack was not followed up. The defence was a simple form of respirator but gases such as mustard gas and phosgene were more sophisticated, attacking the skin and obliging defenders to wear protective clothing, so restricting their movement. After the war the Geneva Convention of 1925 banned the use of gas in warfare, although the Italians employed it in Abyssinia and the Japanese in China before World War II – both times against unarmed civilians, to cause panic.

The nerve gas tabum – a cyanide-based compound that poisons the nervous system – was available to the Germans in 1945 in sufficient quantities to kill the world's population several times over; fortunately it was never used, probably through fear of retaliation. More modern research has produced organophosphorus agents, related to insecticides, which cause the bronchial passages to fill with mucus, the vision to be dimmed, uncontrollable vomiting and defecation, convulsions leading to paralysis, respiratory failure and death within a few minutes. The best-known of these are sarin and VX, both of which are contact and respiratory poisons, of which one milligram would be lethal. Both can be made from chemicals quite readily available. On the battlefield these would be delivered by shells, bombs or landmines, but the attack in a Tokyo subway was delivered through plastic bags and this method could be used once again. The antidote is a gas mask, skin protection and the injection of atropine citrate and oxime, which reverses the effect of the gas.

Bacterial warfare has been used over the centuries to poison water supplies, but bacteria-based diseases can now be dealt with by antibiotics. Even more serious is the risk of a scenario set out by Tom Clancy in his book *Executive Orders*, in which a power-hungry Iranian Americaphobe sets out to destroy the US through spreading the ebola virus through aerosols left in strategic exhibition centres. It is possible to inoculate against the virus but it can only be stopped from spreading through isolation.

Anthrax has been used against media and political figures in the US, spread by envelopes sent through the mail. It is a bacterial organism which by itself cannot last long in the open but when existing as spores can contaminate pastures and soil for many years; it is thought that the strains used could only have been developed by a state apparatus – possibly Iraq. Anthrax has a history of affecting grazing animals going back to the Book of Exodus; it is most commonly caught from handling infected skins that cause lesions which develop rapidly into malignant pustules and, if not treated, septicaemia. Its most deadly form for humans is through inhalation, where only a tiny dose of a few thousand spores could be lethal; the toxins attack the lungs and the heart and death follows in days. It can be cured with antibiotics if caught early enough.

Another potentially lethal disease for those not vaccinated is smallpox, which also has a long history; it killed Rameses V in 1156 BC. It is a highly contagious virus that, after about fourteen days' incubation, causes a fever, skin blotches, then a haemorrhagic rash which is usually fatal. The virus is unfortunately very stable and can survive, for example in bales of cotton or laundry, for many months. There is protection through vaccination but there is no way of stopping its spread other than quarantine of the infected person. The last outbreak was before 1977; it was then declared eradicated and only a small quantity is kept in secure repositories; vaccination was discontinued but stocks of the serum are being built up. Like anthrax, it could be very dangerous if infected so-called 'martyrs' were distributed in crowded public spaces; US models show that an attack could kill 1 million people within two months in three American cities. This is why the President has offered vaccination to all citizens.

The present danger of disease now comes from five directions. First, as we have seen, there is a chronic shortage of water in many countries due to rising populations demanding increasing quantities and outrunning supplies of both stored water in aquifers and the ability to collect rainwater. Already an increasing proportion of land is becoming saline through over-irrigation, so there could be major grain shortages. People with malnutrition are more likely to catch diseases, 80% of which are water-based. By 2025 the UN estimates that forty-five countries, including China and India, will suffer acute freshwater shortages and the disease rate could soar. Put in another context: at present the world uses 25% of the available rainfall; if the global population continues to grow at the present rate, then by 2020 this proportion will need to rise to 70%.

These problems are not confined to the Third World. The migration from the countryside to the cities has accelerated since the Second World War. Countries like Russia and China had up to 80% of the population living in the country until the 1930s, with only a small proportion in the cities employed in manufacturing. Now the percentages there have switched dramatically, as they have in many developing countries.

The second danger is from the climatic oscillations described in chapter 7. These are denying water to areas of the Far and Middle East and Africa, causing drought in northern China, central Asia, Afghanistan, Iran, Southern Arabia and East Africa. This alone is causing refugees to move away from their homelands towards towns and cities. In 1950 there were only two 'mega-cities', London and New York, but by 1990 they had been joined by Buenos Aires, Rio de Janeiro, Sao Paulo, Mexico City and Los Angeles in the Americas; those in the East include Beijing, Shanghai, Calcutta, Bombay and Tokyo. Only a few of these are wealthy enough regularly to update their sanitary systems – quite apart from keeping the malarial mosquito at bay. Their unfortunate inhabitants could suffer increasingly from water-borne diseases such as cholera and typhoid.

Thirdly, the refugee problem has been accelerated since the events of 11 September. Only a few weeks after the outrage there were 7 million Afghans in Pakistan, even before hostilities had begun. Many more could be added to those displaced if there is a conflict between India and Pakistan. As we have seen, refugees can carry diseases into a host country from which the inhabitants have no immunity. Migrants not only carry disease but also possibly increase crime when moving from countries such as Albania where drug smuggling is rampant. Included in this category should be Severe Acute Respiratory Syndrome (SARS) that travelled from China and the East to Canada – not unlike, but not thankfully as severe, as the Spanish 'Flu after World War One. Although people living in close proximity are more likely to pass on the H5N1 virus should it be directly communicable by humans. Fourthly, as described earlier, the West is vulnerable to chemical and biological attacks, but these could be difficult to mount unless they were sponsored by a nation state. The material may not be all that difficult to come by; there are reports that there is enough anthrax buried on Vozrozhdiye Island in the middle of the Aral Sea to kill every person in the world. Apparently the spores were taken from a biological weapons processing plant in great secrecy during the dying years of the Soviet Union and buried in drums only a few feet below the surface.

Fifth, there is the danger from blights such as those that destroyed the crops during the Irish Potato Famine and forced virtually an entire nation to migrate. With the world poised on the edge of a probable water shortage, the destruction of a wheat, soyabean or corn crop could create worldwide devastation. There are also animal diseases such as swine fever and foot and mouth scourges.

When looking at such evidence, it is hardly surprising that the most dangerous biological agents identified in a scientific review are anthrax, botulism, tularaemia, the plague, smallpox and haemorrhagic fever.

The modern threat

While some killers have been dealt with and removed, strains of mosquito are emerging that are immune to DDT and the parasites that cause malaria are becoming resistant to chloroquine. Tuberculosis, which was thought eradicated, is now returning with a mutation resistant to main-line remedies, and new mutations of gonorrhea have made that STD expensive to treat. In addition, new strains of influenza are emerging. But perhaps the most dangerous are the potentially untreatable scourges, like the haemorrhagic diseases described earlier, which have no known reservoir or vector apart from man. Already it is reported that hanta virus, a potentially fatal disease spread by rats and mice, is sweeping the war-torn terrain of the Balkans.

To make the prognosis even more disturbing, hospitals are becoming once more a focus for incubating bugs. A survey produced by the *Journal of the American Medical Association* showed that half the patients in 1,500 European hospitals were on antibiotic treatment for infections they had acquired as patients. As we have seen, the most worrying of these is the staphylococcus MRSA, which can only be treated by a drug called Vancomycin – and even this may soon be ineffective.

One has to be confident in mankind's ability to adapt and survive, despite every attempt by the Four Horsemen of the Apocalypse (war, famine, pestilence and death) to destroy us. Local conflicts are bad enough but the horrors of an international war have been drastically reduced by responsible nations being armed with nuclear weapons. Famine is still a major factor, killing hundreds of thousands, particularly in the Sahel region of Africa.

It is the contention of this chapter that the real danger to millions of the human race will come from hunger allied to disease, which is unlikely to be contained by international agencies. Perhaps many, sensing the danger from STDs, will not just take better precautions but practice abstinence like our Puritan forebears; this could well be coupled with a religious revival that preaches the sound principles of Moses' Ten Commandments and Christ's teachings. People may also move from the danger of diseases in Western cities as modern technology enables those with a suitable skill to practise their trade or profession away from a central office.

Perhaps we should also be comforted by the expanding science of bio-technology, which seeks to identify the human genes whose malfunction is responsible for specific diseases; once recognised, they may be replaced through gene therapy. The techniques can also be used to test whether a patient either has, or is at risk of contracting, an ailment in time for corrective steps to be taken. Experts in this science also believe that bio-technology can be used for testing drugs much more rapidly than at present by creating organic systems that closely resemble human metabolisms.

Even if there were a catastrophe on the scale of the fifth-century plague or the Black Death, nature seems to have a way of compensating the human race, and modern medicine is far from being defeated. True, those weakened by the scourge are often themselves so debilitated that they fall prey to other diseases but there are compensations for the survivors. As we have seen, the Italian Renaissance was stimulated by those who survived the Black Death, and, in England at least, freedom came for the serfs. Nothing is permanent. Man's spirit will always overcome tragedies – perhaps in ways not yet dreamt of.

References

Brown, L.R. (ed.), *The State of the World* reports (Worldwatch Institute, 2000).

Burnet, Macfarlane, and David White, *Natural History of Infectious Diseases* (Institute of Biology Studies, 1971).

Garrett, L., *The Coming Plague* (Virago, 1995).

Hobhouse, H. *Forces of Change* (Sidgwick & Jackson, 1989)

Hobhouse, H., *The Seeds of Change* (Sidgwick & Jackson, 1985).

Karlen, A., *Plague's Progress* (Victor Gollancz, 1995).

Dynamic Five

9

The Greatest Credit Bubble Ever

'All the business of war, and indeed all the business of life, is to endeavour to find out what you don't know by what you do; that's what I called "guessing what was at the other side of the hill".'

The Duke of Wellington

It was probably the span of two generations that encouraged the biblical Jews to keep the fifty-year Jubilee. Leviticus 25 explains how they worked on a seven-year cycle and the fiftieth year was seven cycles plus one. At this point all debts and onerous contracts were rendered void, leases were set at market value and the nation spent a year recovering from the previous excesses. The Mayans had a similar rhythm of fifty four years that was a signal to rebuild their temples, homes and lives.

The fifty-year idea was resurrected by a British Enlightenment thinker, William Jeavons, who rediscovered the fifty-year rhythm; then in the late 1920s the Russian economist Nicolai Kondratieff correctly foretold the 1930s Depression. Working in the Moscow Academy of Agriculture, he was one of the very few who forecast that the West would suffer a great depression in the 1930s.

He was proved right, and his Communist bosses were delighted. They were less pleased when he also predicted that the West would recover, and poor Nicolai was banished and died in Siberia. His work was published in German and achieved some circulation but it only won acclaim when the Austrian economist Joseph Schumpeter wrote his great work Business Cycles, and named the long wave of around fifty years after Kondratieff. Now, fifty years after the Second World War, we are faced with economies that are even more extended than those of 1930. This chapter describes how the same cycle might impact on the over-extended West.

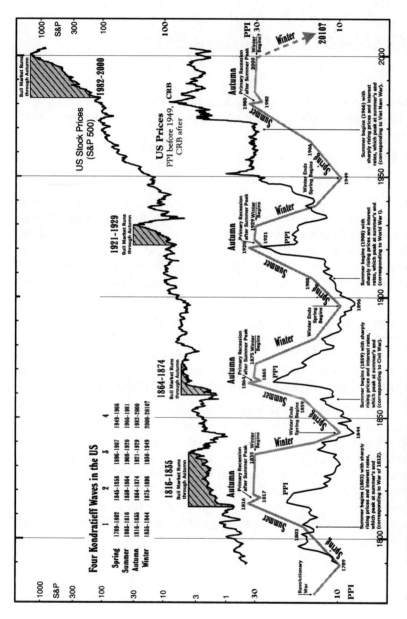

Chart 2. THE KONDRATIEFF WAVE June 1798 through February 2003 showing waves K1, K2, K3 and estimates of K4 – see text *Courtesy of The Long Wave Analyst and Topline Investment Graphics*

The fifty-year cycle mentioned in chapter 5 is now shown graphically by courtesy of The Long Wave Analyst and represented in Chart 2. There have been three complete cycles so far, starting in 1789, called K1, K2 and K3; they all show a similar pattern and have lasted between forty-five and sixty years. Supporters of the cycle have designated the present rhythm, which started in 1949, as K4. The irregularity of the cycle makes an excellent analytical, but a poor predictive tool.

The first stage of the rhythm is the up-wave or spring-summer phase. It starts from a previous recession at first slowly and then with a more or less a continuous upswing in economic activity, usually lasting over half the length of the cycle. Towards the end of this phase there is a build-up of debt, prices rocket and inflation is rife. There is then a financial crisis followed by a sharp recession; some early analysts believed that the last up-wave ended in 1974, but it is more likely to have been 1980.

The plateau (or autumn) phase is a relatively short period of apparent stabilisation. The economy comes out of recession and markets continue their upward trend but, despite this, debt continues to rise. The length of the plateau varies. It was twenty years from 1816 to 1836 during K1, and ten years in both K2 and K3; the Long Wave Analyst believes K4 lasted around twenty years.

The cycle is completed by the down-wave (or winter) phase, which lasted from only ten years in K1 to the more normal fifteen to twenty years. It has always been accompanied by rapidly falling stock, commodity and finished-goods markets. At the same time triple-A and treasury-bond markets have boomed while the remainder of the debt markets have collapsed. The story of Japan from 1990 is an example of what could happen. During that decade the value of Japanese houses declined sharply and the Nikkei Dow by 75% – implying that cash has increased in value, as always happens in a deflationary environment.

However in times of crisis currencies themselves crash, leaving gold as the only ultimate store of value. The chart also shows the movement of the bond market, the price index and stock market at each stage of the three completed cycles. There is a regular pattern of bond yields, rising then falling, with the price index and stocks blowing off during the autumn phase. There is compelling evidence that the winter phase of K4 started in 1999/2000.

While the Kondratieff Wave is primarily economic, other events may follow. Wars of aggression seem to be associated with the upwave part of the K-waves. The Napoleonic Wars were in the early years of K1, the Franco-Prussian War was near the top of K2 and the First World War approached the peak of K3. It can be argued that communism collapsed near the top of K4.

Conversely wars of liberation and civil conflicts appear to coincide with the troughs. Greece, Mexico and others gained their independence near the first low-point. The 1848 European rebellions occurred at the low of K2 in a period known as the 'Hungry Forties'. The Boer War occurred at the trough of K3 and the Second World War during the downwave of K3. While this clearly was a war of expansion, historians argue this was a continuation of the First World War.

Some modern economists criticise the relevance of Kondratieff's work to the modern world because he used the price changes of basic materials such as iron ore, coal and pig iron as well as interest rates to arrive at his conclusions. He also gave no reason why the waves actually happened, unlike Schumpeter, who believed they were caused by an innovation cycle of fifty years. However, this in turn is somewhat incongruous to modern eyes, used to product cycles of a few years or even months. A much more recent indicator will surely be debt as was mentioned earlier.

Will the events of 11 September now accelerate the K4 down-wave? In boom times they might not, but unfortunately they hit a world already sliding into recession from a separate cycle discovered by a French economist named Clement Juglar. In 1864 he analysed a nine- to eleven-year cycle of booms and busts going back to the late decades of the eighteenth century.

The Juglar Cycle also seemed to apply in the twentieth century, identifying a recession at the end of every decade, apart from the 1940s, when war distorted the cycle. If the Juglar and Kondratieff cycles are considered together, there is a progression of deepening recessions from the late summer to end of the autumn phase of the cycle. Dr Iben Browning, who described how exceptional tidal forces trigger volcanoes, gave the analogy of bursting a boiler. A similar reasoning applies to how the Juglar cycles precipitates a Kondratieff down-wave after an excessive credit bubble. As Browning puts it:

If you want to burst a boiler [a credit bubble] then screw the valves down tightly and light a roaring fire in the furnace [create a mountain of debt]. If at some point you hit the boiler with a hammer [a Juglar recession] you have arranged to be present at the explosion [a credit collapse].

During the nineteenth century the free world was on the gold standard which meant that the Juglar Cycle, and to an extent the Kondratieff Wave, were largely controlled automatically. For example, if any economy overheated and prices rose, foreigners, fearing a loss of value of their paper currency (which was gold-backed), sold their paper holdings for metal. If interest rates were then raised, the gold loss would be reversed, prices would fall and the currency would be in demand once more. The system self-corrected quite well.

In the twentieth century matters changed. The US Federal Reserve Bank was formed in 1913, the year that Britain left the gold standard and floated the pound. After the First World War Britain went back onto the gold standard in 1925 at too low an exchange rate and was obliged to keep interest rates higher than other countries to avoid a loss of bullion. This forced the economy to slow down and precipitated the General Strike the next year. In an attempt to help Britain stem the gold loss, the Governor of the Federal Bank of New York, Benjamin Strong, lowered interest rates – a policy that, some held, encouraged the Wall Street bubble and the Crash of 1929.

The Great Depression was the most profound in history for it affected all parts of the world and was a complete reversal of the boom in the 1920s, known as the 'Roaring Twenties'. It pricked the mountain of private debt that had built up in previous decades and caused many companies to fail. The rise in unemployment was the worst in modern history, forcing governments to become nationalistic and to erect protective tariffs. World trade collapsed. But probably the most serious effect was the breakdown of democracy in the larger European countries, which became dictatorships. Could it happen again? Apart from the timing, a number of factors are in place that have a similarity with other cycles.

US governmental and private debt is the highest in history at around $33 trillion – three times the GDP and the same level as the crisis point in 1932 before the collapse of credit. In addition there are estimated to be open derivative contracts of over $150 trillion, which are largely not shown on balance sheets. Economists may argue that these are zero-sum contracts, where one liability is set off against a credit elsewhere, but these rely on the solvency of the parties – as the shareholders of Enron and the holders of Argentina interest-rate swaps discovered. Banks are the first to be hit when derivative exposure is suspect.

Company failures caused by high rates of debt and falling demand are rising – as are personal delinquencies on both sides of the Atlantic. The largest have been Enron, with debts of over $70 billion, WorldCom, with liabilities of $103 billion and more recently Parmalat which, relative to the size of Italy compared to the United States, was as big as Enron. These will not be the last. With private sector debt in the US at 170% of GDP in 2005 and the bond ratings of major companies diminished, any hint of negative growth would plunge many concerns into insolvency.

All these are typical of a down-wave and doubts are already being cast on the viability of some derivative contracts. The revelation of 'creative accounting' in Enron and WorldCom, the seemingly fraudulent behaviour among senior executives, who sold shares while encouraging others to buy, and the apparent laxity of the auditors and investment analysts, are typical of a bursting bubble. The recent Sarbanes-Oxley Act, an attempt to make senior executives directly responsible for accounting errors, could have the unforeseen impact of repelling the brightest from taking responsibility .

In this situation there is a history of revulsion against those in high places, in business, in politics and the professions, who abuse their position during the down-wave. The present cynicism about the motives, competence and veracity of governments is very much part of previous patterns. The noted columnist Dorothy Parkers described the situation in the early 1930s which has relevance for us today:

Two souls dwell within the bosom of the American people. The one loves the Abundant Life, as expressed in the cheap and plentiful products of large-scale mass production and distribution. The other soul yearns for former simplicities, for decentralisation, for the interest of the 'little man';

they revolt against high pressure salesmanship, denounce monopolies and economic empires and seek means of breaking them up.

We can now consider some of the other similarities and dissimilarities comparing the early 1930s with the early years of the twenty-first century.

There was rampant industrial over capacity at the late 1920s in the US and elsewhere after the 'Roaring Twenties' boom. Now the same problem is widespread in the US, Europe and in the Far East where, even in expanding China, capacity has outstripped demand leaving highly indebted enterprises. Of major worry must be the motor industries where excess capacity put Rover into receivership. There must also be concern for the solvency of the banks should borrowers be unable to repay their debts or even the interest. Even booming Australia has suffered the failure of the airline Ansett and two insurance companies, HIH and UMP.

Unemployment reached a peak of 25% in the US in 1933 which saw a mass exodus from the land to the cities when farmers mechanised and dust bowl conditions made large areas of land unworkable. Now, despite large monetary stimulation and historically low interest rates, there are falling levels of utilisation and, even more sinister, depressed levels of incomes and salaries that remain largely static.

There was rampant land speculation in the US during the late Twenties, and in Florida it was not uncommon for the ownership of land to change hands twice in a day. The boom ended and the price of houses halved in the early 1930s forcing many householders into negative equity. The federal government, fearing the electoral consequences of dispossessed householders, was obliged to introduce the Home Owners Loan Corporation that refinanced mortgages at lower rates of interest. In the 1990s, Tokyo land values fell by 70%.

The national index of US house prices has risen 40% in real terms since 1996 deriving from low real rates of interest and the move out of rented accommodation to homeownership, that in 2004 neared 70%. This has generated a massive demand for mortgages and re-mortgages that, in 2005, comprised around $7.5 trillion or 70% of GDP. This considerably exceeds the position in the early 1930s and must be a major potential political and economic concern should the economy reverse.

As suggested earlier, debt is the real concern for the US. In 1929 the debt to GDP ratio was 190% before it soared to 300% when the GDP collapsed. The equivalent figure today is 300% implying that should the GDP fall dramatically once again, the ratio could rise to 400% before a dramatic drop as the credit bubble finally bursts.

The US provided the economic engine driving the rest of the world in the 1920s then again in the early years of the Twenty First Century. Other former leaders such as Germany, France and Japan are still in, or approaching recession while China, which many believed could take the lead, has itself problems of overcapacity and falling demand. Should the US falter there is no other country or grouping able to take over growth leadership.

With the fall in incomes, individual households have been obliged to borrow against the rising levels of their homes to maintain their expenditure that constitutes some two thirds of all spending in the US. By 2005 there was evidence that higher oil prices are causing uncertainty, retail spending is weaker and the stimulus from cashing in the rising value of houses may be falling.

In the 1930s Roosevelt's programme aimed to stimulate America through investment in the infrastructure. As chapter 10 explains, this was directed to hydro-electric power generation, ports, canals, roads and so on. There were also labour intensive projects to clear neglected areas, restore national parks and lay power and telephone lines.

This down-wave will probably demand a major concentration on energy sufficiency through investment in tar sands and the like. Elsewhere there will be different priorities and are likely to be less extensive than the 1930s as governments are so highly indebted. Instead it seems probable that should the conditions suggested by Toffler's Third Wave (chapter 4) be present, local initiatives will predominate as the federal state becomes less centralised.

As already mentioned, one difference from the 1930s is that currencies were then often gold-backed, although one after another country floated to remain competitive. The US dollar remained on the gold standard until 1971, but by 2006 only the Swiss Franc can claim to be backed by gold. Should sluggish growth continue then one could anticipate competitive devaluations and rising protectionism. One must hope that these moves are not the start of another Hawley-Smoot Act which in June 1930 raised tariffs on many imported foodstuffs – an action that plunged the world into a trade war and an even deeper recession.

From the panic of 1920 to the dust bowl worries of 1935 there was a secular decline in commodity prices in the US. It hit farmers particularly badly where, in many cases, the sales price of grains was below production costs. The farming lobby was very strong in 1930 and was directly the reason for President Hoover becoming protectionist against his will to avoid the Republicans being humiliated in the mid-term elections. There has been a collapse of commodity prices in each of the previous down-waves.

However, starting in 2001 commodity prices are in a secular rise across the board including the grains, energy, precious metals, base metals, steel, freight costs and so on. Most commentators put these rises down to the demands of a booming China although that may be slackening. Others recognise that the poor weather conditions described in chapter 7 in Northern China and in the American West as being a restriction on the supply side. The poor growing weather may also have something to do with the need for oil exporting countries to pay for food imports. Perhaps investors, worried by excessive money creation, are moving out of financial and into tangible assets to avoid politicians and bankers destroying their wealth.

Another difference is that in excess of 40% of the US GDP growth in 2004 came from refinancing of homes: half the cash extracted. This is a time bomb under US growth should the housing market collapse.

State pensions and welfare provisions were in the infancy in the 1930s although there were a number of private pension schemes that largely suffered in the Wall Street Crash. Government sponsored programmes proliferated in the upwave of K4 that were largely unfunded on the principle that economies would always grow and that the working population would support those who had retired. Both assumptions have been proved wrong and now states have liabilities that represent several times their GDP. Even privately funded programmes will be put at risk with any decline in the stock market and in any down-wave companies will be unable to make up the losses.

Three scenarios for the US economy

As the American economy is driving the world in the early years of the twenty - first century, anything that transpires in the US will impact on global health. We could be contemplating at least three scenarios: steady as she goes, stagflation and deflation.

Steady as she goes. This assumes that the economic position is not as serious as the cycles suggest. Difficulties with Chinese production or currency devaluations will start to revive US manufacturing with lower costs for the US manufacturing to become more competitive. Individuals, frightened of unemployment will start to pay off private debt. As banks balance sheets recover, the debt burden falls. Belt tightening by governments and rising income from taxation will bring budgets back to balance and even create surpluses – allowing public debt to be retired. This would constitute a 'soft landing'.

Stagflation describes a deflationary economy coupled with rising prices in a number of important market sectors. Something similar occurred in the early 1970s when a negative output gap of –6% in the US implied that economy was working well below capacity. This was coupled with rising commodity prices that reached nearly 300 on the Goldman Sachs Commodity Index. To counter this dire combination, the money supply M2 was raised to 14% in an attempt to reduce unemployment that forced the price deflator to reach its highest post-war peak at 10%; in the UK inflation it reached in excess of 25%!

The commodities rise in the 1970s was weather driven that forced up the price of grains so that by 1972 the CRB Futures Index had risen by 20%, the move continued into 1974 when the index had risen by 120%. Crude oil lagged the grains but rose steeply from $2 a barrel in 1972 to over $10 in 1974, driven upwards in part by the Yom Kippur War. As oil constitutes around 7% of people's income, more had to be spent on energy and other commodities that only added to a decline in private spending.

In economic terms the 1970s reversed the course of the 1950s and 1960s in the US. Unemployment grew steadily from 4% to 6%, inflation peaked at over 6%

on average in the 1970s, productivity declined from 4% annual growth to less than 2%, hourly wages declined as did GDP growth from 5% to 3%. Governments tried to stem the inflationary tide by imposing keynsian-type controls on incomes and prices but this was found to be ineffective so that in the late 1970s, monetary measures were taken.

By mid-2005 we could be approaching similar conditions with the output gap again over 6% (taking into account productivity gains), and capacity utilisation down to below 75%, a similar level to 1974. As suggested earlier, commodities are in a secular rise from the weather, and conditions described in other chapters and the US Fed has already created the most liquidity in the history of the Union in a short period.

However, unlike the 1970s, the money supply is falling implying that the banks are restricting their lending to create even more deflationary pressures that, if allowed to continue, could plunge the economy into a deep recession. To quell deflation there is reason to believe that the Fed would need to ease convincingly, despite the added risk of inflation from rising energy and commodity prices – the precise recipe for stagflation, but on a considerably more dangerous level than the early 1970s. Already there is the threat of stagflation in Europe and in China, South Korea, Indonesia and in other parts of Asia where there are fears that rising energy prices, that would normally be deflationary, would be accommodated.

Any sign of stagflation in the US would force the dollar to a steep decline that would reverberate around the world. This would force other countries to devalue or face being swamped by US goods and services. This would cause a rush out of fiat currencies and fixed interest stocks into tangible assets such as real estate or precious metals that would rise as cash attempted to find a secure home. As a bonus, inflation wipes out debt. This would be a very difficult time for politicians attempting to balance the disintegration of society against international commitments such as the EU and NAFTA. Most will be obliged to learn that any attempt to regulate peoples' habits in times of stagflation would be doomed to failure. Please read the Weimar experience in chapter 11.

Although many businesses would be placed in jeopardy there would be some relief from the strengthening of balance sheets caused by a reduction in capital expenditure in the West. The key to survival would lie in generating pricing power by dealing in items forcing price rises such as energy, food, commodity processing and distribution. As many people's income declined they would be obliged to concentrate more on essential items implying less discriminatory income for non-essential items such as leisure and the environment. The fortunate few able to retain, or even increase, their income would find the world camped outside their door.

Initially government employees supplying essential services such as health and education would have leverage but this would be unlikely to last as government revenues would fall from a lower tax-take from declining income and profits. There would also be collection problems even if politicians tried to increase taxation from sales as this would only add to inflation. In the late 1970s, governments were forced to cutback on cherished public services and would undoubtedly have to do something similar this time.

Manufactured items tend to have the least pricing leverage during stagflation and as the standard of living declined most buyers would tend to seek simple products with a wide range of optional extras. As salaries would still be a large expense item, there would be an even greater drive to outsource from cheaper suppliers.

The response of individuals to a mild inflation is to alter their habits somewhat by buying less expensive items and foregoing things they cannot afford. A quite different approach is needed with hyperinflation where everything tangible is precious for either bargaining or bartering. It was said in the hyperinflation in Germany of the early 1920s that defrauding – particularly the government – became the prime concern of the middle classes.

Deflation. The interest rate rises needed to quell inflation and stabilise currencies after excessive money creation plunge the economy into a depression and efforts are now directed towards recovery. As the monetary squeeze bites, and amidst the general uncertainty, personal and corporate failures rise and bank lending plunges as the future of advances becomes hazardous. At this point, the off-balance-sheet derivative markets will attempt to unwind their positions but it will be too late. Failures such as Long Term Credit Management, Enron and Argentina become more frequent and unemployment rises as firms scramble to reduce costs. There is a rising political crisis which can only be met by local initiatives as central revenue falls and the federal government loses authority. The debt to GDP ratio rises rapidly then plunges as the remaining debt defaults. As always, the recovery out of deflation is led by individual initiatives with government initiatives generally only making matters worse as you will read from the case histories in chapter 11.

References

CNNMoney, *Shades of Stagflation*

City Journal by Steven Malanga

High Beam Research, The Free Dictionary

Houston, W., *Riding the Business Cycle* (Little, Brown, 1995).

Kirkland, W. and D., *Power Cycles* (Professional Communications, 1985).

The Long Wave Analyst, publication of Canaccord Capital (604) 643 0280, with Topline Graphics (303) 440 0157.

Wopec, *A Monetary Explanation of the Great Stagflation of the 1970s*

Wikipedia Free Encyclopedie, Stagflation

Investor Words

Theories of Stagflation, University of California.

Money Magazine, Shades of Stagflation.

Ludwig von Mises Institute, *The Return of Stagflation*.

10

The Road Map of Cycles and the Markets

The major thesis in this work is that cycles and events, well beyond the control of man, dictate his liberty, prosperity and the opportunity to pursue happiness. Here we are particularly interested in how these cycles come down to affect the stock, bond, housing, and commodity markets.

We have for many years constructed maps of what to expect from the stock market controlled by cycles in the underlying economy. This has been driven by Joseph Schumpeter's analysis to include the earlier work of Kitchin, Juglar, Kondratieff, and to some extent Kuznets described in earlier chapters. Some economists have argued that these business cycles are no longer relevant, but we find to the contrary that they are very much alive and well, and working in the real world.

It is true that the economy of early era was dominated by agriculture, and so by the weather cycles of wet and dry climate leading to feast and famine. This also related to disease cycles and to weak immune systems described in chapter 8 and tendencies to revolt and migrate to new areas to escape onerous conditions. These fit well into the patterns described by Dr Raymond Wheeler and George Modelski in the Afterword.

Now let us see how these relate to the economic cycle that we are more familiar with. The Juglar wave described in the last chapter can vary between 7 and 11 years so can be taken as a decadian rhythm as the variations tend to smooth each other out. The economic data shows that there is a strong tendency to at least a mild recession every decade. Coupled with the Kondratieff cycle described in the last chapter; as the Juglar progresses the GNP becomes increasingly negative until the cycle ends and the next long-wave begins.

The four year cycle of Kitchin is often more measurable in the stock market than in the economy. When Harold Wilson was prime minister in the UK there was a clear stop-go era with recessionary conditions every four years. Since then GNP has not become negative so often but the dips have been more relative than actual – for example the Presidential four years election cycle in the USA. It seems that Presidents cannot resist tampering with monetary and fiscal policy to try to influence the result, which locks the cycle in place.

This means that if two or more cycles are naturally tending towards a low point at about the same time, they will lock together. This may actually have altered the Kitchin wave over time and now makes it more likely to be a four-year wave, and have less variance in length than in former times. There is certainly some evidence to support this view. Our Road maps are based on the idea that this is so.

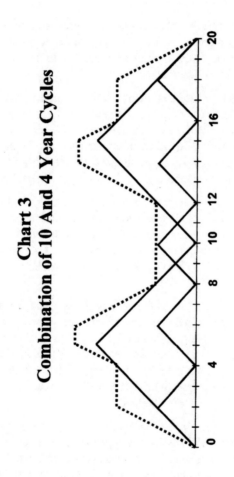

Chart 3
Combination of 10 And 4 Year Cycles

Chart 4
Alternative 10 Year Cycles

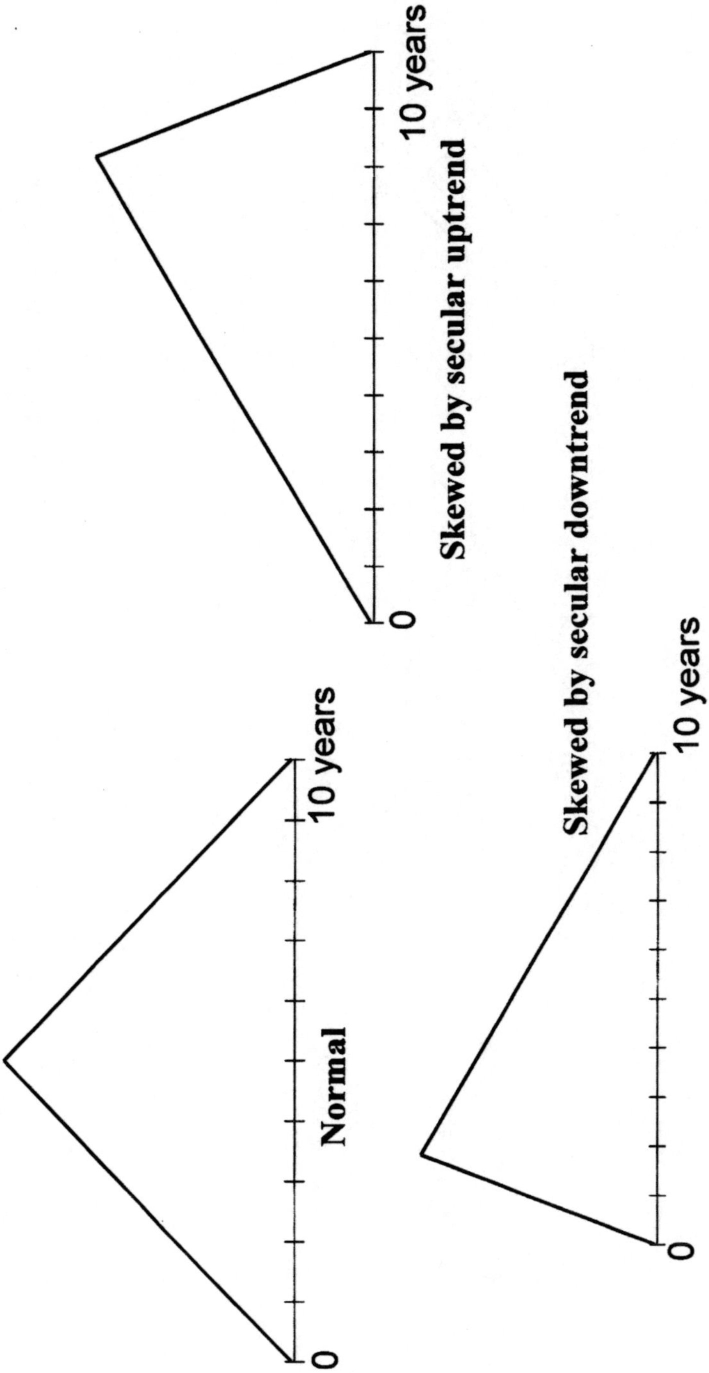
Normal
0
10 years
Skewed by secular uptrend
0
10 years
Skewed by secular downtrend
0
10 years

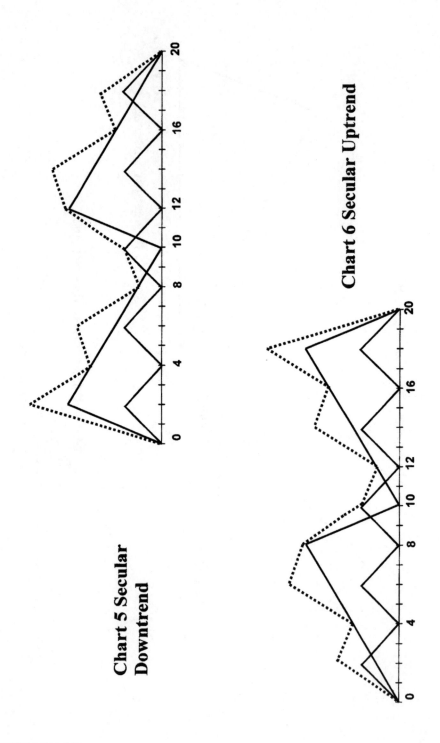

Chart 5 Secular Downtrend

Chart 6 Secular Uptrend

The result of the above means that in looking to the future we can put the ten year cycles perfectly into the short cycle of Wheeler, making lows on the zero year in each decade.

The four and ten year cycles do not fit well together, only being perfectly in step every 20 years. Because of this, as the two cycles interact with each other a complex shape develops giving a different pattern in one decade to the next. The whole pattern repeats on a twenty year basis as shown in Chart 3.

There is another complication. The long cycle can become skewed both positively and negatively as shown in Chart 4. There are therefore three basic conditions. In periods of sustained above average growth, such as China is having today, the skew is positive. After a bubble, as in Japan for the past 12 years the skew is negative. Some times the four and the ten year cycles are both up together, and sometimes down. At others they are in conflict. This leads to the ability to predict super strong period, super weak and neutral periods. The diagrams show how these come about.

There is one more assumption. The cycles we have been talking about are economic and can be measured by normal economic data streams. The stock markets are presumed to discount these events, but with a catch. The markets always move ahead of the underlying cause to discount expectations of what will happen. The markets are however crowds of people – and tend to heard and be subject to moods of irrational exuberance – both positive and negative. Stock market swings become overdone.

The markets sometimes discount something that is not going to occur and then have to correct. In a way it is like the pendulum in a clock. If the clock stopped it would hang straight down. In practice it spends a minimum of time in that position, but is always rushing too far to the left or right. This process leads to three road maps for stock price movements, Standard, Secular Uptrend, and Secular Downtrend.

In essence all stock market indices are on one of these road maps, and many are strongly positively correlated with one another as shown in Chart 5 and 6. This is especially true if they trade a lot together, or are in the same geographical area. In the period of the last giant cycle from 1500 to 2000 the West was favoured and had many markets in secular uptrend. Now the dominant growth has switched to the East so it is China and related markets that are most likely to be positively skewed.

It is vital to notice that the strongest declines occur within secular uptrends of Chart 6. Even with the cycle positively skewed the last two years in the twenty-year period are likely to produce crash type conditions. This is precisely because so much sustained growth has become overdone and needs to have a pause that refreshes.

This pattern has been especially relevant in the west on the rise to the year 2000 with the seemingly unprecedented growth since 1980 and the dot com and Y2K situations. It was also relevant from 1910 to 1930.

The forecast that follows from this in future is that the growth in China and India will not go in a straight line. After a twenty year run these markets will be expected

Chart 7
Combination of the Drought Clock with the Juglar & Kitchin Waves

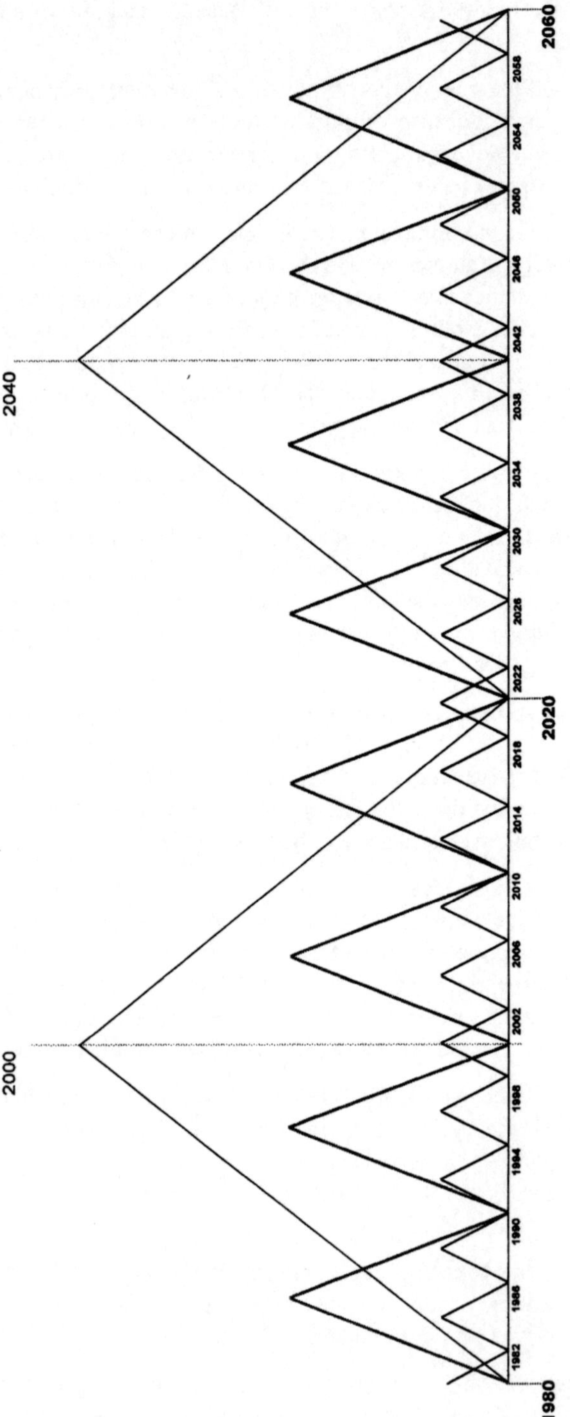

to have a significant bear phase, if not a crash. Whether these will be patterns similar to 2000 to 2002, or like 1929, will depend on how excessive the top of the growth goes in the meantime. Apart from the weather conditions described in chapter 7, the rise in commodity prices is linked to the growth of these two large countries and they too will be likely to have a substantial correction. The likely date for this is 2020.

In the West a secular uptrend clearly started in 1980 and topped out in 2000. It is likely that a secular downtrend in Chart 5 follows and is now under way. This leads us to expect that the S&P index will not make new all time highs for some time. The PE ratio – the index that measures the number of years, earnings related to the share price – is probably going to be trending negatively till at least 2014. The multiple could start to expand again then but the cycles indicate that there is a greater probability of going into standard road maps until roughly 2020. Then a sort of renaissance period could follow up to the warm and wet period expected in 2030.

Extending the Road Map into the future

We can now zoom in on the map shown in Chart 7 to enlarge just the first half of the current up cycle that reaches a low point in 2020. From this we can start to relate the macro weather and drought cycles described in chapter 7 to the normal economic and stock market cycles that derive originally from the work of Joseph Schumpeter. The small fluctuations in investment markets are too small to show up on this scale of things, but what we refer to as secular trends and indeed the ten year cycle or Juglar wave can be mapped quite well with a period of recession at the end of each decade. The start of the next up cycle is always in the time period between 0 and 02 of each decade.

Some of the predictions that follow are that the trend towards Eastern or Asian markets will continue. China and related stock markets, and India should continue to grow in secular uptrend, whereas those in the mature western world will be suffering a secular downtrend. It is easier for emerging markets to grow rapidly and sustain above average growth for a long time. This long-term build-up of China and India towards super power status will not go in a straight uninterrupted line. The north of China and eastward to Central Asia particularly are due to have a rather vicious cooling period right now partly because of the chronic drought in the north.
   Another factor is the risk of a global recession becoming a depression if the housing bubble, which itself seems to be almost global, comes to an end soon. History indicates that such bubbles never have a soft landing, and eventually fall back to lower levels than the one from which they started to rise from originally. Housing may well be in negative equity for at least a decade. This will affect the period up to 2014 and possibly till 2020.

During that same period, starting with the tsunami in 2004, we expect more earthquake and volcanic activity from the closest perigee for two hundred years in 2008. This, together with the Atlantic and Pacific oscillations described in a previous chapter, could be big enough to cool the earth by several degrees. This could well last through to 2020.This cooling would considerably reduce any further melting of Arctic ice and prevent a diversion of the Gulf Stream that at present allows Great Britain, and northern Europe to have tolerable winter weather.

Diagram 7 shows a 2030 low in economics but a high in terms of the weather; then the Wheelers cycle predicts warm and wet times. In this period it is quite possible that India will outperform China, because of the likely extreme conditions in Northern China described in chapter 7. So far India has lagged China but this period will allow the former to build up its infrastructure almost regardless of what goes on elsewhere.

By comparison China is intimately linked to any slowing in the West – the USA economy – that could slow the drift of manufacturing jobs across the Pacific and might, for a while, produce profitless prosperity. From about 2020 on however we expect China to be making much more progress again as the weather gets hotter and wetter.

The year 2065 is likely to have warm wet conditions and also be an economic high point and presumably bull market or bubble top in the stock market. This will then be followed by a vicious cold and dry period in 2080 that will be an economic and stock market low point. Although by this time both India and China should have grown to super power status in the world, the growth will not be smooth and linear. However the macro trend still indicates a tendency for the East to prosper over the west all the way to 2235, which the road map indicates should be warm, wet and buoyant economic conditions, it will still have to endure another period of major dry and cold conditions between 2150 and 2180 along the way.

We can now zoom in with greater detail on the next 50 years with the four-year Kitchin Cycles added in Diagram 7. As suggested earlier, these are phase locked with US presidential election cycles that drives the next set of major stock market lows in 2006, 2010, 2014, and 2018. Somewhere between 2018 and 2022 should be a major economic base pattern and then a boom period develops with the weather getting warmer and wetter up to a peak in 2040. This will help both the emerging east and the west.

In the USA this period will be driven by the children of the present ageing baby boomers. From a demographic point of view the USA remains strong and should by 2040 have almost another 100 million people compared to today. This is in marked contrast to Europe which already has an ageing and shrinking population. The revival in the US will benefit India and China.

If there is to be a Kondratieff winter that follows the bursting of the credit bubble described in the previous chapter, then the maximum period of risk is from 2005 till 2014 coinciding with the collapse in house prices. Calling the top of such bubbles is difficult but when houses change hands in a day – as during the Florida land boom in 1927 – these are signs of a top in place.

A downtrend in house prices, and a pay-back of credit takes time to work through. Our road map indicates a secular downtrend in western markets till about 2014. Europe may carry on in trouble for longer, but the USA can start to build a base pattern. The main difference is demographic. The population of Europe could start growing again especially if massive immigration takes place. To some extent this is occurring but not in enough size to alter the overall position. Secondly many of the immigrants are of the Muslim faith and this might aggravate the tensions in the region.

Apart from conflicts over water, it is entirely possible that there will be Age Wars. Europeans of the baby boom era have grown up believing that they are entitled to work only 32 hours a week, take all of August as a holiday, have free health care, and still retire early on 75% of their final salary. Even when they retire they will still vote, and their interests will count large at election time. The young doing the work to try to pay for all these benefits does not make for a peaceful or stable outcome.

It is wrong to look into the future and assume that life remains the same as today. Technology moves too fast. As Schumpeter spelled out –the process of creative destruction means that some industries that we take for granted will disappear, whilst others that seem like a dream today will become commonplace.

Motor cars will continue to become more economical over the forecast period. The current trend to smaller size and diesel engines will dominate early years, but later give way to Hybrid, pure electric and Hydrogen Fuel cell cars. There is a clear move in manufacturing from the west to the East. Only partly in jest we might think that General Motors will become a Chinese company.

High technology will be used to dramatically lower the cost of health care. This will be partly linked to the coming Robot age. These do not have to be R2D2 but will be much more exciting than a Bank teller machine. Nano and Bio tech are currently embryonic. They might remain in the Jam-Tomorrow category for many years, but over the time period of our forecasts should become very real and important.

The growth of China and India and the weather oscillations will inevitably push up commodity prices for the next ten to twenty years but after that glut conditions could prevail again. Especially in energy the present chronic shortage will lead to the development of Tar Sands, Coal Liquifaction, Fuel cells, wind, solar generation, but the big one will be Nuclear. Price rises in oil will lead the pressure to substitute a better system. Just as mankind gave up collecting firewood, and moved to coal and then oil, so these new forms of power will become the norm.

Over the time span we are looking at Moore's famous law that will have developed cheap computing power well into the realms of Artificial Intelligence. Machines will be able to do things that we can only presently guess at. As Arthur C Clark reminded us, "any new technology is initially indistinguishable from Magic." We will in the time forecast reach that point in time that scientist Ray Kurzweil has called the singularity. Up to that point life will seem broadly similar to the present with all its troubles that we have been talking about. After that date however it will be so radically different as to be unrecognisable to our present minds.

11

One Inflation and Three Deflations

Only a few people can now remember with any clarity the terrible events of the early 1920s in Germany, when the mark was worth a billionth of its value three years later. More will be able to remember the 1930s, when unemployment soared in most Western countries as businesses failed, many elected governments were replaced by dictatorships and only the threat of war breathed any life into economies. Argentina has been in the grip of runaway inflation and Japan is currently suffering from deflation, so perhaps it is timely to review the earlier events to remind us what can occur, how people behave and what happens when politicians lose control of events.

Germany and Austria in the 1920s

It was a common belief in Germany that the First World War would be over in a few months at the most – as the 1870 Franco-Prussian War had been over forty years earlier. After another victory, reparations would be levied on France and her colonies absorbed. Little did Finance Minister Helfferich know that the war would actually cost 110,000 million in pre-war gold marks, to be funded not by raising taxes, which was the chosen method in Britain, but mainly by issuing debt, plus minor taxes on war profits. Thus three-fifths of the war was paid for by eight tranches of war loans plus issues of treasury bills – to be redeemed from newly printed money, which increased the notes in circulation by five times in the three years to 1917.

Wars are always inflationary and the Allied blockade added to rising prices by drastically restricting imports; this meant that for every 100 men at the front, double that number were required at home, where they attempted to stave off hunger in impoverished households whose standard of living had halved since 1914. After the war, the Versailles Treaty greatly disadvantaged Germany for it ceded Alsace and Lorraine back to France, the French occupied the Saarland and swathes of Prussia were passed to Poland. The worst was the reparation, set at 132 billion gold marks, over fifteen times the figure after the 1870 war. This might have been realistic in terms of the war's cost but it would have meant repayments continuing until the end of the century and was quite impossible for the highly indebted Germany to deliver. By the summer of the same year, Germany had repaid 1 billion marks but only by printing paper currency and converting it to gold in the open market. It was never allowed to try this again.

The centre parties then in power were determined to create a new type of republic, where the state had an overwhelming responsibility for directing people's lives. (After the Second World War the same political agenda created a benevolent state that rigidly controlled the movement of labour.) One of the leading political philosophers in 1919 was Dr Walter Rathenau – a friend of the disgraced Kaiser – who said, 'In future the citizen will look with proud pleasure at the state's power, wealth and superabundance . . . Individual incomes would fall, but the new state would dispose, no longer of millions, but of milliards [billions].'

At the start of the First World War, the German mark, the British shilling, the French franc and the Italian lire had almost the same value. At the end of 1918 £1 (20 shillings) would buy 43 marks; by June 1919 (when the Versailles Treaty was signed) the exchange was 60 marks. There was a further collapse to 185 marks by December 1919, but by the end of 1923 £1 could be exchanged for 20 billion marks.

By the end of 1920 the cost of living had increased twelve times since 1914 (compared to three times in the US, four in Britain and seven in France). Food, which comprised half the family budget at the start of the war, rose to nearly three-quarters, reaching almost the levels which added such fury to the French Revolution in 1790. However, despite the 1920 recession, German industry, which had been almost untouched by the war, was starting to recover, its exports greatly assisted by the depreciated currency. Even the unions co-operated in supporting the rising business activity. Unfortunately taxes could not be collected, for many of those who could pay refused to keep accounts and even if they could pay, it would be in a devalued currency. This caused the value of the mark to continue its fall and the budget deficit kept on widening. The deficiency of the railways alone was 17 billion marks.

In Austria, inflation wiped out those on fixed incomes – retired judges and generals could be seen breaking rocks beside the Danube to earn a few additional kronen for their ravaged pensions. By July 1922 the cost-of-living index had increased 124% a month and looting became widespread. This was a signal the Chancellor, Dr Ignas Seipel, could not dismiss and to his great credit he applied to the League of Nations, offering to accept any discipline in exchange for stability.

The reply was surprisingly swift and should be a blueprint for latter-day rescue missions. The League prepared a Geneva Protocol within a month and offered decisive action. In return for appointing a Commissioner General with total authority to return the country to equilibrium, the League guaranteed Austrian political, financial and territorial integrity. There were two other conditions: the first was that Austria should cease discounting treasury bills (redeemed with printed money) and that Britain, France, Italy and Czechoslovakia should underwrite a loan of 650 million gold kronen.

Amazingly, it worked. The price index fell 20% from September until the end of the year, and although inflation continued, the krone, later the schilling, held firm against the dollar. The Commissioner General, a Dr Zimmerman, stopped the printing presses, contracting the amount of money in circulation. Almost immediately it was no longer a sellers' market with high margins, and prices fell. As with Germany, most of the money previously created had been associated with funding a budget deficit to maintain overheads – in Austria's case she had an administration to manage an empire of 50 million souls, not a country of 6.5 million.

Other problems have a more modern ring; for instance, tax collection was totally inadequate. The civil service had to be radically pruned, as did the railways, for one-third of the budget shortfall was from losses on the state system. For example, three men were employed for each mile of track, compared with two in Switzerland. While railwaymen's wages had kept up with inflation, rail tariffs were 20% of the equivalent level. Subsidies were widespread, even extending to cigars, which were being retailed far below the production cost.

The withdrawal symptoms were terrible. Whereas unemployment pre-Zimmerman had been only a few thousand, it rose rapidly in 1923 to around 160,000, half of those being in Vienna on the maximum dole – the equivalent of around five British shillings a week. The post-inflation recession hit overstaffed manufacturers in basic and fabrication industries. It also affected the banks, where there was one official for every £2,000 in deposits compared to £18,000 in London. However, the standard of living did not return to pre-war levels for there were now no subsidies and a state pensioner had to exist on only one-third, in real terms, of their earlier spending power. The redundancies in the public sector followed those in industry and commerce. About 20% of people relied on the state for their salary or pensions and much of the over-manning was on the same scale as the railways. Overall, 23,000 were made redundant in the last quarter of 1923, with a target of 100,000 by the end of 1924. However, by March 1923 the worst was over for most and unemployment was falling quite rapidly, to reach 79,000 in November 1923 as the krone became stable against firmer currencies.

Meanwhile in Germany businesses, like ordinary citizens, became adept at avoiding tax on profits by under-invoicing exports to an overseas subsidiary, which then re-invoiced at the agreed sale price. This dodge also had the advantage of avoiding the 26% tax levied on exports by the Reparations Commission. Only those monies needed to finance the business were remitted home, the balance being held in a foreign bank account. This meant that a company's costs were held down just when the employees' incomes were being squeezed by the collapsing mark.

By October 1921 the government outgoings were 113 milliard marks, while estimated revenue was 90 milliard marks (the sum owed in reparations to the Allies at an estimated rate of 13 marks to 1 gold mark – a gross overvaluation). Try as it would the government was unable to raise taxes to fill the deficit – once more proving the principle of the Laffer Curve, which states that when the burden of taxation becomes too onerous, ways will be found to avoid payment and the state's revenue falls.

By November 1921 £1 would buy 1,040 marks, which incited unrest in the Ruhr as wages failed to keep pace with rising prices. The middle classes, who had so loyally supported the war-time Reich by buying the war loan, were in a worse position. For example, bonds worth 1 million marks when they were bought were now worth only £1,000. Likewise pensioners on annual fixed incomes which had been equivalent to £500 before the war, now had the purchasing power of only around £30. Just as the Russians were forced to act during the 1990s, those on fixed incomes sold such things as furniture, pianos, jewellery and furs just to survive. To make matters worse these were often bought by foreigners at ridiculously low prices. Outsiders were not the only ones buying. Frightened by the continual rise in prices and the onset of winter, people were laying in stocks of everything they needed for fear that it may not be available during the hard cold months. As the mark fell to 1,300 to the pound, there were food riots in Berlin.

Politics came a long way down the list for most people. Their major concern was the price of food, with most commodity prices rising by more than fifteen times (beef up seventeen times, pork by nearly twenty-eight times and butter up by a crazy multiple of thirty-three). The lowest was rye bread, with a thirteen-fold rise in the eight years from 1913. Deficiencies, made worse by the continuing blockade, were beginning to affect children's health. Anxious mothers were seen retrieving scraps of food from the detritus of wealthier neighbourhoods in an attempt to supplement their families' nourishment.

Of course black-market costs were much higher than the official prices. Hyper-inflation (defined by prices rising at 50% per month) was reached in May 1922. Up until then, the unions had been able to extract wage rises in line with prices but the new situation took even them by surprise, and for a time they had difficulty in pitching their demands. Bankruptcies declined: before the war there were normally some 9,500 failures a year, but this fell to just 150 by November 1921. This was a sort of never-never land, for no one anticipated that the pack of cards could collapse once the printing presses were shut down.

Inflation, of course, had wiped out any debt contracted before or during the war. For example the debt of the Stinnes Group, which owned one-sixth of German industry, had fallen to 2% of its previous level by 1922. While it would be expected that its owner, Hugo Stinnes, would welcome hyper-inflation, it is astonishing that it was also welcomed by Dr Havernstein, the Reichbank's director. Like other German bankers he held the position that printing notes had little to do with hyper-inflation; he put it down to the mark falling against other currencies.

Even a relatively poor foreign visitor to Germany could eat in the best restaurants and could be excused for believing that Germany was booming. One English student, wanting to change a £5 note (a lot of money for her), was astonished to see the bank manager himself in his morning suit coming out to transact the exchange. As the demand for currency increased, private banks could no longer process money and cheques fast enough, which meant that a pending cheque declined in value before it was cleared. At about this time some states, local authorities and companies issued money tokens called 'Notgeld' that had a guaranteed value if spent within a day.

By September 1922, as the collapse accelerated, the mark had fallen from 9,000 to 13,000 to the pound in six days. People held notes for as short a time as possible. Before the war the gold value of currency was equivalent to £300 million but by November 1922 it had declined to £20 million. As in Austria, this caused people to change their behaviour drastically. The collapsing currency benefited country people as the value of land and its produce increased pro rata. Those who borrowed to buy farm or building land when the mark stood at 2,000 to the pound could easily pay off the loan when it collapsed to 13,000 – often from the output of one or two fields. People found that houses, property, commodities and artefacts were the best stores of value.

As cash became less valuable, barter was more widespread. The practice of issuing Notgeld increased as large industrial firms and municipalities paid their employees partly in the coupons, to be spent at local shops and redeemed within a short time. An interesting investment offer was called the Rogenmark. It was based on the current price of 125 kilos of rye, to be redeemed in the first quarter of 1927 at the present market price. The instruments were bearer bonds secured on the issuing bank's assets that could be traded like a modern commodity.

In mark terms the stock market rose 13.4 times from July 1914 to July 1922, but had declined in real terms by one-third, and by October 1922 its value in US dollars was 3% of that pre-war. By that time total stock-market capitalisation was equivalent to around £200 million, which concerned the authorities, because much of German industry could be bought for a song by foreign owners.

Some of the more shrewd operators became currency speculators. In early January 1923, someone could borrow nearly 2 billion paper marks and convert these into $100,000. Three months later he could sell some $80,000 to clear the mark loan, then with higher stakes repeat the exercise, enabling him to clear $250,000 by June. This was an excellent deal provided the profits were kept in a hard currency. Arbitragers were widespread, operating from back-street dealers called 'Winkelbankiers'.

Hyper-inflation also changed people's perception of education, for in this situation academic brains were less useful than manual skills or a 'nose' for trading. Pensioners and those on fixed incomes were very badly hit but professional people like teachers came a close second. Even the unions lost influence as their demands failed to keep up with the rise in prices and they lost power to Communist agitators, resulting in riots and looting.

Hyper-inflation often turned previously upright citizens to fraud. Those with the greatest opportunity were, of course, government officials, whose incomes failed to keep pace with rocketing prices, but the practice was widespread and in some cases reached the highest level of government. It was a time when it was unwise to demonstrate the fruits of success. The most successful entrepreneurs sometimes could not conceal their ostentation – much to the anger of less financially talented citizens.

Matters were made infinitely worse by the French and Belgian occupation of the Rhineland, after Germany was deemed to have defaulted on her obligations. The idea was to seize coal, iron, timber and finished products in lieu of reparations. As the troops went in, the whole area virtually shut down: no transport ran, coal production (85% of resources) ceased and iron smelting stopped. This enraged the already over-stretched German government, which had to print even more money to underwrite the now totally inactive industrial heartland. By the end of January 1923, the rising inflation succeeded in depressing the mark to 227,500 to the pound.

The Ruhrkampf, as the seizure was known, was a disaster for it ended up convincing Germany that it should re-arm. Some historians argue that the occupation of the Ruhr was the turning point that led to the rise of Hitler, but amongst all the privations suffered by the German people, it is hard to identify any single trigger event.

The final slide into the abyss happened in June 1923, when the government could raise only the equivalent of £30 million to cover expenditure of £80 million. By then the exchange was 800,000 marks to the pound and workers were paid twice a day, the money being spent immediately, for items could double in price within twenty-four hours. Petty crime grew as copper plaques were unscrewed and lead disappeared from roofs. Everything removable was liable to be stolen and exchanged for barter. A lump of coal might buy a cinema seat and a gallon of petrol might be exchanged for a shirt, that might be bartered for a bag of potatoes. In situations not unlike those occurring in some parts of Russia in the 1990s, thieves stole the contents of shopping bags but left the cash behind.

Foreigners had a field day. A Swiss student was able to buy up a terrace of houses on his Swiss-franc allowance and one US dollar enabled four men to buy a night out in Berlin including dinner and night-clubs – and still leave money in their pockets. Sometimes banks simply didn't have the cash to honour foreign visitors' notes.

While the Ruhrkampf experience was uniting the German people, hyper-inflation was tearing them apart financially. Hard times concentrate minds and, as the nation descended into chaos, it became every man and state for himself. A prosperous area like Prussia had no compunction about finding foreign customers for its agricultural and other exports when fellow Germans were starving further west. People west of Cologne became more aggressive. Bands of protesters started ravaging the countryside, destroying crops and burning farm buildings. In Bavaria, when food was short in the towns, the farmers refused to take notes in payment after the mark had collapsed from 300 million to 500 million to the pound in twenty-four hours. The country people referred to them with derision as 'Jewish confetti from Berlin'. Linz, Hitler's home town, was plundered by looters who ransacked shops, burned farms and stole cattle.

Although matters were still relatively calm in Berlin, crowds with wheelbarrows and sacks surrounded the Reichsbank demanding notes after reports of yet another note-printing strike. The dispute had held up essential foodstuffs because the producers insisted on being paid. The despair that overwhelmed much of Germany was made worse by rumours of the French army marching on Berlin – which the generals did nothing to deny. As chaos descended into anarchy the country polarised into two divisions: Communist and Fascist. Strikes became widespread.

In desperation, the government attempted such futile gestures as confiscating foreign currency held by people on the streets and – in a throwback to the French Revolution – jailing anyone found hoarding food. They went so far as to compel shops to stay open and accept notes. But nothing worked. With the mounting problems of civil disorder, the Ruhrkampf absorbing over 60% of the rising debt, the sheer futility of printing further notes and the rising anarchy, the government declared martial law.

Matters proceeded, not unlike the way they did during the French Revolution, with the authorities interfering at will with communications, organising house searches and confiscating property. Inciting civil disobedience became an offence and ringleaders could be liable for penal servitude if lives were at risk. The death penalty was introduced for leading armed mobs, treason, arson or damage to the railways.

By late October 1923, the mark had fallen from 24 milliards to the pound to 80 milliards in three days. Lord d'Aubernon, the British Ambassador to Germany, rather wickedly calculated that this was the number of seconds from the birth of Christ. But there was nothing amusing about the plight of all classes of people; in the chaos, factories closed and the workers, who had kept up roughly with inflation, now suffered alongside the bourgeoisie. By November 1923 nearly 5 million people were out of work and the state could not afford adequate dole support.

It is hard to believe the position at the end of 1923. While the printing presses were turning out 74 milliard marks a week (quadrupling the previous issue in six weeks), the townspeople starved while the warehouses groaned with food. But help was at hand from the unlikely source of the banking sector – the very people that had condoned the prolific printing of notes.

The inflation was halted when Hjalmar Horace Greeley Schacht was appointed the first Commissioner for National Currency. This remarkable man later became head of the Reichsbank, saved Germany from anarchy, and helped Hitler stabilise the Third Reich's finances until 1939. He was cleared of war crimes in 1946 and died in 1970 aged ninety-three.

His first act was to stop the Reichsbank redeeming treasury bills with printed notes. Next he issued notes against the security of German land, building and factory assets, replacing 20 billion of devalued money with one Rentenmark (RM); Schacht reported that the unissued old notes would have filled 300 ten-ton railway wagons. Amazingly his policies worked, and with the new confidence the US and, to a lesser extent British, banks raised short-term loans throughout the 1920s to generate a rapid recovery. Unfortunately these same funds were withdrawn just as quickly after the Wall Street Crash of 1929, thus playing a fateful role in the subsequent German depression and the rise of Hitler.

And three deflations

Accounts of modern slumps invariably focus on the Great US Depression of the 1930s. How could a nation whose armaments had won the greatest war in history and whose industries were the most efficient in the world, seemingly lose all confidence? Yet the events that were to trigger the collapse started in Germany, the loser of the Great War and the country that was to dominate much of the later decade. The incubus first spread to America and then Britain. Each country dealt with deflation in its own way.

By November 1928, the German economic boom had reached its peak. There had been a strike in the steel industry and the intense cold from December 1928 to March 1929 (the lowest since records began in Berlin) shut down construction, greatly hindered transport and forced up the price of energy. By the summer, unemployment was at 1.9 million, inventories were stubbornly high and failures were rising.

After 1929 industrial output reversed rapidly, falling 14% in 1930, 18% in 1931 and a further 15% in 1932; in all, over 47%. The rigidities in company structure and labour policies made it more difficult than in Britain and America to reduce costs in line with demand. As companies failed, banks were forced to reduce their loans, and from the summer of 1930 the money supply contracted, falling 17% to June 1931. At the same time foreign banks were being obliged to redress their own balance sheets and withdrew funds after their losses following the Wall Street Crash.

The cash crises, coinciding with the economic slowdown, forced inventory levels to rise rapidly – putting even greater strain on already stretched balance sheets. At the same time companies were forced to reduce their investment spending and to divest assets, the industries worst hit being chemical, engineering, construction and textiles. The credit squeeze required companies to exchange debt for capital, which placed large amounts of shares into the hands of banks. In this situation the banks themselves only avoided failure by being bailed out by the state, an ideal situation for later Fascist control.

Germany was not the only country to be in financial difficulties. Three banks failed in France, which resulted in funds being withdrawn from London and shipped to Paris. In Italy a banking failure was avoided by hushing up a central bank rescue and there were similar problems in Belgium and central Europe. Probably the most critical failure was that of the Viennese Credit Anstalt in May 1931. Despite the rescue programme described earlier, Austria had never really recovered from having to call in the League of Nations in 1922. The unemployment that was a feature of the stabilisation programme continued at a high level during the 1920s, averaging between 10 and 15% during the decade. The banking system was also weak, obliging the Bodenkreditanstalt to take over the Unionbank and Verkehrbank in 1927. The acquirer was itself merged with the Credit Anstalt in 1929, bringing with it 80 million schillings of capital but 140 million of accumulated losses.

Buying a failed business without first clearing the bad debts is a hazardous policy in the best of times; for a bank to make the acquisition on the eve of a recession is a recipe for disaster. When, three years later, the American Federal Deposit Insurance Corporation was set up to effect bank rescues, the bad loans were inevitably cleared before the remaining assets and goodwill were sold on. Failure to do this left Credit Anstalt fatally vulnerable. It was widely held that French withdrawals of deposits triggered a run on the bank, and by 5 June 1931 its reserves were exhausted. The failure of Credit Anstalt created uncertainty in the solvency of all European banks, including those of Germany such as the Danat, the Dresdner and the Deutsche Bank, which between them lost over RM220 million of reserves. The Chancellor Brunning attempted to balance the budget and allay the crisis by lowering the salaries of civil servants, cutting unemployment benefit and raising taxes, but these only hastened a crisis when the Danat Bank failed.

After frenzied meetings of politicians and bankers, similar to those in 1998 during the Asian crisis, individual nations eventually refused to lend any more money to Germany; it was the end of the line. On 13 July there was a general run on German banks, when depositors were thought to have stashed RM1 billion in their proverbial mattresses. This action closed all financial institutions for two days. After they reopened, 91% of the Dresdner capital, 70% of the Commerz Bank and 35% of the Deutsche Bank were taken into public ownership as the price for restoring balance sheets. There was an effective moratorium on foreign loans which, for British and American creditors, were usually in revolving three-month bills, discounted by the accepting bank outside Germany and then sold.

The action spread to Britain, where a report had shown the extent of foreign balances. The initial selling pressure seems to have come from commercial banks in the smaller European countries such as Belgium and Sweden, which converted sterling balances into gold to redress their own losses. The withdrawals continued after a report by Sir George May, the Secretary to the Labour cabinet, warning of a UK budget deficit of £120 million. Further losses forced the Bank of England to raise its discount rate from 2.5% to 4.5% during the month. There was a general election and the new administration balanced the budget by raising taxes and cutting the salaries of all government employees by 15%. The greatest protest came from the Home Fleet at Invergordon, which refused to sail. This finally destabilised holders of sterling, forcing a devaluation of 25%, carrying with it a number of countries whose currencies were linked to the pound.

Back in Germany unemployment had risen to 6 million as GDP imploded. This polarised politics between left and right and in a November poll the National Socialist Party won the largest share of the votes, although not a majority. On 30 January 1933 the then Chancellor, with President Hindenburg's agreement, brought in Adolf Hitler as Chancellor. One month later, an emergency decree "For the Protection of the People and State" was proclaimed suspending basic constitutional rights. The first attempt at German rule by a democratically elected government had finally failed.

Hitler had made his priorities quite clear in *Mein Kampf*, but first he introduced measures that enabled the Third Reich to reduce unemployment from 6 to 1.8 million. He was also determined to re-arm within a centrally directed state. Industry, although not nationalised, was obliged to follow party dictates, banks were given lending priorities and, after the labour unions were dissolved, employees were placed in a straitjacket regarding their working conditions. To achieve his aims Hitler needed to avoid printing money and to keep the Rentenmark steady. His measures to reduce unemployment were much more successful than those in the USA.

The first aim was achieved by issuing certificates for work undertaken which could be offset against future Reich taxes. In the meantime the bills of exchange, which had a state guarantee, could be discounted within the banking system. To conceal the rearmament programme after 1935 a new financing institution was formed called the Deutsche Bau-und-Bodenbank. It paid contractors using bills of exchange carrying a Reich guarantee which had state acceptance. Both methods relied on increased revenues from an expanding economy but were clearly inflationary. However, when this was pointed out by Hjalmar Schacht, the Reichsbank Chairman, he was fired by Hitler.

Next, the mark was kept from inflationary free-fall by allocating foreign exchange by priority. Rearmament had top priority; 'necessary' expenditure up to RM10,000 was the second category; the third category, including such things as tourist foreign travel, was rated 'unnecessary'. Probably the most important for Hitler's subsequent expansion was to create a set of 'client' states which provided preferential access for imports against exports; for example, raw materials or food for steel. This was arranged with countries like Romania (which had oil), Hungary and Yugoslavia, and was managed by a huge bureaucracy.

The results, although based on rearmament, were not unimpressive. Taking a base of 100 in 1929, industrial production nearly halved to 53 in 1932 and had just begun an upswing in 1933, the year Hitler assumed power. Thereon, output increased steadily to reach an index of 126 in 1938, while wholesale and retail prices were kept steady. Hitler also ordered the country to become self-sufficient through synthesising part of oil, rubber and chemical production, and with strict controls on foreign exchange. German exports were almost ten times the level of imports by 1938.

Roosevelt's New Deal

Unlike Britain, Germany and France, the United States ended the First World War stronger than when it began. Its productive facilities were modern; emigrants and the war had provided it with a spate of energetic workers and it was the biggest creditor on earth. It was also a major importer of goods whilst exporting agricultural products, raw materials and finished goods. Unfortunately the war had also made the nation protectionist, which encouraged the Republicans on Capitol Hill to reject both the Versailles Treaty and involvement in the League of Nations that was set up as an international forum to solve disputes.

The boom kept going through the 1920s, increasing the national income by 40% in 1929. Over the same period productivity rose by 43%, exports by 28%, and there was heavy investment abroad. The benefits showed not only in profits but also in wages, which rose by 40%, so generating demand for such things as cars, domestic appliances, radios and houses. The housing boom reached a peak in 1925 with an expenditure of $5 billion, then started to slow down, as did industrial investment.

After this stellar performance it is surprising that the Great Depression hit the USA so hard but the symptoms were already present. Commodity prices had fallen since 1920, there were record debt and credit levels, a feverish stock market and signs of markets like housing slowing down. By June 1929 industrial production peaked and then fell some four months ahead of the stock-market crash on Black Thursday, 29 October.

The President in 1930 was Herbert Hoover, the third in a line of Republicans, who believed completely in the free market and the ability of business to adapt. This very able administrator realised the nature of deflation and put in place several remedial programmes for the benefit, not of people, but of business. The first to be created was the Reconstruction Finance Corporation (RFC) in 1932, designed to bail out banks. This initiative later became detested when failed bankers were seen as the enemy of society after depositors lost their credits. Hoover also instituted public works programmes which put the budget into deficit but did little to relieve the gloom, coinciding as they did with the cancellation of other projects.

The international trade position deteriorated in 1930 when American farmers (who dominated the House of Representatives) prevailed upon the President to sign the Hawley-Smoot Act or lose the mid-term elections. This legislation raised the import tariff of foodstuffs by 30% and, when other countries retaliated, world trade slowed down.

The failure of the Austrian bank Credit Anstalt in May 1931 caused virtually every overseas country, with the exception of Britain, to default on their debts to the US; this forced the closure of a number of US banks. The banking crisis reached a peak early in 1933, when one of the first acts of the new Democrat President, Franklin D. Roosevelt, was to call a bank holiday to avert the run becoming a rout. In all some $90 billion of credit was destroyed – a sum nearly equal to the national income of the USA. The destruction of credit was made worse by a flight of money as foreign lenders repatriated funds to shore up their own depleted balance sheets. In turn US credits were withdrawn from European banks, so reversing the capital exports of the late 1920s.

The credit collapse accelerated the deflation and in the four years to 1933 American GDP collapsed by nearly 30%, despite the US remaining the most wealthy nation on earth, with 28% of the world's gold reserves. In the climate of national despair, Herbert Hoover fought the 1932 election on a ticket proclaiming 'the business of America is business', although by then most believed that only Roosevelt was capable of delivering a recovery.

The scene was thus set for the biggest experiment in peacetime government intervention ever experienced by a democracy. The inauguration of the new President was on 4 March 1933 – only a few weeks after the appointment of Adolf Hitler as Chancellor. But unlike the calculated actions of the Third Reich, most of the New Deal policies were not guided by a set of theories; they were pragmatic, created by the perceived needs of the time. The measures contrasted with those of Britain (described later) on the assumption that it was the government's job to revive the economy, not that of individual entrepreneurs.

The first task of the Roosevelt administration was to stem the banking crisis in March 1933 by declaring a week's bank holiday. He then passed an Emergency Banking Act which required banks to hand over gold and foreign reserves in exchange for supplying additional cash to keep their business customers trading. Later the Federal Deposit Insurance Corporation (FDIC) was set up. It collected insurance premiums from member banks in exchange for protecting depositors in the event of a failure. At the time the more left-wing members believed that a better solution would have been to nationalise the banks but they misread the methods of Roosevelt, who was no socialist.

Next, to make American exports more competitive and imports more expensive, the dollar was devalued relative to gold, and the Emergency Banking Act made it an offence for individuals to own the metal. Although the dollar fell naturally by 17%, this was deemed too little so the next step was to use the RFC to purchase newly minted metal. By January the price of gold had risen to $35 per ounce, a devaluation of nearly 70%. Overall it had little effect for in the four years to 1935, US exports fell by around 60%.

Most countries adopted a policy of cheap credit to encourage entrepreneurs to borrow and the banks to lend. But, as Japan has discovered once again during the 1990s, cheap credit is not enough to spur an economy back to growth while there is still a mountain of bad debt and the banks cannot lend. Once again the Roosevelt administration used the RFC, funded by banks with insufficient customers, to make loans at subsidised rates. The clients were mostly companies, railways and farmers who would otherwise not rate a sound credit. By 1937, 46% of all loans were being subsidised by the federal government, the RFC itself lending more than $5 billion.

There were hints of Nazi Fascism in the next US legislation, whereby the government hoped to regulate the economy through the National Recovery Administration (NRA). In concert with consumer groups, unions and industrial organisations it was hoped to establish a regulatory code for commerce and business. These were to cover such matters as wages, commercial practices, industrial output and prices in the hope that entrepreneurs would be able to generate enough profit to start an enterprise. Other aims were to increase consumer spending power and, to an extent, introduce social reforms such as shorter working hours.

Some industrialists and unions who enjoyed a monopoly welcomed the NRA. There was also a subsequent rise in employment, but on balance the rigidities in the system hindered progress. It was destroyed by its own contradictions, for what entrepreneur would attempt to invest with so many regulations and restrictions? In the end it was ruled unconstitutional by the Supreme Court, after a case in which the Schechter brothers were given short jail sentences for disobeying a nitpicking regulation that if a buyer did not want to buy a full coop of chickens, he was not allowed to pick out the better birds.

It is perhaps too facile to explore whether the NRA could have worked should the federal government have wanted (or been allowed) to introduce some of the directives that made the Nazi recovery programme such a success in peacetime. If it had been possible to create some sort of national assent to a programme for famine or poverty relief, then there could possibly have been agreement for a limited time. But then could the people trust the leaders to give up power gracefully?

Nevertheless, the much-despised NRA did have one successful programme called the Public Works Administration (PWA), which had over $3.5 billion to spend on public works projects approved by the federal government and other public bodies. Not all the funds were spent on public works per se, as some went to the Highways Department and to Farm Credit, but the biggest programme was the Tennessee Valley Association (TVA), based at Chattanooga, which set up a series of barrages and hydro-electric works on the Tennessee river. Later a second tranche of $4 billion was allocated to be administered by the PWA.

The agricultural equivalent to the NRA was the Agricultural Adjustment Act (AAA), which was designed to raise prices through regulation. By March 1933 one quarter of the American people – the proportion engaged in farming and as important consumers – were deemed to be destitute, squeezed between high costs of production, low prices and the inability to fund their mortgage payments. The AAA aimed to restrict agricultural production by paying farmers to take land out of production and then slaughter animals on an agreed scale. This would be partly compensated by the national treasury but also through a tax levied on processing (such as flour milling) which fell upon the non-farming consumer. The main products were corn, hogs, wheat, rice, tobacco and cotton. There was an outcry when it was learned that piglets were being slaughtered with baseball bats.

Unlike the NRA, the AAA was largely successful in raising farm incomes, which increased from 55% of their pre-war level in 1933 to 111% by December 1935, but whether it succeeded in raising incomes overall is debatable. The programme was inadvertently helped by the extreme dust bowl in states around Oklahoma, the Texas Panhandle and Kansas, which is estimated to have destroyed some 75 million acres, and damaged a further 24 million. By 1935 the drought was so bad that corn and wheat had to be imported.

The debate over a policy of deliberately restricting some food production while encouraging other types continues with today's EU Common Agricultural Policy. The AAA was regionally based so that farmers who were discouraged from growing wheat in one area could turn to cotton while the reverse would occur in another part of the US. Also, instead of being confined to a small group of products, the AAA might have cast its net more widely to include vegetables and dairy products.

The most important question is whether a nation should attempt to be self-sufficient in essential items such as food when, in times of low prices, the surplus of one nation tends to be dumped on another. Modern Western nations now employ only 2% of their workforce on the land instead of the 25% 70 years ago, so the producer argument at the core of the AAA hardly applies. However, as the dust-bowl conditions showed, it was climate and not man that was ultimately the most crucial element for increasing incomes.

Public works programmes were considered a means of reducing employment and stimulating the economy; the other alternative was directly to pay individuals' wages as was the policy in Nazi Germany. Public works such as building roads, harbours, river defences, airfields and hydro-electric programmes created something permanent but took time to design. They employed heavy equipment but the numbers of people needed were relatively few. The Nazi principle of direct payments and central control of prices and wage rates reduced unemployment much more rapidly but would not be acceptable to a democracy.

As the Japanese discovered in the 1990s, public works programmes do little to stimulate the economy but are extremely expensive if paid out of increased borrowings. Another way of funding would be to increase taxation, but this only deters entrepreneurs, upon whom politicians rely to stimulate the economy. Reflation through effectively printing money was used by the Reichsbank in 1922-3, but is no longer effective when entering a credit cycle, as shown in Japan during the 1990s and more recently in the USA.

Apart from the RFC, two other funds were set up, this time to help farmers and mortgage-holders. The purpose of the Farm Credit Administration (FCA) was to refinance farm mortgages by reducing interest from 5% to 3.5%, thus relieving interest by more than a quarter. By 1937, government credit agencies held 37% of all farm debt. A similar fund was set up for home owners when repossessions were running at 1,000 per day. The Home Owners Loan Corporation (HOLC) refinanced loans at substantially lower rates of interest by buying troubled mortgages from lenders such as banks, trusts and Savings and Loans. By 1936 the HOLC had loaned $5 billion and by 1942 was wound up at no cost to the taxpayer.

But the main relief programme of the New Deal was the Federal Emergency Relief Act (FERA) of May 1933 which authorised the federal government to make direct grants of up to $500 million to states and local authorities. Its purpose was similar to the Nazi programme of paying individuals for local projects. Like the later US Workfare plans, there was no payment unless work was done locally. This obviously had a social purpose that was later codified in the Civil Works Administration (CWA), providing direct relief from poverty. In addition, Roosevelt initiated what was probably one of the most imaginative work-generation and human programmes ever undertaken by a democracy. The Civilian Conservation Corps (CCC) took young men from deprived homes and gave them the opportunity to learn trades, perform useful work and to earn money. Millions of young men were given the chance to lead healthy and useful lives at a time when millions were out of work.

By the next presidential election in 1936 over $12 billion had been spent on public programmes – around 20% of a depleted national income. After rising to an index of 103.6 in 1929, the GDP fell to 73.8 in 1933 and only regained its 1929 level in 1937. Unemployment which had been some 3 million in 1929 was up to over 12.8 million in 1933 (25% of the working population) and only recovered when the nation started to rearm. With low rates of plant utilisation during the 1930s, capital was only expended to reduce costs, until 1940 when the nation geared up for war.

In Britain

In its own pragmatic way, Britain achieved more growth and lower unemployment than almost any other country. By adopting the principle of cheap money, a balanced budget and a stable currency, the government encouraged the expansion of new industries. Among these were the manufacture of domestic appliances and cars, radio, electrical and chemical engineering, and an aircraft industry that was later to challenge the Luftwaffe in the Battle of Britain and outbuild Germany and its satellites. However these measures did little to alleviate unemployment in areas such as south Wales, the north of England and Scotland, which contained the staple industries of coal, steel, textiles and shipbuilding. These industries were heavily unionised and there was much bitterness.

The 1920s were not a good time for Britain, probably because of unwise policy initiatives. One was the decision to return to the gold standard at the pre-war rate which required a higher rate of interest to avoid loss of gold reserves. It was directly responsible for the deflation which triggered the miners' strike that later led to the General Strike of 1926. The policy error was somewhat rectified by Benjamin Strong, the Governor of the New York Federal Reserve Bank, who tried to reduce the loss of Britain's reserves by keeping US interest rates low. Unfortunately this action led directly to the Wall Street bubble by allowing excessive speculation.

There was also the uncertainty created by the election of a Labour government in 1928, which weakened the stock markets while those in the US were still booming. The lower stock prices in London were held to be the direct cause of Clarence Hatry's steel empire failure, an event that many in New York blamed for the precipitous fall of the Dow Jones Industrial Index in October 1929.

The US recession was catastrophic for Britain's external finances; between 1929 and 1931 merchandise exports halved and overseas investment income declined by 40%. The loss of earnings created a major external deficit and in May 1931 an official report recommended major economies and tax increases to repair the imbalance. The report posed a dilemma for the government over whether to deflate or devalue. Being unable to agree, the Cabinet resigned and a few ministers, including the Prime Minister and a few members of parliament, joined a newly formed national government. In the end the decision was made for them by the German default, which triggered a run on Britain's gold reserves on 20 September. The next day the pound was taken off the gold standard and devalued by around 25%.

British governments of the 1930s have been vilified for allowing despondency in the coalfields, the shipyards and the cotton mills, but the country was divided geographically. While conditions in most of Wales, Scotland and the north of England were bad, the Midlands and south were booming; in fact GDP rose by around 25% from 1932 to 1939 and during the early part of the 1930s the budget was balanced, until in 1938 rearmament was ordered, when it went strongly negative.

The measures that led to this result were relatively simple and were based on the principle that, given the right economic conditions, entrepreneurship and innovation would revive. Despite his later failure as Prime Minister, the credit for this should go to the Chancellor, Neville Chamberlain, who introduced a balanced budget to allow private enterprise to flourish. This was achieved by severely reducing government expenditure, including civil service pay, by 15% and lowering the coupon on war loans from 5% to 3.5%. Other savings were made in expenditure on roads, education and grants to local authorities. At the same time direct and indirect taxation was raised and employers were levied to pay unemployment compensation.

The pound was kept stable by an exchange equalisation fund which allowed interest rates to fall rapidly, permitting the government to borrow long term at 3.5% and the banks to lend commercially at a small premium of over 0.5%. This did little to reduce unemployment, however, and like most other countries Britain raised general import tariffs by 10% on items including food and manufactured goods; iron and steel were protected by at least 20%. At the same time, the Ottawa Conference in 1932 was negotiated to allow Commonwealth countries preference for imported foodstuffs while manufactured exports were given the same treatment. A similar deal was negotiated with the USA in 1938.

Bilateral deals were also negotiated with large importers outside of the Commowealth. Denmark was given preference for importing bacon in exchange for taking British steel, textiles and manufactured goods. Other arrangements were made with Argentina and Scandinavian countries.

The stable currency and low interest rates stimulated new businesses but, unlike the NRA in the US, the government gave little help to industry. However the Export Credits Guarantee Department was set up to protect export payments to viable countries, and older staple industries were given subsidised loans to replace obsolete machinery and to generate exports. This was little help to those who had been made redundant – they had the unpleasant option of either staying put and living off benefit or moving to the prosperous parts of the country.

Because it was not regarded as a strategic resource, as it was in Germany, British agriculture had to compete with cheap Commonwealth food, although meat, poultry and fish were given some subsidies. Milk production was helped by setting up the Milk Marketing Board for co-operative distribution, and a wheat fund was set up in 1932 to encourage growers.

Would prior knowledge of the long-wave cycle have prevented the Great Depression? For a few people who knew their history, maybe, but only someone following the Chief Rabbi in Leviticus 25 could have avoided the build-up of credit that has been such a constant feature prior to its destruction during a down-wave. It comes down to human nature. Otto von Bismarck once commented that 'other men learn from their own mistakes while I learn from other people's mistakes'. How can we learn from the 1930s?

Public works do not launch a recovery, as America learned in the 1930s and Japan in the 1990s. The PWA did little to reduce unemployment, although some worthwhile infrastructure projects such as the TVA, harbours, canal and road programmes were undertaken. Less concentration on public works in Britain reduced the cost of government, allowing innovators to thrive. In future recessions, the most propitious environment for recovery would be a regime of minimum taxation, low interest rates and few regulations.

Only enterprise can offer worthwhile job opportunities, although there is a government role for encouraging programmes like the Civilian Conservation Corps described earlier, to be run by the private sector. Even so, there are likely to be calls for tariff protection and competitive devaluations should unemployment start rising rapidly. This is now impossible for countries within the Euro, but the demand for individual countries to act could break up that union. Dictatorships might be seen as an alternative but are likely to end in war or major geo-political dislocation.

References

Adcroft, D.H., *British Economy Between the Wars* (Philip Allen, 1982).

Alford, B.W.E., *Depression and Recovery* (Economic History Society, 1972).

Arndt, H.W., *The Economic Lessons of the Nineteen-Thirties* (Cass, 1944).

Brendon, Piers, *The Dark Valley* (Jonathan Cape, 2000)

Brinkley, A., *Voices of Protest* (Vintage, 1977)

Capie, F., *Depression and Protectionism* (Allen & Unwin, 1983).

Congdon, T., *The Debt Threat* (Basil Blackwell, 1988).

Constantine, S., *Unemployment in Britain between the Wars* (Longman, 1980).

——————, *Social Conditions in Britain 1918-1939* (Methuen, 1983).

James, H., *The German Slump* (Clarendon, 1986).

Kindleberger, C., *The World in Depression 1929-1939* (University of Kindleberger, 1973).

McElvaine, R.S., *America 1929-1941* (Times, 1984).

Morgan, T., *FDR* (Grafton Books, 1985).

Morris, M., *The General Strike* (Journeyman, 1976).

Perrett, G., *America in the Twenties* (Simon and Schuster, 1982).

St Etienne, C., *The Great Depression, 1929 to 1939: Lessons for the 1980s* (Hoover Institute, 1984).

Stevenson, John, and Chris Cook, *The Slump* (Quarter Books, 1977).

Watkins, T.H., *The Great Depression* (Little, Brown, 1993).

Zahorchak, M., *Climate: The Key to Understanding Business Cycles* (Tide, 1983).

12

An Anatomy of Fascism

The historian A. J. P. Taylor argues that the right sort of history tells us things about human behaviour that we did not know before. Now, in the early years of the twenty-first century, there are increasing signs of right-wing movements in Norway, Denmark, Austria, Switzerland, Spain, Italy, Germany, France, Holland and Belgium, and we should be aware of what could arise should economic and climatic conditions deteriorate. In addition, we should also focus on the rising fundamentalist Islamic movement, which is every bit as nationalistic in outlook and as dictatorial as Fascist states. To learn what this means we should review the 1930s, when Germany, Italy, Portugal, Japan, Hungary and Croatia – and later occupied France – elected a single party with a dominant leader; in Spain, General Francisco Franco won the civil war and similarly imposed his own order.

Unlike Communism, there is no one blueprint or theory for Fascism and, of the two, it is easier for a country to recover from the latter than the former. The concerns of terrorism and migration have caused even liberal cities like Hamburg to elect a nationalist mayor committed to reducing the influx of foreigners into his town. The real danger is that politicians of the centre will become sidelined, while those advocating some mutation of a nasty and inefficient creed will seem to provide a solution that the nice, politically correct liberals do not satisfy.

Until the collapse of the Berlin Wall in 1989, the world was obsessed with the evil influence of Communism, a regime that at one time seemed to threaten the very existence of the West. The creed was based on the apparently inevitable domination of the workers through confiscation, common ownership and violent revolution, due to their own apparently inevitable domination of the middle classes. It took over seventy years for those it was supposed to liberate to realise that they were suffering from despotism, incompetence, venality and an inability to deliver a better living standard.

Communism's sister doctrine of Fascism ostensibly lasted twenty-three years – from Mussolini's march on Rome in 1922 to the end of the Second World War – except in Spain, where a milder form ended with Franco's death. Like Communism, it thrived on the breakdown of society, but unlike Communism, Fascism actually brought order and, initially, an increase in people's living standards before they again descended into the abyss. Fascism dominated the 1920s and 1930s, but may once again be used as solution to chaotic conditions early in the twenty-first century.

Most historians blame the work of Friedrich Nietzsche, the nineteenth-century German philosopher, for providing the intellectual base for Fascism. An atheist who despised the growing cult of democratic ideas, Nietzsche preached the need to create an *Übermensch* – a superman and superior being who had achieved self-mastery and a higher morality. An Italian, Gaetano Mosca, who stressed the role of leadership and strong authority, expanded these ideas.

Other strands of both Fascist and Communist thinking originated in the work of Georg Hegel who, with others, was responsible for rallying German morale after the crashing defeat of Prussia by Napoleon at Jena in 1806. Hegel and others postulated the ideal of Frederick the Great's Prussian era, which glorified the state as supreme in human life and the highest revelation of the 'world spirit'. The philosopher held that war creates the 'ethical health of peoples corrupted by a long peace'. He also believed that Germany had the God-given genius to regenerate the world, overruling Christian virtues of modesty, pity, humility, forgiveness and forbearance – a heady brew indeed for would-be dictators.

Other writers extolled the work of Charles Darwin's doctrine of the survival of the fittest and encouraged racial purity through nationalism, the glorification of war and violence. The racial ideas were expanded by a French aristocrat, Comte Arthur de Gobineau, who argued that the white Aryans were superior to other races, particularly those with a Semitic or Slav background. However, it was a Germanised Englishman – one Houston Stewart Chamberlain – who glorified the Aryan racial stereotype and affirmed a 'race soul'. It was he who defined Jews as the bitter foes of the Aryan and so promoted the notion of a race war. He also developed a romantic notion of the German people as the *Volker*, a people who had a unique relationship with nature and the cosmos, and could develop human nature free of corrupting influences.

All Fascist cultures stressed the need to create a 'new man' by emphasising youth programmes and fitness as the way to build a new race – something the democracies failed to do in the 1930s. After the fall of France it was noticeable that the captured British soldiers, raised in the 1930s depression, were in relatively poor physical shape compared with the Hitler youth, reared on fresh air, an outdoor life and exercise.

At the beginning of the twentieth century several strains of nationalism were becoming evident. There were those in Germany, Spain and Portugal, where the monarch could dismiss prime ministers or elected representatives. In Germany there was a belief, even amongst liberals, that the state should create a *Rechtsstaat* – a modern, civilised 'state of reason' where the rights of the many would take precedence over the individual. France had already experienced the dictatorship of Napoleon I and his nephew Louis-Napoleon, until the latter was deposed in 1870 after the disastrous Franco-Prussian War. There followed a 'League of Patriots', who vowed national vengeance and became anti-Semitic after the Dreyfus Affair in which a French-Jewish army officer was falsely convicted of treason. Italy also had devotees of Fascism early on.

The different routes to Fascism

In Italy, the first modern dictator was the disreputable but surprisingly able individual Benito Mussolini, who was to become Il Duce. He was born in 1883 of working-class parents in the region of Romagna, fifteen kilometres from the nearest town of Forli. His father, a blacksmith, bequeathed to him a legacy of drunkenness, violence, womanising and fecklessness; he was also one of Italy's first socialists and passed his creed to his son.

By the time Mussolini left school there was something of the intellectual bohemian about him. He was a mixture of an anarchist, international socialist and revolutionary. He was also a congenital liar who found difficulty in holding down a job. Surprisingly for one who hated discipline, he joined the army for a short time, but then left it to teach – an odd profession for a man who preached violent insurrection and boasted of spending time in jail. His mother, a staunch Catholic, must have been horrified by her son's life.

His enthusiasms and increasing powers of polemic brought him into contact with socialist groups in his home town, where he edited a four-page weekly magazine called *La Lotta di Classe* ('The Class Struggle'). As well as being anti-clerical, he was also anti-military, seeing the army as the protector of capitalism. As his attitudes and haranguings became increasingly more vitriolic he deliberately split from the socialist party in an attempt to lead his own revolutionary group, which succeeded in attracting a few malcontents.

Mussolini's journalistic career advanced when he became the editor of a socialist newspaper, *Avanti*, which had as its art critic a rich Milanese called Margherita Sarfatti. She became his mistress, weaned him from socialism to Fascism, and later wrote his biography. His mistresses described him as being scruffy, untidy and unshaven in private, then changing rapidly into a silk-faced coat and patent leather shoes for his public life. They confirmed his superficiality and ambition to be 'a man of destiny, a celebrated writer whose name would be on everyone's lips like Napoleon, but greater'.

The declaration of war in 1914 was his turning point. Convinced after the Battle of the Marne that the Allies would win, he did another volte-face by attempting to change *Avanti*'s socialist neutrality to supporting the Allies, and was promptly fired. Then, with the encouragement of wealthy, belligerent contributors, he started *Il Populo d'Italia* as his own launch-pad into politics. From being anti-war he became a national imperialist, demanding as a war aim the return of Trieste and Fiume to Italy, and justifying the Libyan campaign which he had previously castigated. His was the genuine voice of Fascism and he later boasted that he was responsible for Italy declaring war on Austria. He was later called up, and though his service was undistinguished he was apparently resolutely cheerful, despite the squalor of trench warfare. After being wounded he was invalided out to rejoin his paper where, it was said, he increased the daily circulation to 60,000 by 1917.

By now a seasoned journalist, he adopted a hard-hitting energetic style, writing sensational headlines in an appeal to the malcontents who felt let down after the war. In this way he attracted readers from a hodge-podge of futurists, anarchists, Communists, anti-clericists and ex-servicemen who made up his group the Ardenti – the first of his 'blackshirt' henchmen. They were armed illegally and cheaply from the quantity of equipment available on demobilisation. Like Hitler's support for the SA, he planned that the Ardenti would give him the manpower for armed insurrection, although in early skirmishes they were easily bested by the police.

Mussolini was now becoming quite well known for his attempts to return Trieste and Fiume to Italy, and in 1921 his Fascists, allied to the liberals, won thirty-five parliamentary seats with 7% of the vote. He then showed his true colours by promptly voting against his political allies to prove his revolutionary colours and to encourage the diverse factions making up his blackshirts.

In the post-war chaos the power of the Ardenti increased, with continuing polarisation between the far left and right at the expense of central coalitions. This was the situation he had been waiting for and he used the political vacuum to direct his Ardenti, replacing socialist local authorities with his own people. Even more importantly he had growing support from industrialists, who feared Communism more than a Fascist dictatorship, and in the political paralysis he attacked other strategic cities and trade-union premises, using his brutal henchman Italo Balbo to lead the insurrections.

However much of a devious buffoon he appeared to be, Mussolini prepared his coup with considerable care by cultivating those in the police and army who would be sympathetic to his Fascist views. His time came in October 1922 when he took control and rallied a mass meeting of his supporters at the San Carlo theatre in Naples; there he explained the advantages of Fascism for an Italy drifting towards anarchy, depression and lawlessness, much of which he had fostered. He than incited his henchmen to march on Rome. These events were widely reported, but ministers failed to declare a state of emergency to quell the rebellion – until even they were forced to prepare a document for the king's signature.

Amidst rising rumours of an insurrection, Mussolini kept a low profile in Milan, hoping he would not be arrested as groups of his supporters were duly taken away. Then in one of those curious turns of fate, the king refused to confirm the state of emergency, fearing that yet another government would fall. In a fit of desperation, the outgoing premier actually recommended the monarch call upon Mussolini as his prime minister.

It is typical of the man that he planned to enter Rome at the head of his 'troops' on horseback. However, fearing that he might look ridiculous leading a ragged mob, he quietly took the night sleeper and arrived on 30 October to find the Avanti had already closed down left-wing newspaper offices and socialist clubs. To a capital grown weary of political decay, it was something of a relief to have a supposedly benevolent right-wing, anti-Communist government and the people came out onto the streets to welcome him.

Showing once again considerable political astuteness he then formed a government from a wide range of politicians, knowing that he needed a parliamentary majority

– something impossible with his small number of Fascist deputies. In what must have been an expression of relief following the recent chaos, he won a huge majority in both houses on a bill to improve the lot of the poor and a demand for full powers to change the law to stabilise the country. Perhaps not surprisingly for one who had travelled little, his first official visits were to conferences in Lausanne and London, accompanied by a bodyguard of *Fascisti* to impress on foreigners that he and Italy were a force to be reckoned with.

Back at home his previously illegal groups, now part of a militia and paid for by the state, continued their reign of terror against left-wing opposition and critical newspapers – their obstinate editors often being jailed on trumped-up charges. Despite the violence, two ex-premiers, Giolitti and Salandra, supported him, encouraging the police and civil service to support the anti-Communist administration. He also renounced all previous anti-clericism in a bid to gain the support of the Catholic Populari party in the assembly and insisted religious teaching be made compulsory in schools.

No dictator likes to be challenged and, prone to paranoia, only feels secure when in total control. Although the lower house would have given him emergency powers for a year, Mussolini proceeded to call an election in the spring of 1924, insisting, however, that any party winning 25% of the votes would be given two-thirds of the seats. This should have been no problem, for he had wide-ranging anti-Communist support, but he still directed a reign of terror against anyone courageous enough to offer opposition; not surprisingly, he won a thumping majority.

Despite his parliamentary success, Mussolini was still paranoid about opposition and his campaign of violence, vilification, incarceration and threats of exile continued. In one area his repudiation of law worked well: under the liberals the Mafia had been able to intimidate witnesses and manipulate the system. Mussolini locked up 2,000 known brothers – some on slender evidence – and the rackets stopped.

By 1925, wearying of dealing with parliament, he informed the deputies that he was taking personal executive authority and then dissolved the assembly. Later a directly appointed rubber-stamp chamber called the Grand Council was formed, made up of people from a wide range of society but having no power to initiate action. With all the power in his hands, Mussolini allowed King Victor Emmanuel to remain as head of state.

Mussolini's public mien was that of a hardworking family man who planned his every moment, worked partly from an instinctive genius, appeared ahead of everyone in his thinking and was disdainful of riches. Probably only the latter was true; apart from his salary he derived income from ownership of newspapers and journalism but, despite having as many benefits as he liked from the state, he actually gave much money away to charities. Although of short stature he was proud of his physique and liked to pose with his head thrown back, hands on hips and legs apart. He was a vain man who hated social events and used bad language, but he could be engaging and even charming company.

Surprisingly for such a strong anti-Communist, he recognised Soviet Russia, explaining that he had always admired Lenin. These links were tested when Italy attempted to occupy Corfu but was forced to retreat – the Soviet Union being the only uncritical country in the League of Nations. With her colonies in Somalia and North Africa, Italy mixed the arrogance of the master race with a surprising commitment to improving health, abolishing slavery and solving inter-tribal conflicts. Later however he aroused the world's ire by conquering Ethiopia with the help of mustard gas.

At home he continued to support capitalism while the economy boomed and tax concessions helped to retain the support of industrialists, who liked the freedom from strikes and official support for exports. Under Il Duce, the first motorway in Europe was constructed and he boasted that the Italian trains were the best in the world. Another useful contribution was marsh-draining – especially the Pontine marshes near Rome, which had been a source of malaria for centuries.

Industrial liberalism did not last long. A creed that held an individual to be subservient to a state had no difficulty in concluding that the government was the unifying force for the whole economy. Gradually companies were brought together under a ministry of corporations, which was to be the directing force and 'cornerstone of the Fascist state'. Unlike the Communist creed of nationalisation, Mussolini retained the principle of individual ownership, concluding that capitalists could at least support the Fascists financially. Unlike Hitler, Mussolini wisely never attempted to bring the Catholic Church under direct control, although he absorbed the lands of the Papal Estates.

During the 1930s, and perhaps taking a leaf out of Hitler's book, Mussolini stepped up his attempts to create the 'new man' by introducing Fascism and fitness into elementary schools; by 1939 the party had grown to 5 million people. The Ministry of Culture built new stadia and the Italian soccer team won the World Cup in 1934 and 1938; at the same time, over 11,000 sports arenas were started, cinemas opened, orchestras formed and libraries built. Everywhere the themes were of labour, sport, motherhood, struggle and physical perfection.

If Fascism was meant to increase employment, it failed: there was a 20% rise in unemployment in the early 1930s and those out of work rose to 1 million by 1933. The response of the government was to set up the Instituto Mobiliare Italiano (IMI) to buy shares in bankrupt banks and virtually nationalise the banking system. Another innovation was the Instituto per la Ricostruzione Industriale (IRI), a holding company which rescued failing industrial companies and injected funds. It became a permanent institution which eventually bought 21.5% of all public companies. The country was eventually taken out of recession by the rearmament needed to fight the Ethiopian war in 1935, which caused the economy to grow even faster than that of Germany. Surprisingly, by the mid-1930s the proportion of income taken by the state was 27.6%, which was modest by post-war standards, although there was also a sales tax.

Both Germany and Italy strove to create a greater state and encouraged a rising birth rate in an attempt to confirm and expand the 'new breed' of individual. Both countries improved health services, which boosted the longevity of those of sixty-five and above but had little impact on the younger population – the age group they so desperately needed to fight wars.

Although Hitler and Mussolini 'compared notes' in the 1930s, it was not until June 1937 that Germany and Italy became allies assisting Franco in Spain. Thereafter, and to Hitler's eternal gratitude, Mussolini stood aside during the Anschluss, which integrated Austria into Germany; Italy only declared war against the Allies in 1940 when Hitler was the dominant power in Europe.

The Second World War was a disaster for Italy, for they lost all of their African colonies and much of the country was ravaged by the fighting – although the historic cities were barely touched. But however unpleasant Fascism may have been in its later racial policies and the growth of state control, there is little doubt that in Italy it created the industrial base which was the launch-pad for the country's post-war economic growth.

National Socialism in Germany

In Germany, the man who came to power was as clever a political operator as Mussolini and can only be described as an evil genius. In *The Rise and Fall of the Third Reich*, William Schirer describes Adolf Hitler as having 'uncommon shrewdness who led Germany to such dizzy heights and to such a sorry end'. The future dictator was born on 20 April 1889 at a town called Braunau am Inn on the Austrian-German border. His father was an illegitimate minor customs official whose name was Schickelgruber, until his paternity was recognised and he took the name Hitler. (Schirer doubts whether his followers would ever have greeted each other with 'Heil Schickelgruber'.)

Unlike Mussolini, Hitler was a thin, pale and sickly looking child with piercing eyes who hated the schooling that was intended to make him into another minor official. In any case he made poor grades in all subjects and to the horror of his father announced he wanted to become a painter. He was released from paternal strictures when his father died in 1903 and his mother moved to an apartment in the nearby town of Linz. Although his mother found it difficult to make ends meet, Hitler describes the next few years as the happiest of his life, reading, walking around towns and the countryside or lazing by the Danube.

Despite his intention to become a painter, Hitler was already becoming politically conscious, spending all the hours available reading (usually German history) in libraries. At about the same time that his mother died, he was turned down by a Viennese art school for having insufficient talent. In 1908 he returned to Vienna and spent what would be formative, but unpleasant, years living as a vagabond.

Vienna was an enchanted capital city in the last days of the Habsburg dynasty, especially for those who could enjoy the music, gaiety, waltzing and dining. There was, of course, a less fortunate group who were poor, ill-fed and living in hovels, but this was in some cases by choice, for there was paid work everywhere. Hitler was never one to submit to a steady job so he spent his time shovelling snow, doing odd jobs and using what drawing talents he had to make sketches, signs and other daubs. In those days he wore a long, black, shabby overcoat, a greasy hat and had dank unwashed hair.

Unlike Mussolini, he read avidly from Fascist literature, and by now he was crystallising his thoughts on politics. As a fervent German nationalist he hated the social revolution that was destroying the Habsburg unity by demanding workers' rights; however, he was interested in why the unions appealed to the masses, and to this end studied socialist and social-democratic literature, read their speeches, investigated their symbolism, and absorbed their propaganda. But the movement he wished to create was quite different: a German-speaking empire that would dominate the Slavs, Czechs and other 'inferior' races.

At the start of the First World War, Germany was an unusual blend of the traditional and the modern. Since its unification in 1871 it had inherited the Prussian ideals of militarism, authority and discipline. It was also a dynamic centre of capitalism, excelling in technology and culture with a growing, educated middle class which absorbed liberal political ideas. As in France there was also a strong radical element among the working class that was international in outlook and detested the ideas being absorbed by their future dictator.

In 1914 the traditional overcame the radical as Germany mobilised to meet the Russian threat. Like others, the Austrian vagabond was swept along and was recruited into a Bavarian regiment after petitioning King Ludwig III. The future Führer was apparently a model soldier, who never complained about the discomfort of the trenches and, after volunteering for the dangerous task of a regimental runner, won the Iron Cross, first class – an unusual award for a lance corporal. His active service ended in hospital after a gas attack and it was there he learned of the German surrender, which he subsequently described as the 'greatest villainy of the century'.

Hitler's political life really started when, as an educational adviser to the army in Munich, he was sent to vet an extreme group called the German Workers' Party. So taken was he with their views that he became a member and was soon nominated as its leader. Among the group was Captain Ernst Roehm, a stocky, bull-necked professional soldier who had a genius for organisation and later helped propel Hitler to power as leader of the brown-shirted *Sturmabteilung* (SA).

The Germany of the young agitator was perfect soil for his brand of idealism. Under the Treaty of Versailles the nation had lost around 13% of both its population and its land, including a greater proportion of its farms and the heavy industry of the Saar basin. Inflation was rife and after the successful Allied blockade food became very expensive, claiming around 80% of the average pay packet. There was also the conflict between forces of the left, which owed allegiance to Moscow, and right-wing dissidents, who were increasingly attracted to Hitler's view of Germany's dominant place in the world.

At this point all Hitler's previous reading and experience was focused on setting out the principles of the now re-named National Socialist German Workers Party – or the Nazis. He developed special party uniforms, badges and emblems, including the Swastika, an inversion of an ancient occult design implying 'the art of the self'. All these were displayed at party meetings, which were elevated to ceremonial events. By 1923 the party numbered 55,000, plus the 15,000 members of Roehm's SA. As the mark collapsed, Hitler believed the time was ripe to take over the government of Bavaria. A year after Mussolini's 'March on Rome' he mounted a rally in the capital's largest beer cellar, then led his followers to the streets. The march became a fiasco when it was easily dispersed at the first rattle of militia musketry and Hitler was imprisoned for five years; this was subsequently reduced to twelve months by a benevolent and supportive judge. It was in jail that he wrote *Mein Kampf* – 'My Struggle' – his political blueprint.

In 1925 the new government under Chancellor Gustav Stresemann restored the value of the currency, the crippling reparations had been scaled down and loan money poured into the country to create boom conditions quite different from the post-war poverty and tension. Nevertheless Hitler and his henchmen started rebuilding the Nazi party as a racially pure, nationalist group dedicated to *Lebensraum* – the need to create a living space to the east; although at that time the party's racial policies were toned down. There was some attempt to develop the socialistic side of the party in the northern cities but Hitler swept this aside. Unlike the Communists he was determined to achieve power through legitimate means so as not to frighten the increasingly supportive middle classes and capitalists, who were essential to party funding. By 1929 the party had 178,000 members and was able to attract 18.3% of the votes in the election a year later.

The Nazis demonstrated considerable organisational abilities in delivering their message to various groups. Foremost there were the financial backers, but at the lower end Hitler needed the bullies who were attracted to Roehm's SA. There were also other groups, including women, farmers, professionals such as teachers, the law, the armed forces and veterans, who were attracted by Hitler's pledge to rebuild military strength. Added to these were the sundry intellectuals and writers who were disenchanted with the liberal Weimar government and were attracted to the German dream described by Hegel and others. Of particular importance were the young who become the Hitler Youth; because of First World War losses, this age group greatly outnumbered those in their thirties and forties.

As suggested earlier, physical fitness for this age group became one of the greatest Nazi successes. Young men and women were required to spend at least 15% of their school curriculum on physical exercise and those who could not pass the test were denied graduation. Curiously for a technically advanced nation the education standards, particularly in maths and physics, actually declined while the politicisation of the teaching profession grew.

The onset of the Great Depression in Germany had thrown 6 million out of work. While many of the displaced blue-collar workers were attracted to the Communists (whose vote increased to around 10% in the 1930 election), by far the greater number voted for the Nazis – both left and right parties pushing out the discredited centre. The downturn also created disarray among politicians, who had advanced the welfare state but could no longer afford it. Unable to raise taxes, the government was forced once again to borrow.

The crisis proved a blessing for the Nazis, who had formed alliances with powerful interest groups like the industrialists, attracted by Hitler's anti-Communism. By now numbers in the party had risen to 450,000, plus 400,000 Brownshirts – now a force larger than the army. In the election of July 1932 the Nazi proportion of the vote rose to 37% and it became the largest single party. Reluctant to appoint Hitler, the aged President Hindenberg instead chose Franz von Papen – an aristocratic right-winger – who called yet another election in November, when the Nazis were again the largest party. In despair, von Papen persuaded the president to appoint Hitler as Chancellor, believing that the non-Nazi cabinet members could bind him 'hand and foot'. The appointment was confirmed on 30 January 1933, but von Papen had grossly misjudged his man.

Like Mussolini before him, Hitler was determined to observe a veneer of democracy and persuaded the president to call yet another election in a month's time. In the meantime he used the Brownshirts to foment trouble in one region after another, quelling the disruption by appointing his own henchmen. Hitler's men also framed a half-wit Communist for starting the Reichstag fire, which was used as an excuse to arrest the Communist leadership and ban the party from elections.

After vigorous campaigning, the Nazis gained 43.9% of the votes, and, with their right-wing allies, gained a clear lead. Hitler then won the necessary two-thirds majority for governing by decree for the next four years. The Nazi programme now took on new vigour and by July trade unions had been outlawed and their offices occupied, gauleiters had been appointed in the regions, non-party cabinet members were ousted and the Nazis declared the sole party in Germany. So much for binding Hitler 'hand and foot'.

The only power that could unseat Hitler was the army. In the 'night of the long knives' over 100 potential opponents, including Roehm, were murdered by the SS, Hitler's special police force. The Brownshirts were then merged with the army – their fire-raising days no longer needed. When Hindenberg died in June 1934, Adolf Hitler, the erstwhile Bohemian corporal, was endorsed as Führer, combining the offices of President and Chancellor. All military personnel and public servants were required to declare an oath of loyalty, not to the state, but to Hitler himself.

The workings of the Nazi state were now becoming clear. Hitler, who showed no interest in economics, left the management of the country to Hjalmar Schacht – the Chairman of the Reichsbank – and others. Their first task was to get people back to work. Compared to the democracies this was highly successful; when France tried something similar, the work-creation measures destroyed the currency, while in Germany the mark remained steady against the dollar.

In 1935 the Fuhrer ordered a progressive increase in rearmament and at the same time planned to make the Third Reich as self-sufficient as possible in food to guard against another wartime blockade; the supply was increased when farmers were later resettled in conquered territories. Germany also needed oil, which was produced chemically from heating coal under pressure in the presence of hydrogen. By 1939 the chemical firm IG Farben AG was producing one-third of German needs and by 1943 the proportion was nearer three-quarters. Later Hitler secured oil from Romania, although he failed to capture the Baku oil fields in his drive through the Ukraine. A substitute for rubber was also developed.

Large-scale industry that had so loyally supported the party was not nationalised but tightly controlled by bureaucratic decrees. This was made somewhat tolerable by having a workforce that was virtually tied to its firms, and whose wages could only be raised by increased productivity. Investment was directed more and more towards rearmament in the larger firms, but small companies, which provided much innovation, were severely starved of funds.

Hitler's primary interest was the armed forces, over which he effectively acted as the combined Chief of Staff, leading to intense inter-service rivalry. War production was initially put directly under the control of the associated armed service; however as each demanded numerous modifications, mass-production wasn't achieved until Albert Speer was put in charge. The result was that despite huge initial losses, by 1943 the Soviet Union was easily outperforming the might of Germany and its captured territories.

The media were put under the control of the evil and clever Joseph Goebbels. In their attempt to produce a heroic 'new man', no effort was spared to present the regime in graphic and stark terms. The themes were the romantic and heroic; they highlighted epic battles, valour, the strength of labour, discipline, cleanliness and joy. Every event, from the mass rallies at Nuremberg to the torchlight marches and industrial achievements, was beamed to people who were banned from listening to foreign broadcasts. But later in the war nothing could disguise the food shortages, the constant power failures and the hand-to-mouth existence of most people. For them war was an unending drudgery.

One of the reasons for their compliance was the sinister force of the black-uniformed *Schutzstaffel* (SS) or 'Defence Squads', formed in 1925 from the SA to be a personal bodyguard for party chiefs. In 1929 Hitler appointed Heinrich Himmler, a former chicken farmer and a fanatical Nazi follower, to be its leader and the SS started to become a state within a state. Himmler proved an able organiser and the SS grew rapidly to become a private police and security force which performed high-profile assassination tasks such as the 'night of the long knives'. Later it administered the concentration camps, provided elite troops for the Waffen SS and created its own political intelligence services, the SD. At its peak, its numbers reached around 1 million.

The SS manifested all of the necessary brutality foreseen by the nineteenth-century philosophers. However the Nazis also exhibited a strong environmental streak which lauded the countryside and detested the conditions that drew people to live in dirty cities. Their culture of youth fitness was a part of this message, as was the romanticism of womanhood that forbade them from working for the war effort, even though production lagged behind the Allies. They were also modernists, extolling German technology as the product of the 'new man', and they championed anti-pollution measures.

In the end, Nazi Germany was unable to generate a warlike state dedicated to conquest and warfare for it failed to mobilise its resources as effectively as the Soviet Union and the Western Allies. Despite the production of sophisticated weapons and the fine fighting ability of all the armed forces, the system was a disaster. This was mainly due to control being divided between the party and an arthritic state administration – each jealously guarding their own authority. This more than anything else stunted the war machine, which at one time had most of continental Europe's productive capacity under its control. Even though new leaders may embrace nationalism as a policy, surely nobody would wish to emulate the brutality and incompetence of a Nazi state.

Austria

It will be recalled that Hitler learned his political and racist ideas in Vienna before the First World War. Later, the same groups readily accepted the Austrian Nazis in the fruitful ground provided by the chaos of the Great Inflation of 1923, and the country was split between the socialist parties on the left, who looked to Moscow, and a right wing, primarily Catholic, which looked to Mussolini. The latter was supported by the extreme nationalist *Heimwehr*, or home guard, a group similar to Roehm's Brownshirts who vowed to protect Austria from socialism.

Initially any union with Germany was denied by the Chancellor Engelbert Dollfuss. He was then killed in an uprising, but the state held intact and many of the Nazis who did not flee were executed. Support for the Nazis was still strong, however, and in 1936, once Mussolini had withdrawn his protection, Hitler was able to invade and unite the two countries.

Spain

Insulated partly by the Pyrenees, Spain had not been engaged in European conflict since 1814, when the Duke of Wellington's forces cleared the French out of the Iberian Peninsula. This isolation, though providing some protection militarily, was little help economically; by the start of the First World War its industry was probably a generation behind that of Italy.

After neutrality during the First World War the country was split politically between the left and a national movement which started life in Catalonia before moving to Madrid. At about the same time as Mussolini gained power, a Spanish general, Primo de Rivera, became the country's first right-wing dictator; but his rule lacked direction and failed in 1930, also bringing down the monarchy.

There was then an attempt to bring together republican groups, but they sought to exclude the Church and a more right-wing government was elected in 1933. This alienated the left, which adopted a militant form of 'Bolshevisation' and the next year attempted a coup in which over 1,000 died. There was another election early in 1936 when the left was victorious, causing each side to take positions; after the assassination of a leading nationalist, Calvo Sotelo, who admired Mussolini's brand of Fascism, this later resulted in a bloody civil war.

The party of the right was led originally by José Antonio Prima de Rivera, the eldest son of the late dictator. Calling themselves the Falange Española – 'Spanish Phalanx' – they drew support from business and industry in preparing a programme that had 'authority, hierarchy and order'. Like Mussolini, they idealised the 'new man' but unlike the Italian model, the Spanish created the traditional Catholic hero in a twentieth-century guise. Unlike the warlike, pitiless new Nazi, Primo de Rivera's man had all the Christian virtues. In the final elections in 1936, the Falangistes only polled 44,000 votes, the lowest in continental Europe. Even later the Catalan and Basque regions never accepted Franco.

After the start of the civil war, the party leadership was taken over by General Francisco Franco, a young officer who had rallied nationalist troops in Spanish Morocco and crossed with them to southern Spain, ferried by German JU52 transport planes. The new leader criticised Primo de Rivera for being too much like a South American dictator and promptly drew together the dissonant right-wing groups to create a party that differed little from Mussolini's Fascists. This leaning towards Italy was of considerable help during the civil war, when Mussolini provided by far the greater number of supporting troops. Although Hitler provided the Condor Legion, his prime objective was to use the conflict as a live testing ground for his new weapons. Foremost in this was to test the JU87 Stuka dive-bomber, which flattened Guernica, but Hitler also tested the ME109 fighters, which were deployed in the Battle of Britain. Their enemies were Soviet machines sent in to support the Republicans.

Both sides used brutality against their enemies and dissonant civilians, with the death toll in the tens of thousands. But, as in most Latin countries, the real blood-letting reprisals took place after the Fascists prevailed, with thousands being forced into exile. Politically, however, Franco's regime diverged from the Fascism of Mussolini towards a Catholic, corporative and less military administration. Unlike all the other dictatorships, Franco reintroduced the monarchy, and on the death of the dictator, there was a relatively smooth transition to democracy.

Japan

Unlike the European Fascists, Japan's right-wing dictatorship in the 1930s had its roots in the cult of Shinto, the doctrine of the gods that went back over 2,000 years. This was a mixture of Confucianism and Buddhism, and deified the ruling dynasty as descendants of the sun-goddess, the emperor's source of power. It made a comeback in 1853 when Commodore Perry and his US squadron of 'black ships' disgraced the ruling Tokagawa regime. This was the signal for the emperor to regain leadership of a divine country destined to be the world's ruler. However, before that could happen, Japan had to achieve economic parity with the West.

In a fascinating story of adaptation, a group of young Samurai sent officials to the USA and Europe to understand the sinews of a modern state. They were helped by a close relationship with politically aware industrialists called the Zaibatsu (links not dissimilar to the strong national bond between Hitler and the German industrialists). The binding force for the new Japan was the Shinto religion, which emphasised the power of a centralised state to even the meanest peasant. The faith in Japanese armed might was strengthened after the Russo-Japanese war of 1904-5 which ended in the crushing naval victory over the Russians at Tsu Shima and the recognition of Korea's independence. Certain territories were ceded to Japan (including Taiwan, renamed 'Formosa') and Russia was obliged to part with an indemnity of gold.

The new imperialism found confirmation after the First World War when the political theorist Kita Ikki wrote his plan for the reorganisation of Japan. This was a programme of national socialism which aimed to control swathes of industry, foster economic modernisation, break up the large estates and introduce an element of worker control. The primary purpose of the new-found wealth was to free Asia from Western imperialism, after which Japan could realise the Shinto aim of becoming an enlightened world ruler. Heady stuff for a nation that was just becoming industrialised.

However, while there were some leanings towards Marxism, Ikki's nationalistic and imperial ideas were taken up by a group of young army officers – the latter-day Samurai – who were the most enthusiastic supporters of the new right. Like Hitler's Aryan model, they sought the cult of will and primacy of morale to win the ultimate victory. The most important of these groups was the 'Cherry Blossom Society', organised within the general staff in 1930; they were followed by groups such as the nationalistic trade unions.

Their aims were crystallised in 1931 when the prime minister was assassinated and military-supported politicians took over. Thus began what Japanese historians call the Fifteen Years War, which started in Manchuria, where the last Chinese emperor Henry Pu Yi was declared regent. Like Hitler's *Lebensraum*, Manchuria and Korea were areas designated to relieve population pressures at home and help feed Japan's population, which had grown to nearly 65 million by 1930. On the pretext of a supposed Chinese incursion at Mukden in 1937, Japanese forces swept through the mainland, inflicting terrible massacres at Nanking, Hankow and other cities.

Amidst rising international tension, the Japanese government declared a national mobilisation in 1938 and took sweeping economic measures directed by a national government based on Hitler's Nazi party. Under Prime Minister Prince Konoye, a 'new political order' ended the independence of political parties and introduced bureaucratic control. The government became more like that in Germany when

General Hideki Tojo became prime minister in the autumn of 1941 and set about creating 'East Asia for the Asiatics'.

Japan was as inefficient in producing arms as wartime Germany, showing little of their post-war efficiency. For example Britain, with a much smaller population, out-produced Japan in aircraft in every year of the Second World War except 1944 (with 26,461 units compared with Japan's 28,180); in the same year America produced over 96,000. Japan was also the smallest producer of tanks, turning out under 2,000 at their peak, compared to over 8,500 in Britain and nearly 24,000 in the USSR.

The rest of Europe

In Europe many countries followed Italy away from representative governments. Poland also went down the Fascist route in 1926, Portugal in 1926-36, Greece in 1929, Yugoslavia in 1933 and Romania in 1938. All these resulted from the chaotic conditions after the First World War, the fear of Communism or the 1930s Great Depression. Each country tended to follow the lead of Mussolini, but there were many variations – such as those in France.

It is held that some of the Fascist movements (as opposed to ideas) originated in France late in the nineteenth century, with groups called the League of Patriots and the Anti-Semitic League. Although they were largely absorbed during the Great War, one group was reconstituted in 1925 under Georges Valois Le Faisceau and claimed 60,000 members, mainly from the middle classes. Another was the Croix de Feu, which was popular amongst veterans and supported moral values; it was later reorganised and by 1939 had 800,000 members. It should be remembered that the right-of-centre parties in France voted to accept Hitler's peace terms in 1940, so creating the Vichy Government.

The Low Countries and Britain also had small Fascist parties, the largest probably being the Dutch National Socialist Movement, which attracted nearly 50,000 members (it is interesting that, on the other hand, Holland also produced the most formidable resistance against the Nazis). In Britain, Oswald Mosley, an ex-socialist, formed the British Union of Fascists; they wore brown uniforms, gave the Fascist salute, preached discipline and nationalism, and aimed to correct perceived social wrongs. At its height Mosley's party attracted some 50,000 members and through their marches caused several breaches of public order. The movement was dissolved in 1939 and its leaders detained.

Among the most prolific Fascist states were those in the Balkans. Hungary spawned the largest number in the 1920s after the Treaty of Versailles broke up the Austro-Hungarian Empire. Probably the most vicious was the Croatian Ustashi state, which arose after King Alexander of Yugoslavia imposed a dictatorship. Its aim was to create an independent Croatia led by a *ustanak*, or armed insurgency, and to propound Catholic values. Its enemies were Turkey and, more closely at hand, the Orthodox Slavs. The movement culminated in the assassination of King

Alexander in October 1934, but, after a pause and like many of the Balkan states, became much more aligned to Nazi Germany.

Unlike Communism, where the patterns were originally set by the Soviet Union and China, the road to extreme nationalism has undergone many mutations, stemming probably from Napoleonic France. While there are many common features with Communism one can pick out what Fascism meant in practice.

There was always a one-party state and a central dictator, who in most instances was xenophobic. In some cases, as in Italy or Germany, the ruler was elected to power but in others, like Vichy France and Croatia, the president ruled by the suffrage of the conqueror – in both cases Germany. In Spain the dictator was established by conquest but unlike all the others there was a peaceful transition back to democracy. The state was controlled by a secret police, totally dominated the media, and existing laws were usually suspended where they were deemed to be 'against the public interest'.

The economy was ruled through regulation but, despite several Fascist parties calling themselves National Socialists, there were few attempts at outright nationalisation. Instead every facet of the state was regulated through an inefficient bureaucracy, with restrictions on movement. There was regulation of labour and trade unions were made illegal. Probably because of this, democracies out-performed the managed economies during wartime.

Germany was most successful in attempting to make a 'new man' – the pitiless Aryan warrior bent on imposing a German culture and the blonde mother joyfully producing healthy young Teutons. Spain also tried to create a new hero in the image of the valiant El Cid. Perhaps the only thing democracies could learn from Fascism is from their programmes to improve the fitness and health of young people.

In every case the state was highly nationalistic and despised other races. Yet despite his brutal attack on Abyssinia, Mussolini greatly improved the infrastructure and public services of the North African colonies. However, states can be nationalistic but not Fascist. Britain and America became inward-looking, raised tariff barriers and obliged importing states to negotiate bilateral trading deals.

Germany and, possibly, Japan had more effective policies for reducing unemployment than the democracies during the early part of the 1930s depression. In both cases the methods would not have been accepted in a democracy and each was militaristic in nature but was accepted as an alternative to unemployment. As part of the programme all countries restricted migration, and Germany and France were actively anti-Semitic.

If there is to be a dictatorship it is probably better it be Fascist than Communist, for it is easier to revert back to democracy from the former. In Germany the reversion was helped by the break up of the large Nazi chemical, metallurgical and engineering cartels into new independent units and industrial unions. In Japan, MacArthur's control and reforms set the scene for the world's most dynamic economy from 1970 to 1990. A similar re-entry was impossible for Russia, where state control and attitudes were absolute.

Is Fascism still alive?

It is almost inconceivable that economic considerations could encourage a return of Fascism, but variations on the idea are not dead. The worst excesses of the 1930s will probably not be repeated but nationalism is certainly alive and would resurface if economies deteriorated. In the early years of the twenty-first century there are nationalist movements in Austria, Switzerland, Spain, Italy, France, Belgium, Holland, Denmark, Norway and Germany to restrict, or even repatriate, emigrants; in the first two countries, right-wing parties increased their support to 25% of the vote between 1994 and 1999.

Even in normally liberal Hamburg, the mayor points to a high proportion of migrants being drug dealers, murderers, criminals and welfare recipients. In France, Jean-Marie Le Pen was supported by 5 million voters – some 18% of the electorate at the last election. Hitler achieved 33% and that was in the depth of a depression. These movements will surely grow should uncertain climatic conditions assert themselves, and politicians of the centre are unable to meet the aspirations or assuage the fears of the people.

While the right is strong, ex-Communists are still powerful in East Germany: in two states the vote reached nearly 30% in recent elections, and both extremes gained votes from the centre parties.

The more extreme form of Islamic state was introduced in Iran by Ayatollah Khomeini in 1979 and the Taliban in Afghanistan; both were a form of Fascism that was every bit as intolerant as a 1930s dictator. As they try to create a model Koranic state, there is more concern about the length of beards and the cut of burkas than the economic well-being of the people. In addition there are two movements in the Central Asian Republics called the Islamic Movement of Uzbekistan (IMU) and the Hizb ut-Tahrir al-Islam (HT). Both are attracting young men (those under twenty-five comprise 60% of the 50 million inhabitants) to train for setting up a new Islamic state to include Xinjiang, currently part of China. They are likely to start as a guerrilla force that could become a powerful army. Their eventual aim, like Osama bin Laden's, is to unite all Muslim peoples in a world-wide jihad.

There would surely be moves towards economic nationalism should conditions similar to the 1930s return. In this case any political party offering a national programme of raising tariffs to protect domestic concerns would attract the long-term unemployed (including many of the middle classes). This could also attract any group accepting that the loss of some personal freedom was worth it for added security. As many of the nationalist movements are in the EU, moves to take power away from the unelected European Commission and return them to national governments could be very popular. This was shown dramatically in the French referendum for the European Constitution on May 29th 2005 and the Dutch a few days later.

The US has not been immune to directive tendencies. The economic regulations imposed by the National Industrial Recovery Act in 1933 became a happy hunting ground for monopolist industrialists, ambitious trade unionists, busy-body bureaucrats and well-meaning intellectuals. Later a similar group tried to implement President Johnson's 'Great Society', which aimed to end poverty by imposing increasing costs and bureaucratic regulations on taxpayers. By the turn of the century there was still poverty, and even more bureaucracy from programmes concerned with drugs, energy and the environment. None achieved their objective but freedoms have been diminished.

The US is not the only country being throttled by bureaucratic control. In the EU the French state spends around 53% of the country's GDP and extracts 24% of its taxes from business; Italy spends just under 50%. It is no accident that these two countries have the high rates of unemployment. When such a high proportion of the electorate are dependent upon state subsidies, these governments can become self-perpetuating. After all, how many individuals vote for policies that cut off their financial lifeline?

References

Beevor, A., *The Spanish Civil War* (Cassell, 1999).

Mack Smith, Denis, *Mussolini* (Weidenfeld & Nicolson, 1981).

Overy, R., *Why the Allies Won* (Random House, 1995).

Payne, S.C., *A Brief History of Fascism 1914-1945* (University of Wisconsin Press, 1995).

Shirer, W.L., *The Rise and Fall of the Third Reich* (Secker & Warburg, 1959).

Taylor, A.J.P., *British Prime Ministers and Other Essays* (Allen Lane, 1999).

Thomas, H., *The Spanish Civil War* (Eyre & Spottiswood, 1961).

Welch, Robert, 'Republics and Democracies', *The New American*, 1 February 1999.

Wheeler, Dr J., *None Dare Call it Fascism* (Council for National Policy, Montreal, 1997).

Dynamic Six

13

The Threat to Energy Supplies

Since the beginning of the twentieth century, the Western world had grown up with the anticipation that the supply of oil was limitless. To be sure there were oil shocks in 1973 and 1980, but these were regarded as being political and did not herald shortages.

In fact there were already straws in the wind from a report by a geologist called M King Hubbert* who stated that the US – and probably the world oil output – peaked around 1970 and would slowly decline. At the time, the global demand was 45 million barrels per day and the report was dismissed by the industry but it gradually became the accepted view that although Hubbard's timing might be out, for every ten barrels of oil consumed only four barrels were being discovered, such as the area around the Caspian Sea – see reading list.

By early in the twenty-first century the total world demand is 80 million barrels of oil a day with supplies from Saudi Arabia, still the largest producer, at 8.2 million barrels a day (mbd) followed by the USA with 6.8 mbd, Russia 6.7, Iran 3.5, China 2.9 and so on. Of these Iran, although not a major supplier to the West, is vulnerable to military strike action over its nuclear programme and Nigerian supplies could be at risk through insurgency.

The three largest Western oil companies and their outputs are Exxon/Mobil 4.2 mbd, BP/Amoco 3.6 and Royal Dutch Shell 3.9 but, compared to national oil companies their reserves are small. The chairman, and another senior executive, of Shell were obliged to resign after admitting his reserves were overstated and it is suspected that some oil producing countries are falsifying their potential capacity to enhance their borrowing power.

By the end of 2005 Saudi Arabia was also what is known as the 'swing supplier' – that is able to make up supply should there be additional demand or an interruption of supply. The problem is that the giant Saudi Ghawar oil field can only meet its quota by pumping in increasing quantities of water so that by late 2005 this was over 55% and increasing; it is reckoned when this reaches 75%, the limit will be approached. The difficulty is that the oil is embedded in porous rock and, when nearly pumped out, water instead of oil fills the interstitial spaces in a process called 'coning'. By the end of 2007 some estimates suggest that the Ghawar field output will fall to 7mbd.

This is called depletion dynamics. Saudi Arabia is not the only country to suffer loss of output. Suppliers such as Australia, Gabon, the UK, Indonesia, Venezuela and probably China are all showing signs of falling output and there is little indication that major discoveries are being made probably because only fourteen fields in the world deliver 20% of the total output. At the other end of the scale, over 4,000 fields generate 53% of the total.

In addition to present world demand there are estimates that increased off-take from China and India could push this figure up by two thirds – over 50 mbd by 2015. Of this some 60% will come from the transportation sector and nearly 30% from industry – that is before any other factors set out in this book are taken into account.

Where is this extra supply to come from? It is anticipated that the energy balance will be made up from liquefied natural gas (LNG), from tar sands, coal gasification and nuclear power; the contribution from wind farms and solar radiation – the latter making only a marginal contribution in temperate climates.

At over $40 a barrel, it makes economic sense to develop tar sand extraction found extensively in Canada and Alaska. The centre is Lake Athabasca where very extensive investments have been made to extract and refine the heavy shale oil from reserves that are estimated to last for decades, if not for a century. The oil is heavy and costs from $10 to $15 to refine and investors are looking for an output of between four and five million barrels a day within the second decade of this century.

There are abundant sources of coal in many countries but it has fallen out of favour for electricity generation due to its costly plant and its high emissions of sulphur dioxide and carbon dioxide. With impending oil shortages, its use is being reviewed including the capacity to produce oil from SASOL, a process developed in South Africa.

Conventional power stations pulverise coal before firing a boiler but in a gasification plant there are several purification processes. After pulverising the dense mixture is gasified with oxygen in the presence of water after which solids are removed and the gas is passed to the next phase where hydrogen is extracted (for possible use in fuel cells) and sulphur is washed out and can be sold. After preheating, the gas is passed to a gas turbine. Typically these plants almost eliminate the discharge of sulphur and reduce carbon emissions by 60%. Another other alternative is Liquefied Natural Gas (LNG).

With the US consuming around 20 mbd and importing 60% of its energy needs, it was one of the first countries to be interested in LNG. Unlike oil that can be pumped unmodified into tankers and out into refineries, LNG – normally a waste product – must be first liquefied before being loaded into specially constructed pressurised tankers; after shipment it is warmed back into a gas. However at an estimated expense of $100bn only the major oil companies, such as those listed earlier, could afford the investment likely to be made over 6-8 years. Although Russia has by far the largest reserves of LNG, sources such as Trinidad and Qatar will be the first to be developed to reduce political risks. As it is, guarding critical pipelines could be an added military load on the West.

The big one going forward for China and India that fills the gaps in requirements and does not put CO_2 into the atmosphere is nuclear fuel – as demonstrated by the unusually large order China has placed with Australia for uranium ore. The new Pebble Bed reactors are smaller and safer than old technology, are cheaper and faster to build and have a built in safety factor that shuts the reactor down about a temperature limit.

On the downside, the climatic problems described in chapter 7 could throw energy supply from the Arctic regions into jeopardy. As the Wermacht discovered in its invasion of Russia, it is very difficult to keep machinery running in conditions of extreme cold. Should major volcanic action occur in 2008, the extraction of tar sands and the Russian oil and gas fields could become too cold for operations.

It must be said that Hubbert's oil prognosis is not universally accepted. The prime reason for optimism is that discovery techniques are such that two thirds of all drillings are successful. Another is that technology enables successful wells to be dug in deep water such as the untapped fields in the Gulf of Mexico. Also there is great hope for tar sands that are economic with the price per barrel over $40.

For strategic reasons governments are likely to employ a multi source strategy for energy rather than relying on just one technology. At the margin, wind can probably give some of electric grid needs and is now cost competitive with other types of power. Also at the margin is an additive to gasoline called methanol made from corn or sugar that power flexi-fuel engines. The problem is they are in effect energy sinks because fuel has to be used for land clearance for ploughing, sowing, harvesting and processing. Also with the likely water shortages in many parts of the world, this may not be an attractive use of rainwater.

Much has been made of the potential for fuel cells that generate electricity directly form feeding oxygen and hydrogen to electrodes in a sort of reverse battery-like process. It is an attractive alternative with water as its only emissions, but its general use is unlikely in the near future. Possibly in the end the most attractive source of energy is likely to be cold fusion that harnesses the power of the fusion bomb in a controlled manner.

This chapter suggests that the world is not running out of ideas for keeping it moving and powered, but of the alternatives coal, tar sand oil, LNG and nuclear are likely to be the best alternatives. However the search to stay on oil is likely to generate as much controversy and conflict in the near term as water is in the longer term.

References

Leggett, Jeremy, *Half gone; Oil, Gas, Hot Air and the Global Energy Crisis* (Portobello Books, 2005)

Roberts, Paul, *The End of Oil, The Decline of the Petroleum Economy and the Rise of a New Energy Order* (Bloomsbury Books, 2005)

Kleveman, Lutz, *The New Great Game, Blood and Oil in Central Asia* (Atlantic Books, 2004)

Afterword

The dynamics unlocking the future

When the past no longer illuminates the future, the spirit walks in darkness

Alexis de Tocqueville, *Democracy in America.*

When reading through the material in this book we began to understand Winston Churchill's dictum that 'the further back you look, the further forward you can see'. What particularly arrested our attention was the unusual combination of forces that has not been present since around 1500.

Then Europe was frantic about the Ottoman Turks about to threaten Vienna and there had been a communication break-through with Gutenberg's printing press that made the Reformation possible. Technology was becoming available that made the Industrial Revolution inevitable and the climate was unusually cool causing famines in England in 1500-03, 1520-2, 1527-28, 1556 and 1586-8. Commodity prices rose throughout the century probably driven by the appalling weather helped by the release of Spanish gold onto the market and the population recovery from the Black Death.

Having read the previous chapters, does this sound familiar?

Five hundred years ago they reacted in various ways. With the invention of the magnetic compass and the astrolabe for finding latitude, Prince Henry the Navigator of Portugal and Ferdinand and Isabella in Spain initiated greatly extended voyages of discovery to the west and to the east. These opened new sea borne routes to by-pass the landward spice and pepper caravans now controlled by the Ottomans. In England, Henry VIII followed the lead of the Augustinian monk Martin Luther, to defy the most powerful human force on earth, the Roman Catholic Church. Militarily the heavy cannon had been designed for shipboard use enabling the piece to be loaded from inboard. In the latter stages of Elizabeth's England, the first ever Poor Law was passed to help those made destitute by famine.

In essence, although they could not have realised it at the time, they established the groundwork for the later Industrial Revolution. In England, in particular, the dumping of the rule from Rome cleared away many previously forbidden practices that freed up commerce and gave individuals greater liberty. For many, of course, life was still miserable but at least there was some relief from abject poverty. Although the Spanish and Portuguese were the first to make voyages of discovery, the two great seafaring nations of Holland and England, that had embraced the Reformation, created lasting colonies in North America and in the East.

The question we asked ourselves was how could and should the modern world respond to the present formidable dynamics to create another Elizabethan golden age? Although we have endeavoured to look ahead in some fashion in chapter 10 using cycles, no human has the foresight to envisage how everything will turn out but at least one can rate the dynamics and from these create different scenarios. For simplicity these are ranked on a scale of one to three – the least to the greatest.

The First Dynamic – the terrorist threat

The first chapter considered the history of Islam and how the word of the Prophet Mohammed – who died in 632 AD – changed the face of the then world twice, seven hundred years apart. The first Jihad had swept through North Africa and Spain to be stopped in 732 by Charles Martel at Tours, near Poitiers. In the east, they swallowed three of the five Christian Metropolitans at Alexandria, Jerusalem and Antioch and advanced into present-day Turkey, Iraq, Iran and into India. Their power was formidable.

On cue seven hundred years later, in the early part of the Fourteenth Century, Osman, the ruler of a small province in Anatolia, conquered the surrounding states and by 1354, his successors had invaded Gallipoli. After beating the Serbs at Kosovo in 1393, there was a hiatus while the Ottoman army was defeated by Tamerlane but the momentum was re-ignited shortly afterwards. Under Mehmed and his successors, the Ottomans occupied the Balkans including Greece, had captured Constantinople and circled the Black Sea. By 1529 they were at the gates of Vienna and it took over a hundred and fifty years to dislodge them.

Now after another seven hundred years the West is facing another Islamic militancy from countries like Iran that were independent before the First World War; followed by Saudi Arabia, Lebanon, Iraq and Syria, after that war ended. Many more were given their freedom after the Second World War including Pakistan, Malaysia and Indonesia. Since the fall of the Soviet Empire, countries in Central Asia have become independent. These are probably the most dangerous for both China and Russia because they share a border of thousands of miles and are driven in part by religious fanaticism that can only become more acute with the climatic changes described in chapter 7.

What next?

At best one can expect the occasional outrage such as car bombs outside embassies, trains and soft targets aimed at hurting civilian and political morale – not unlike the IRA campaign in Britain until the mid 1990s. The Madrid outrage succeeded in changing the government in Spain but most countries in the West have increased surveillance and intelligence operations. At this level terrorism in the West would be tolerable but, as suggested earlier, the main concern should be for Russia and China.

At level two, the attacks aim at conceding major advantages to Islam through damaging the West economically. The targets would be primarily installations such as power stations, disrupting communications and control networks though hacking, interrupting oil supplies and creating transportation chaos. This would demand the West increasing resources taken away from more profitable undertakings. 'Anonymous' in Imperial Hubris – see reading list – believes al-Qa'eda has studied the disruption in America caused by the Viet Nam War using relatively few financial resources. This would require a much higher level of vigilance needing voluntary organisations similar to the Air Raid Wardens or Home Guard of the Second World War in Britain.

The most dangerous level would be another armed holy war where terrorists tried to take over countries such as Saudi Arabia or Pakistan or make an all-out attack on Israel in the hopes this could ignite a global conflict. In all cases the West would be obliged to respond. For example, India – and the West – would find it extremely difficult to accept Pakistan's nuclear weapons and their means of delivery in the hands of bin Laden or Wahhabi clerics.

The Second Dynamic – the Information Age

As Abraham Darby's invention of the coke fired blast furnace in 1709 kick-started the Industrial Revolution, so Charles Babbage's mechanical computer followed in 1958 when Jack Kilby's integrated circuits designs made the Information Age inevitable. Then the industrial era concentrated physical, financial, professional and political muscle; now the Information Age has the capacity to create individual freedom not seen since the Reformation. The effect should be considered at three levels.

At the best, the transition would take place over two or more generations allowing time for the loss of repetitive and relatively unskilled jobs to areas of low cost such as India and China giving time for governments and other organisations to retrain managerial and other jobs, and for enterprise to generate higher added-value products and services.

At level two the transition would take place over a generation or less hitting nations like Germany with major manufacturing capacity. The present calls to reverse globalisation, a rise in protectionism and nationalism become stronger – such as France in mid-2005. This might be managed with mammoth government support but it may be no longer possible by politicians with overstretched budgets.

In the worst case, the transition takes place over only a few years to cause maximum political and social disruption.. Amidst rapidly rising unemployment there are acute pressures for protectionism and the break-up of trading and political unions such as the EU and NAFTA. Six millions unemployed pressured Germans to give Hitler's National Socialists the majority party and the chance to rule in January 1933.

The Third Dynamic – weather patterns

The combination of oscillations in the Atlantic and Pacific described in chapter 7 could create an unusual period of around twenty years. There will be some parts of the world, used to receiving adequate rain, which will receive much less than expected; others, usually dry, could expect flooding. The chapter also explained the likely crustal upset to be caused by the closest perigee for several hundred years of which the tsunami of December 26 2004 could be a harbinger.

At best there is tolerable rainfall in the main grain growing areas of critical regions such as the US, China and Korea, Central Asia and the Middle East although shortages will drive up the cost of grain worldwide. After a period of abundant rainfall, there will not be enough food in important poor areas that will cause some migration that can only be absorbed with difficulty because of the worldwide economic slowdown described later.

Should the oscillations impact as in the past, there could be drought in the sensitive grain-growing areas described earlier that are most likely to cause local conflicts and mass migration. Remember that the Korean War occurred during the previous combination of events. There is also a rising number of seismic events starting in 2005 and ending around 2015 from the tight perigee in 2008. These events trigger a rising number of terrified refugees that will absorb an increasing amount of effort and cost to the West.

In the worst case there are widespread famines as the effect of volcanic eruptions lowers the temperature several degrees in northern latitudes. The worst hit will be Russia, Canada, Northern China, Korea, Mongolia and so on to the extent that it will not be possible to live in some areas due to the cold. This will bring an avalanche of refugees with the likelihood of war and disease becoming widespread. A number of these areas are resource-rich that will propel the cost of commodities upwards.

The Fourth Dynamic – disease cycles

The most dangerous form of spreading diseases is for migrants or invaders to carry pathogens for which they are immune but their hosts are not. The record of the 'Conquistadores' and Mongols described in chapter 8 are ample testament. As migrations are often caused by climate shifts as described earlier, then these cycles will be very significant in the early years of the twenty-first century.

Again we can consider three levels; best, potential killers such as bird 'flu are containable and that terrorist attempts to spread viruses such as smallpox are anticipated and countered. At the next level there are outbreaks of epidemics such as the Great Plague of 1665 in England that require a major mobilisation of medical and security services.

The worst condition would be an outbreak of an epidemic such as ebola or a modern version of the 'Spanish 'flu' of 1918 where there is no known antidote. This leads to the death of millions and constitutes a national emergency requiring the equivalent of a war footing.

The Fifth Dynamic – bursting the credit bubble

By 2006 we are living in a most remarkable era when the most powerful nation on earth, the United States of America is also the largest debtor, carries the greatest budget deficit and has potentially one of the weakest currencies. With a consumer kept alive by borrowing on rising house prices, the major suppliers in Europe and the East have felt obliged to buy American securities and hold dollars to keep their own economies from falling into recession. How long can this state of affairs last and what will be the consequence should the bubble burst? This has been considered in chapter 9 but we must now consider the degrees of severity.

At the most optimistic level a state of equilibrium and stability is reached between the US and its major trading partners. Slowly the US manufacturing capacity is able to adjust to globalisation through employees being obliged to accept a lower standard of living in order to compete; this re-ignites investment in manufacturing and the acceptance spreads throughout the West. Gradually income flows within the US start to pay off debts that have been rising exponentially. As the US becomes more competitive internationally, the budget deficit reduces and debts start to be re-paid. The adjustment in global currencies balances out the deficits enabling the overhang of dollars and securities held overseas by central banks to be returned into circulation without causing a dollar collapse. In this scenario, the US does not lose dominance so quickly to the East.

At the next level, the measures to kick-start the US economy into a sustainable recovery fail despite increasingly large amounts of credit. The amount of additional debt to generate an additional dollar of GDP (over seven late in 2006), rises but then stalls and the economy starts sliding into recession. This is a condition that cannot be allowed due to the excessive levels of debt held by individuals in the mortgage and other credit markets – so even more money is pumped into circulation. Despite the Fed's best efforts, bank lending stalls and the external creditors, sensing hyperinflation, dump the dollar and a condition approaching the Great Inflation of the Weimar Republic prevails, although the economy fails to grow. This is known as stagflation and is described in chapter 9.

At the worst, the US sinks into a deep depression as the build-up of credit collapses. There is no longer an economic locomotive so the rest of the world sinks as well. This is a personal tragedy for millions of households, unemployment rises, and delinquencies soar – this will concentrate the minds of not just the US government but all countries affected. In 1933 the Roosevelt administration introduced the Home Owners Loan Corporation that underwrote existing mortgages at minimal interest rates; something similar will be needed now, but on a massive scale and not just to cover housing. As the West adjusts to a reduced standard of living and the value of tangible assets falls, there will be a collapse of the old order out of which a new beginning will emerge. Other nations with a bottom-up society will experience something similar. Some Continental European nations could flirt once again with fascism and the East would suffer major export problems.

The Sixth Dynamic – the threat to energy supplies

Since the beginning of the twentieth century, the Western world in particular has grown up with the anticipation that the supply of oil was limitless. There were oil shocks to be sure in 1973 and 1980 but these were regarded as being political and did not herald shortages.

In fact there were already straws in the wind from a report by a geologist called M King Hubbert (www.princeton.edu/hubbert/links.html) who stated that the world oil output peaked around 1970 and would slowly decline. The report was dismissed at the time by the industry but it gradually became the accepted view that for every ten barrels of oil consumed only four barrels were being discovered, such as the area around the Caspian Sea. The energy balance is made up from liquefied natural gas (LNG) and from tar sands requiring many thousands of tons of sand removed to extract a mixture of oil and water.

By early in the twenty-first century Saudi Arabia is still the largest producer at 8.2 million barrels a day (mbd) followed by the USA with 6.8 mbd, Russia 6.7, Iran 3.5, China 2.9 and so on. Although not a supplier to the West, Iran and China have invested heavily in an oil pipeline to the Pakistan port of Gwadar that would also supply India and Myamar.

The three largest Western oil companies with their daily outputs are Exxon/Mobil 4.2, BP/Amoco 3.6 and Royal Dutch Shell 3.9 but the problems are the reserves. The chairman of Shell was obliged to resign after admitting his reserves were overstated and it is suspected that some oil producing countries are falsifying their potential capacity to enhance their borrowing power.

By 2005, the global demand was around 80 bpd of which Saudi Arabia supplied a tenth; Saudi was also what is known as the 'swing supplier' – that is able to make up supply should there be additional demand or an interruption of supply. The problem is that the giant Saudi Ghawar oil field can only meet its quota by pumping in increasing quantities of water so that by late 2005 this was at 55% and increasing; it is reckoned when this reaches 75%, the limit will be approached. The problem is that the oil is embedded in porous rock and when nearly pumped out, water instead of oil fills the interstitial spaces in a process called 'coning'. By the end of 2007 some estimates suggest that the Ghawar field output will fall to 7mbd – or by over a quarter.

This is called depletion dynamics. Saudi Arabia is not the only country to suffer loss of output. Suppliers such as Australia, Gabon, the UK, Indonesia, Venezuela and probably China are all showing signs of falling output and there is little indication that major discoveries are being made probably because only fourteen fields in the world deliver 20% of the total output. At the other end of the scale, over 4,000 fields generate 53% of the total.

In addition to present world demand there are estimates that increased offtake from China and India could push this figure up by two thirds – over 50 mbd by 2015. Where is this extra supply to come from? At over $40 a barrel, it makes economic sense to develop tar sand extraction, mentioned earlier, found extensively in Canada and Alaska. The other alternative is Liquefied Natural Gas (LNG).

With the US consuming around 20 mbd and importing 60% of its energy needs, it was one of the first countries to be interested in LNG. Unlike oil that can be pumped unmodified into tankers and out into refineries, LNG – normally a waste product – must be first liquefied before being loaded into specially constructed tankers. It must be warmed back into a gas after delivery. However at an estimated expense of $100bn only the major oil companies, such as those listed earlier, could afford the investment likely to be made over 6-8 years. Although Russia has by far the largest reserves of LNG, sources such as Trinidad and Qatar will be the first to be developed to reduce political risks. As it is, guarding critical pipelines will be an added military load on the West.

It must be said that Hubbert's prognosis is not universally accepted. The prime reason for optimism is that discovery techniques are such that two thirds of all drillings are successful. Another is that technology enables successful wells to be dug in deep water such as the untapped fields in the Gulf of Mexico. Also tar sands can be economic with the price per barrel over $40.

The Sixth Dynamic – dwindling sources of conventional energy

Just when the world needs a reliable source of energy to cover the other uncertainties, we are faced by growing problems as described in Chapter 13. We are also faced with a form of state terrorism when a country such as Russia cuts off supplies for political reasons to the Ukraine and shows the potential for curtailing supplies to Continental Europe. There could be additional difficulties should supplies of gas in northern latitudes be unable to pump due to extreme cold.

As with the other dynamics we could conceive of three levels of severity.

At the minimum, the price of a barrel of oil remains in the $40-$50 range within the next ten years due to varying degrees of depletion. There is little threat to supplies either from terrorist action or climatic difficulties that remain at their lowest level.

At some point there is either terrorist action or a rapid increase in demand due to conflicts either over water or indeed oil. This is equivalent to putting out of action the Ras Tannurah oil terminal, a major refinery or a sustained attack on tankers passing through the straits of Hormuz that takes nearly 15% of global output, and would push the price of a barrel of oil up into the $70-$100 range. This will demand a sustained military effort by the West to safeguard oil supplies from the Caspian pipelines, the Persian Gulf and from Venezuela. These measures will have a stimulatory impact on military effort while taking away government support from the deflationary impact mentioned earlier. A rising oil price would have serious downward pressure on prices in major importers such as the US, Japan, China, India or continental Europe.

At its worst, a major war successfully closes the Persian Gulf, major refineries in the West are subject to attack or extreme weather conditions in Russia disrupt oil and gas supplies, particularly to continental Europe. All vulnerable countries will have to introduce rationing when the price per barrel exceeds $100. On top of the severity of the condition described under the Fourth Dynamic, a price rise of this nature would plunge the West into a deep depression. Bin Laden's efforts will have borne fruit.

Checkables

This, we understand, is the name given by the intelligence community to classify information based on its reliability and accuracy. If the Dynamics set out earlier represent the major forces in the early years of the twenty-first century, then these can be put into two categories: those that are an immediate threat and those, though equally important, are more secular in nature.

Of a threat within two to five years

From the earlier analysis we would argue that the bursting of the credit bubble and the threat to oil supplies represent the most immediate checkable threat.

The bursting of every bubble is preceded by an exponential rise in price. This was true of the South Sea Bubble, the Mississippi land scandal, the Tulip Bubble, the Dow Jones in 1929, the gold price in 1980, the dot-com bubble in 2000 and so on.

Now in the US and Britain, house prices have risen exponentially and will surely collapse sometime despite every effort to keep them afloat. House construction represents over 10% of a modern economy and by early 2005 mortgage debt was £850bn in the UK and $7.5 trillion in the US representing nearly 70% of GDP for each country. A collapse in house prices of perhaps 40% would wipe out debt equivalent of around £350bn in the UK and $3 trillion in the US – not far off the total government expenditure in both countries.

It is inconceivable that any democracy could allow a high proportion of its adult population to be made insolvent, quite apart from the lenders that include all the major banks. In 1933 house repossessions were taking place at the rate of 1,000 a day. Worried about rising distress when unemployment peaked, Roosevelt introduced the Home Owners Loan Corporation (HOLC) that refinanced mortgages for distressed borrowers at low rates of interest.

Something similar today would require huge resources to underwrite perhaps 20 million homes in the US and around 3 milion in the UK needing massive borrowings and switching government expenditure away from the welfare state – an action that would accelerate the advent of the Second Dynamic. Any such act would lead to a collapse of already vulnerable paper currencies and require a much-reduced standard of living.

Quite apart from depletion, a major threat to oil supplies is from terrorist action for al-Qa'eda must be aware of the economics of energy as anyone else. A concerted move against refineries and terminals could force the price of a barrel of oil to over $80. Any such move would apply a downward thrust to the West that would push most countries into recession.

How each country would react might be judged by its history. Both the US and Britain adjusted to a considerable reduction in standards of living during the nineteen-thirties and still remained democracies; they also have many public charities such as the Salvation Army to help take the strain away from the state. They could probably do so again although, after fifty years of relative peace, the adjustment would be traumatic for most people and lead to some calls for a centrally directed state. For the more top-down countries, such as many on the continent of Europe, they are likely to seek solutions to prevent the collapse of state institutions – or various forms of fascism – and alliances with like-minded countries.

– and over five years

Although historically climatic changes have been highly significant, the uncertainty of their impact, their extent and duration would put them into a second category of 'checkables'. While oil availability is the most immediate concern, water could become a more important commodity than oil by the end of the decade. The advent of the Information Age, though certain, could take place over several years although the events described earlier would advance the timing.

Scenarios arising from the Primary Checkables

There are clearly a number of alternative outcomes of the dynamics described earlier.

At best al-Qa'eda remains contained, oil remains below $60 a barrel and the credit bubble slowly subsides as debt is gradually paid off – particularly in the US – and a new equilibrium is formed at lower levels of consumer spending. This causes a lower standard of living for many manufacturing jobs, although new higher added-value work is created. The recession in North America is contained and any decline in the housing market is arrested through extensive re-financing of mortgages.

This causes considerable overcapacity for the exporting countries. In Continental Europe the euro, already under pressure from the virtual disintegration of the Stability and Growth Pact and constitutional rejection, is strained as each nation attempts to adjust to lower demand. Where unemployment rises, there will be attempts at protection. In the Far East the creditor nations such as Japan and China form their own relief organisation in place of the IMF while a new balance is achieved. This too causes a recession and a gradual re-adjustment until the embers of growth are re-kindled.

There are a number of different scenarios relating to the severity of each Dynamic until the worst case that could arise from a collapse of the dollar and the US housing market. Both would have a number of serious consequences. Of these:

The US would be obliged to save foreign exchange by pulling back troops from Germany, the Far East and elsewhere although safeguarding oil supplies would still be a strategic imperative. Otherwise the peace in vital areas of interest would mainly have to be kept by the US Navy and allies taking over the role of the Royal Navy in the nineteenth century. Military alliances such as NATO would be put under massive strain and would probably fail.

Areas previously under US control could be plunged into chaos as all but the troops needed to protect oil supplies are brought home in the absence of alternative peacekeepers. The disturbance is likely to spread to Saudi Arabia where, perhaps, as an alternative to al-Qa'eda, the country would come under the control of the Wahhabi extreme Sunnis. There would be calls for united action against Israel.

The dollar would lose its status of the reserve currency needing most commodities to be priced in national currencies including a newly liberated mark, yen, yuan or even a gold-backed currency. This would apply more downward pressure on the US economy.

Nations relying on the US for exports would have no alternative locomotive; unemployment would rise and each country would seek to devalue. This reversion to nationalism would seriously strain trading and political unions and tariff protection would be introduced to safeguard jobs.

At the beginning of the chapter we suggested that we were inflicted with similar pressures to those around the year 1500 and explored some of the consequences. One result of the Turks controlling the trade routes was to launch the voyages of discovery. One implication was to temporarily release the warring countries of Europe from looking inwards to peering over the horizon to new worlds. It changed much of the power structure. Could something similar be about to happen five hundred years later?

International consequences

One of the most helpful suggestions has been provided by international consultant Michael White who argues that a multi-polar division of the world will emerge – not unlike the rivalry between Portugal and Spain centuries ago.

France and Germany could ally themselves closely with Russia. In exchange for cheap energy, they would keep their economies and their social systems intact and in return rebuild Russian industry. Other countries such as Belgium and Spain might join them. This would end the EU, the inclusive euro and NATO.

Diagram 8
Based on the Drought Clock by Dr Raymond Wheeler
(for exact timings see text)

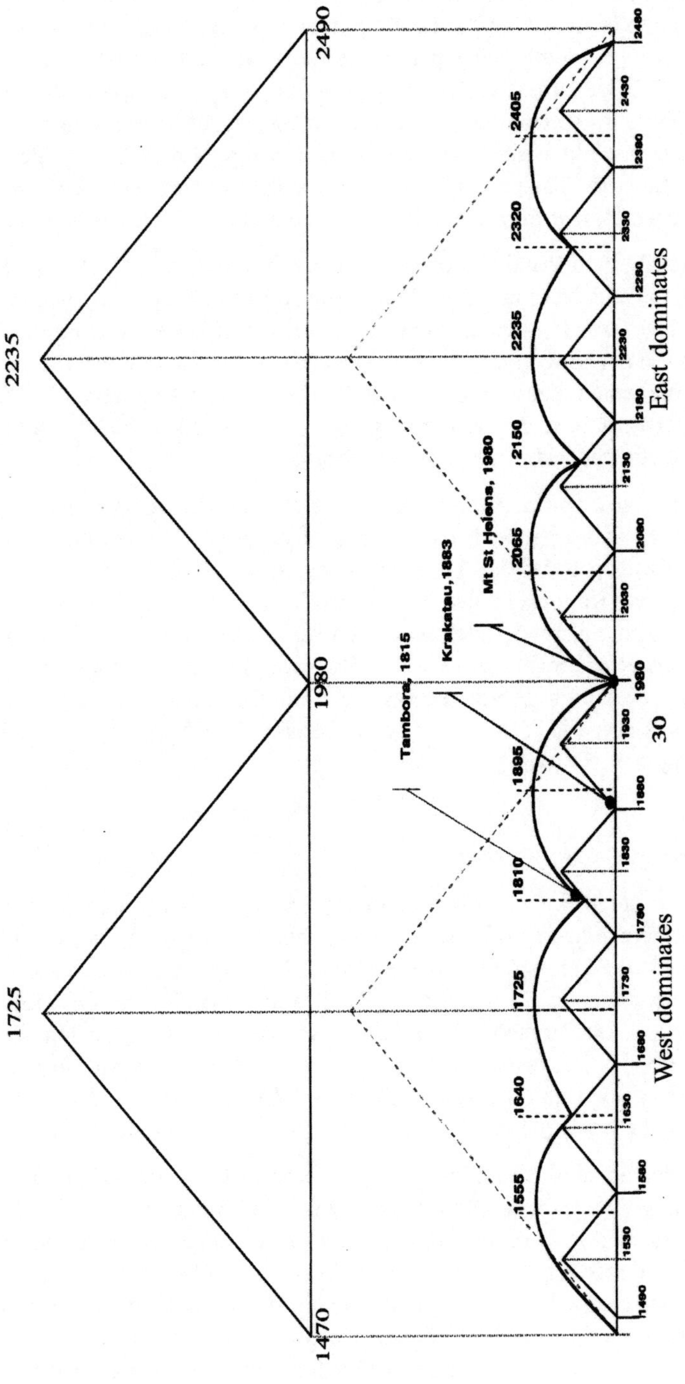

191

China has already sought a close arrangement with Iran that could also include North Korea. The Chinese leaders are brought up to believe in a Chinese Empire before the Opium Wars in the early 1840s that stretched deep into Central Asia and south to Burma. This would bring them into direct conflict with Russia in the west, India in the south and Japan in the East. They are already building a formidable navy. Should the freedom movement in Tyrgyzstan spread to the neighbouring Uighurs in the Chinese province of Xinkiang, repressive action could inflame the Muslim world against their huge eastern neighbour, China replacing Muslim anger for America. This may not be China's only problem because there could be rising internal dissent from the millions of young men who fail to find a bride.

The US, with Britain in the west and Japan in the East, would ally themselves with Turkey and Israel in the Mediterranean. White believes that resource-rich countries such as Canada, Australia and South Africa would keep themselves apart to benefit from competing demands of the new blocs. However concerns about a resurgent China would place themselves in the US camp protected by a US Navy lead force – partly funded by the outlying nations. This would be the pattern foreseen by Robert Conquest in *The Ravaged Century*.

The Islamic world. Although not mentioned by Michael White, this would leave the Islamic countries, with the probable exception of Iran, without any mentors but sitting upon a valuable, but diminishing asset, and a lot of sand. The Wahhabis have long yearned for a unified Muslim world with the Caliph as the combined spiritual and temporal ruler. They would probably also control Pakistan with its nuclear weapons and means of delivery. This would place the other rising superpower of India even more solidly into the US orbit and make a war with Israel more likely. In this scenario it is hard to see a role for the UN that would go the way of the League of Nations.

National consequences

The other major consequence of the 1500s was the break for many counties in Northern Europe with the Roman Catholic Church that led to a breakdown of a powerful administrative superstructure. For America, Britain and other countries, this could entail a forcible entry into what Alvin Toffler describes as The Third Wave, a condition post the Industrial Revolution. With considerable insight Toffler foresaw a time when the decentralisation of much of industry would lead to a diminishing role for centrally controlled finance, government and the like. Not far from the consequential collapse of the housing bubble described earlier.

Earlier in this book, chapter 5 considered alternative models for counties undergoing radical change and suggested that the Swiss Cantonal system represented a working and cheaper form of devolved government with a much reduced role for the centre. It could also form a basis for a citizens' army and its civilian equivalent – both these would be needed both to guard against terrorist attacks and to provide a constructive alternative to unemployment. Like the many Protestant experiments, many different alternative communities could be tried and those that failed discarded. Who would be the greatest innovators? It is likely that the English speaking peoples, who were the clear winners from the events following the sixteenth century, would perform a similar role in the West – to be consolidated later by more centrally organised counties.

Scenarios arising from the secondary 'checkables'

Although secondary in terms of timing, the climatic and disease rhythms are every bit as formidable in their impact as any other Dynamic. As we saw in chapter 7 and above, the end of this decade could provide very serious shocks that could hit economically, socially, militarily and politically.

International consequences

At the best, the onset of the worst combination of the Atlantic and Pacific oscillations, coupled with a likely rise in seismic activity, has only a marginal impact on grain yields. This only somewhat delays the economic recovery. At worst the disruption caused by rapidly rising commodity prices would mean a higher proportion of income devoted to foodstuffs that would delay recovery from the recession described earlier. The help that governments would be able to give at home would be reduced by aid needed for refugees.

Should the impact occur on the new international groupings, this would only increase the risk of conflict over water. In the Far East a drought in Northern China and the Korean Peninsula could put Japan at risk, America's main ally in the area. Another added point of conflict would be between Central Asia, China and Russia; a drought in Afghanistan and Pakistan would add to the existing friction between the latter and India. In the Middle East anxiety caused by a drought on top of an inflammatory political and religious situation could cause extreme tension between the Arab countries, Israel and her ally Turkey.

A shortage of grain would force up the cost of living in the West so adding to the existing deflationary pressure. Could a climatic shift alter the new political groupings? The main problems will be what to do about the millions of refugees and an extreme cold in Russia disrupting the supplies of energy to her new allies: France and Germany.

National considerations

The deflationary pressures felt by the US and her allies to restructure would be helped by being obliged to re-arm to support Japan, Israel and India involved in water wars and also to cope with a flood of refugees – and probably also epidemics. This could stimulate flat economies – as did World War Two.

A reading of history inclines us towards the more radical outcome.

How, then, can business adapt to the new age

It follows from the earlier scenarios, that as governments will be unable to fulfil dreams of a benevolent state so individuals and enterprise will be obliged to take a more leading role within the community, as did the medieval guilds. Although some cities like London and New York, with powerful academic and business cultures, will remain centres of excellence others, which have lost their role as an industrial era power base, will probably fade to become more like Manila or Detroit.

As power dissipates away from the bureaucrats towards the suburbs and country many more local centres will be formed perhaps specialising in a technology or in the quality and skills of the people. It is likely that any bursting of the credit bubble would seriously disrupt centralised banking and give way to a much more dispersed system as found in the United States. The new money centres could form a wider role than at present working with professions such as law, surveying and accounting to offer a specialised and diverse service tailored to local needs. How rapidly this will change the role of enterprise will depend on world events. Again we can consider three levels of severity.

At the most benign level the changes take place over decades to permit a slow and orderly transfer from the large corporation to the more compact enterprise. Jobs will certainly be lost or made redundant but fresh skills will be taught and more work created. The gradual nature of change does not effect globalisation where work will continue to be moved to the cheapest location, leaving the West to concentrate on the higher added-value products and services. In this case banking, foreign exchange, investment, insurance and other financial services remain centralised.

Should the bursting credit bubble bringing with it stagflation then business will be faced with much more serious management and customer problems. In this scenario many manufacturing firms will suffer a squeeze on prices while, at the same time, the value of food and other commodities will rise rapidly. In any case there will be increasing demands from national security.

At its worst case, stagflation turns into outright deflation where personal spending is much curtailed and business will have to adapt to a much lower volume. From 1929 to 1933 the US GDP declined by some 30% followed by a collapse of credit lasting until 1950 that was equal to the GDP in 1929. Something similar would accelerate the break-up and dispersal of many companies and accelerate the development of new industries and technologies – that also occurred in the 1930s.

Life on earth is a continuum

In Chapter 10 we have concentrated on the early decades of the twenty-first century with some incursion into the next centuries – but these should be considered as part of a continuum that goes back to at least to 1500 but in reality centuries in the past. In our view the year fifteen hundred is critical to an understanding of the present and what might lie ahead. The next chart, Diagram 8 extended from the work of

Raymond Wheeler, shows the climatic history from that date with various cycles superimposed.

For the purposes of clarity we have shown the cycles as V shaped moves, but in practice they are more U shaped. Also the cycles did not all start up in 1470. There was a bottoming period between 1470 to 1490. By about 1500 it was clear that a low was in place.

At first sight the timing for the bottom established by Raymond Wheeler in 1980 appears to be nonsense because clearly the cold period did not take place then but, as Iben Browning showed in *Nature* magazine of September 12 1975, there is often hysteresis between the initiating tidal force and it cooling effect thirty years later – as there was during the Sporer and Maunder minimums. At a more practical level, the stock market did not peak until 2000 and the maximum cooling effect is not expected until 2008 – see chapter 7. Within the overall envelope, the cycles are:

Wheeler's 100-year cycle of climate change with variants on cold and warm, wet and dry.

The Sun Retrograde cycle of 178.8 years described in chapter 7 starting from the Sporer Minimum in 1500 through the Maunder Minimum – or Little Ice Age – in the latter part of the seventeenth century and the Sabine Minimum early in the nineteenth century. Records show that Tambora occurred in the Sabine and considerable volcanic action is anticipated towards the end of this decade. In Wheeler's low points, Krakatoa went off in 1883 and Mount St Helen's in 1980.

The Five Hundred Year Cycle suggested by Wheeler and confirmed by others, including William Jevons, shows the shifts from East to West and back again every half millennium – see chapter 10.

We have described some of the events unlocked by the Dynamics but the chart puts these firmly in the context of history and what might lie ahead for our successors. But do we actually care what happens over the next five hundred years? We believe we should because we live in a dynamic world and seeing the trends around us today better helps us to understand a world that is not driven by us but by the forces within the solar system over which we have no control. Let us examine the chart more closely.

Wheeler's hundred year weather rhythm underlies a pattern confirmed by George Modelski, Professor of Political Science at the University of Washington. Within the framework of Western dominance there has been a progression of individual nations. Starting from the left triangle, Modelski argues this was the age when Portugal pioneered ocean exploration until the late fifteen hundreds when the Dutch became dominant and took over many trading posts. After the Dutch Wars in the 1640s, Britain became dominant for at least two centuries until the early nineteen hundreds when the United States started to become the most powerful nation on earth. It is essential to realise that each country became dominant through control of the seas and this will undoubtedly continue into the future.

Finally there is the dominant half millennium that peaked in the middle of the Eighteenth Century with the Enlightenment when reason replaced dogma and the West dominated. It ends with the majority of institutions, and indeed national sovereignty, becoming under threat in the period we are now in.

And the next five hundred years?

As all the evidence suggests the low point will be from around 2010 to 2020, but the switch from west to east may not occur until the weather is more favourable to China, India or indeed Japan while the water shortages described in chapter 7 prevail. These may be mitigated in the future as cheaper forms of energy become available and de-salination could become economical. Also if the present growth in volcanic activity is to continue then eastern Russia is unlikely to be viable because of extreme cold. Together, with a squeeze on oil, this area will be a source of conflict.

But as water and energy shortages pass later this century, the dominant nation will be that in control of the sea. With the exception of Japan, neither India or China has been really comfortable as an ocean power – in the last five hundred years – but we may be sure that one nation will be in the future. If history is to be a guide this will change over time and perhaps one will be the next empire builder. Can we also learn the characteristics of the next superpower?

If the history of the West is to be a guide then the next top nation will have some form of democracy where power genuinely stems from the people. Without it nations cannot easily adapt and change because politicians, almost by definition, look backwards. This has probably led the success of the English-Speaking Peoples that have adapted gradually over time.

Another is the capacity to experiment and innovate perhaps to help fellow human beings, but more likely to follow the profit motive – the drive for much of Anglo-Saxon history. An important factor also must be a stable and thriving home economy with a sound currency without which the brightest citizens will move elsewhere and there will be little spare to invest overseas. The analysis of national characteristics in chapter 6 suggests Japan may emerge as the leader. It has a well-educated people, a climate sufficiently far north to have vigorous winters but an unenviable colonial record. Wheeler believed the next winner would be India.

Does this mean the Dynamics will not apply in the future? Probably religious terrorism will reach a peak then slowly decline in the next few hundred years as the capacity in the rest of the world adapts and counters the threat. However the Information Age will grow and change – like the Industrial Revolution – as the micro-chip does much of the work previously done by humans.

The dominant cycle in the future of course will be climatic with a benevolent period late in the twenty-first century, another low in the mid-twenty-second century and so on. Wheeler believed that warm benign weather weather induced wars of aggression while the dips in the major cycles such as 2250 would trigger rebellions and civil wars. Those living then can expect to have a similar impact on their affairs as in the past. Unfortunately humans seldom learn from history so that our successors will be condemned to relearn the economic and human lessons of Leviticus Chapter 25.

Whatever happens we must hope that the human spirit, that was first set free two thousand years ago then latterly by the Renaissance, Luther, the Enlightenment and even later by men like Oakeshott, will continue to drive the greatest success story of all time – liberty.

Individual liberty and the state

For the last seventy or so years most Westerners have grown up with the knowledge of a powerful central state that was the legacy of a war but was never dismantled. Instead it became an instrument designed by well-meaning politicians, who had little grasp of history but a strong sense of power and a worthy desire to prevent the poorest in society from tasting poverty. However they ended with providing the majority with services they could perfectly well organise much more cheaply and efficiently for themselves. In the process taxes have risen to feed a growing bureaucracy that would be largely irrelevant should the scenarios described earlier come about.

The idea of a centralised state is not new. In China, the Ch'in (221-206BC) emperor introduced a centralised civil service with entry based on recommendations by local officials. Later the entry was decided by a competitive examination based on Confucian ethics and special schools were set up to train would-be mandarins. The system failed to deal with the changes demanded by Europeans and Americans after the Opium Wars of the 1840s and finally collapsed shortly before the Revolution by Sun Yat Sen in 1911. Europe also had collectivist ideas.

Late in France's Ancien Regime, Jean-Jacques Rousseau, concerned about the inequalities in society, introduced the idea of a Social Contract where individuals gave up natural rights in return for civil rights 'forcing a man to be free' within a self-imposed law. He went on to suggest that, as the majority of people do not necessarily represent the most intelligent citizens, it is better to impose the 'general will' of a lawgiver. Napoleon and later Lenin used the concept to legitimise their dictatorships.

In Germany Immanuel Kant followed a similar line of reasoning to Rousseau believing that freedom can only be found in rational action. As this cannot be found in a single individual, it can only be found in a universal law and general will. These thoughts were uppermost in many German minds after the defeat of Prussia by Napoleon at Jena in 1806 and created a yearning to recreate the rule of Frederick the Great.

The idea was taken up Georg Hegel who suggested that the modern state is based on rationally selected principles that would shape the individual who would not consider their own interests unless these were part of a community. Later in the nineteenth century Friedrich Nietzsche suggested that the nation-state ideally was invested with transcendent value of purpose with the ultimate value of brotherhood, democracy and socialism. Nietzsche gave superhuman qualities to the 'will to power', the superman.

These ideas might possibly be acceptable for some peoples used to the idea of centralisation. Initially a benevolent Messiah who reduces unemployment, protects the currency and revives the national morale might be a welcome distraction from self-seeking politicians. Unfortunately, whatever the original intention of a dictator, there always emerges some forms of despotism with its own secret police, control of borders and state media. What then for the rest of us? How are we to think about what sort of society would we wish for ourselves?

In the eighteenth century Adam Smith argued famously for the individual as did Michael Oakeshott, once the Professor of Politics at the London School of Economics, and one of the most profound thinkers of the twentieth century. Unlike many social engineers, Oakeshott cut through all theories of class by arguing that a person's (he called them agents, describing men and women) starting point was an understanding of his own situation and what it meant to him; decisions were made, not as part of a class but were the result of life experiences. In this way individuals cherish the idea of diversity, originality and spontaneity through their own intrinsic freedom and the ideal of human self-development being achieved through a free and harmonious exercise of individual capacities. The outcome was someone who was largely independent of class or creed.

Within this framework people are regarded as adults who can make their own choices in their pursuit of happiness and are under no obligation to justify their preference in making their decisions. In Britain and America this was supposed to find expression either in parliament or in the three elements of the American Constitution through the rule of law without an overwhelming concentration of power.

Clearly, it is very difficult for agents to achieve their aims on their own which Oakeshott describes as intelligent agents seeking the satisfaction of their individual wants. As most needs cannot be satisfied on their own, it follows that there is a requirement for an agreed framework of law within which these can take place.

Oakeshott divided his societies into two main categories: societas and universitas. The societas is a system of laws to be overseen and kept by judicial office-holders who declare the meaning of these rules and are there to settle any disputes. A societas leader is the custodian of the loyalties of the group and is not in any way the director of an enterprise. These were probably the New England societies Alexis de Tocqueville found on his visit to the United States in the early 1800s (chapter 5) and could also be applied to the original 'hundreds' grouping in England.

The state is a societas – what Oakeshott describes as an identifiable collection of overlapping persons, families, groups, corporate associations and so on. These pursue their own distinct and different purposes severally and jointly with complete freedom – to be enjoyed at almost any cost. They are all related to one another in the recognition of a sovereign authority and a system of laws that constitute a civil order. Unless there is a war, the state does not have a unified purpose when it could be described as a universitas.

Politics then becomes how to understand and guard a process of historical beliefs without attempting to impose a moral or directive system such as those following the French and Russian Revolutions that changed entire societies. The laws should be sparingly exercised. This obliges governments to preserve, be the custodian and apply general rules of conduct enabling people to pursue activities of their own choice with the minimum frustration or regulation.

The second grouping is a universitas formed to act for a specific purpose or enterprise and, as a company, acts as a single legal entity. Like a corporation it would be bound by its own set of rules and will have its own seal and identifier such as a logo. New members can be admitted as associates and there is an administrative manager or a director that manages its affairs with the owners taking decisions by a majority that binds the others. The Medieval guild was clearly a universitas, as is any commercial enterprise, a co-operative such an Israeli Kibbutz and probably most religious orders. Like any other group they are responsible to the laws of the country in which they operate.

How then might we judge the best system for dealing with the Dynamics described earlier? Is it the centrally directed state so essential for fighting wars or the bottom-up societies found in Anglo-Saxon countries? History shows that politicians, used to solving yesterday's problem, are not the best engines of recovery but individuals working separately or in groups pursuing their own initiatives with the minimum of interference or regulation. In the adversity of the 'thirties' it was the English speaking countries that created the innovations so essential for the later recovery and it is likely to be the same in the future.

But history suggests that this will be no ordinary liberty because some discontinuity has accompanied the end of a five hundred year period, at least from around 500 BC when the Buddha and Confucius were born. Next there was the birth of the Christian saviour whose life and works have driven those striving for liberty throughout the centuries.

The fall of the Roman Empire in the Fifth Century by Attila was not the greatest act of liberty; it heralded the dark ages but there were signs of enlightenment in Europe. Following the Augustinian tradition, this was the age of Saint Patrick, David and Benedict, among others, who started the monastic tradition. Five hundred years later, when settled national characteristics started to emerge, Cluny Abbey produced one of the great reforming popes, Gregory VII, who encouraged the growth of monasteries and learning. In 1053 the Catholic and Orthodox churches split, with the fault line creating divisions in the Balkans today.

Carrying on the tradition of liberty, five hundred years later Martin Luther successfully challenged the Roman Catholic Church that, by then, had become indolent and venal. He created a new sense of freedom where the individual no longer needed the church to provide absolution.

The five hundred years cycle is not the only one falling due for Platonic scholars point out that there is a cycle of around six hundred and fifty years that creates moves towards fundamental principles. Plato wrote the *Republic* in the Fourth Century BC when he established the principle of universal ideas – concepts followed by other Greek philosophers.

Then around the middle of the third century AD Saint Augustine of Hippo revived Platonic ideas in his great work the City of God. The next Platonic revival was by Alfarabi, a Koranic scholar before 800. Probably the greatest revival of Platonic ideas was during the Renaissance when Cosimo Medici set up the Florentine Academy with Nicholas of Cusa. The work continued with Marsilio Ficino, one of the scholars working with Lorenzo Medici to promote and encourage the work of Plato.

And now at the birth of a new millennium these two cycles coincide to provide a heady break from the past combining a drive towards fundamental thinking with a new found sense of liberty. It is quite possible that the new saviour is already born and we may only discover the message when he or she opens their web site that, in the tradition of Google and e-bay, will sweep the world.

How this person will change our perception of ethics, morals and behaviour we will have to discover. What is not in doubt is that human resilience, ingenuity and sheer grit will see the world through to the next golden age – as did our forefathers five hundred years ago. When Mary Tudor reigned many must have thought England would lose her identity to Spain but then Elizabeth steered the nation through to an age shaped in her image. We must hope our new saviour will sweep away the trivia that so obsesses our media and politicians on our behalf and make us more thoughtful, genuine – even more spiritual – people, liberating the spirit of the individual in the great tradition of this cycle in history.

References

Conquest, Robert, *The Ravaged Century* (WW Norton, 1999)

Houston, William, *Riding the Business Cycle* (Little Brown, 1995)

Oakeshott, Michael, *On Human Conduct* (Clarendon Press, Oxford, 1975)

Index

Fuhrer *see* Hitler
fundamentals
    return to 59–61
    S-curve theory 30
future scenarios 181–200
    climate change effects 96–7
    next 500 years 196–7
    US credit bubble 126–8

G

GAP *see* South-east Anatolia Project
gas depletion 34
Geneva (John Calvin's) 48
Genghis Khan 101
German Workers' Party 164–5
German-speaking Peoples (GSPs) 76
Germany
    1920s 139–45
    Communism 165–6
    fascism 172
    First World War 164
    Great Depression 165–6
    national socialism 163–8
    rearmament 148
    unemployment 147–8, 172
    see also Hitler
germs *see* bacteria; disease; viruses
global warming 83–4
God 9
Goebbels, Josef 167
gold 121, 122, 125
Great Depression 36, 37, 54, 77,
154–5
    Germany 165–6
    USA 146, 149
    world effect 123
Great Dying *see* Black Death
Great Plague 106
Great Society 174
Great War *see* First World War
Greenhouse Effect 83
GSPs *see* German-speaking Peoples
Gutenberg, Johannes 35

H

Harrington, Dr Robert 84
health service 27
Hegel, Georg 158, 197
Henley Centre for Forecasting 47
Henry VIII Act of Supremacy 50–1
hierarchy of needs 71
Himmler, Heinrich 167
history
    discontinuities 75–6
    education 62
    technology 31
Hitler, Adolf 43, 145, 147–8, 150
    fascism 162–5, 167, 168
    see also Germany
Hitler Youth 165
HIV 91
HOLC *see* Home Owners Loan
Corporation
holy war *see* jihad
Home Owners Loan Corporation
(HOLC) 124, 152, 185, 188
Hoover, Herbert 55–6, 149
hospitals 115
house prices 124, 188
Hubbert, M. King 177, 186, 187
human breath aerosols 104–5
human spirit 3
Humboldt, Friedrich von 60
hyper-inflation 128, 142, 143, 144

I

Ikki (Ikka), Kita 170
Il Duce *see* Mussolini
immune systems 102–4
impact of information age 27
IMU *see* Islamic Movement of
Uzbekistan
India 45, 136, 137
individuals
    future 79
    liberty 197–200
    responsibility 67

Toffler, Alvin 41–4, 47, 62, 192
training 77
transport 33
travel effects 104–5
tuberculosis 114–15
twin towers disaster *see* September 11th (2001)
typhus 106

U

unconnected people 69–70, 72
unemployment
    Germany 141, 147–8, 172
    Great Depression 123
    information technology 183
    Japan 172
    numbers 27
United States (USA)
    credit bubble 185–6
    debt 124–8
    deflation 148–53
    education 61–2
    fascism 173–4
    Great Depression 146, 149
    September 11th aftermath 78
    troops withdrawals 190
universitas (Oakeshott) 198, 199
unsustainability 27
USA *see* United States
Uzbekistan 12, 173

V

value, currency 140, 165
Versailles Treaty 139, 148, 164
Viennese Credit Anstalt 146, 147, 149
Viet Nam War 14
viruses 103–4, 107, 110–11
von Bismark, Otto 155
von Humboldt, Friedrich 60
voyages of discovery 181

W

Wahhabis 11, 12
Wall Street Crash 71, 77, 146
wars 32, 55, 112–14
    of aggression 121
    of liberation 121
    on terrorism 59
water supplies 193
water wars 83–97
The Wealth of Nations 53, 64, 73, 74
weather change 83–97, 184
Weber, Max 73–4
welfare state 26, 27, 59
What Comes Next 59–60
Wheeler, Raymond 23–4, 129, 191, 195, 196
White, Michael 190
Wilhelm III of Prussia 60
Wilson, Woodrow 57–8
winners 69–79
Wired magazine survey 69–70
Wolf Minimum 85
women 27, 47
World War I *see* First World War
World War II *see* Second World War
WorldCom collapse 123

Z

Zaibatsu 170
Zimmerman, Dr 140–1